THE AFTERLIVES OF THE TERROR

THE AFTERLIVES
OF THE TERROR

FACING THE LEGACIES
OF MASS VIOLENCE IN
POSTREVOLUTIONARY FRANCE

RONEN STEINBERG

CORNELL UNIVERSITY PRESS
Ithaca and London

First published 2019 by Cornell University Press

Library of Congress Cataloging-in-Publication Data

Names: Steinberg, Ronen, 1970- author.
    Title: The afterlives of the Terror : facing the legacies of mass violence in postrevolutionary France / Ronen Steinberg.
    Description: Ithaca [New York] : Cornell University Press, 2019. | Includes bibliographical references and index.
    Identifiers: LCCN 2018047446 (print) | LCCN 2018048276 (ebook) | ISBN 9781501739255 (pdf) | ISBN 9781501739262 (epub/mobi) | ISBN 9781501739248 | ISBN 9781501739248 (pbk.)
    Subjects: LCSH: France—History—Reign of Terror, 1793–1794—Psychological aspects. | Political violence—France—History—1 8th century. | France—History—Revolution, 1789–1799—Influence. | France— Social Conditions—18th century.
    Classification: LCC DC183.5 (ebook) | LCC DC183.5 .S74 2019 (print) | DDC 944.04/4—dc23
    LC record available at https://lccn.loc.gov/2018047446

For Geneva, whose love, support, and sense of humor have seen me through the writing of this book.

Violent action is unclear to most of those who get caught up in it. Experience is fragmentary; cause and effect, why and how, are torn apart. Only sequence exists. First this, then that. And afterward, for those who survive, a lifetime of trying to understand.

—Salman Rushdie, *Fury*

CONTENTS

List of Illustrations   ix

Acknowledgments   xi

Introduction: Approaching the
Aftermath of the Terror   1

1. Nomenclature: Naming a Difficult
   Past after 9 Thermidor   17

2. Accountability: The Case of
   Joseph Le Bon   43

3. Redress: *Les Biens des Condamnés*   65

4. Remembrance: The Mass Graves
   of the Terror   90

5. Haunting: The Ghostly Presence
   of the Terror   117

   Conclusion   146

Notes   153

Selected Bibliography   195

Index   215

Illustrations

1. Frontispiece, Prudhomme's *Histoire Générale*, 1796–1797   35
2. Prudhomme's "General Table of the Disasters
   of the French Revolution," 1796–1797   37
3. "The Cruelties of Joseph Le Bon in Arras," 1795   58
4. The cenotaph at Brotteaux, Lyon, c. 1795   103
5. The expiatory monument in Brotteaux, Lyon, 1821   113
6. The phantasmagoria at the Capuchin Convent, c. 1798   127
7. Giovanni Aldini's experiments on severed heads, 1804   137

ACKNOWLEDGMENTS

When I was a graduate student, I used to roam the library stacks, wondering whether my own book would, one day, be among these volumes on the shelves. I suppose there was a touch of vanity in this, but there was also a genuine desire to be let into this company of scholars, who have devoted much of their lives to understanding something that, often, only they could see. Now that this dream of mine appears to have been realized, it is a great pleasure and a great honor to thank the people and the institutions who have helped it come true.

This project began at the University of Chicago. I am deeply grateful to Jan Goldstein, Michael Geyer, and Bill Sewell for their support and hope this book justifies the trust they have placed in me. Thanks also to Bernard Wasserstein, the late Moishe Postone, Ibrahim Kaya Sahin, Joyce Cheng, Karin Nisenbaum, Hsia Ke-Chin, Dan Koehler, Ari Joskowicz, and Zhu Jingsheng.

My colleagues at Michigan State University have been a model of support and encouragement. A heartfelt thanks for their general *bonhomie*: Leslie Moch, Lewis Siegelbaum, Karrin Hanshew, Sean Forner, Naoko Wake, Steve Stowe, Ed Murphy, Charles Keith, Heleh Veit, Lisa Fine, and John Dunn. I am very grateful to Walter Hawthorne for his support during his time as chair of the department. An early version of chapter two was presented at the European History Colloquium at MSU. I am grateful to the graduate students and faculty for their helpful comments. Thanks also to Beth Drexler and to the Program in Peace and Justice Studies at MSU.

I have been fortunate enough to receive financial support from various institutions in the course of my research. I am deeply grateful to The Eisenberg Institute for Historical Studies at the University of Michigan, the American Philosophical Society, the Institute for Historical Studies at the University of Texas at Austin, and the Humanities and Arts Research Program at Michigan State University.

The year I spent as a fellow of the Institute for Historical Studies at UT Austin was especially important in the evolution of this project. I am very grateful to the other fellows, the faculty members, and the graduate students for creating such a rich environment for intellectual work: Leslie Harris, Carel Bertram, Dominic Yang, Seth Garfield, Julie Hardwick, James Vaughn, Lina del Castillo, Tarek El-Ariss, Chloe Ireton, Sandy Chang, Lior Sternfeld, Eyal Weinberg, and Courtney Meador. I learned a lot about intellectual history and many other things from my conversations with Tracie Matysik and Ben Brower. Yoav di-Capua has helped me to think through most parts of this manuscript. I am very grateful to him and to Stephennie Mulder for their friendship and hospitality.

In the course of doing my research, I have benefitted from the expert advice of countless librarians and archivists here and in France. I am grateful to all of them, but especially to Marie-Laure Imbert at the *Archives Municipales d'Orange*, Pierre Quernez at the *Archives Départementales du Rhône*, Jérôme Triaud at the *Bibliothèque Municipale de Lyon*, and the staff at the *Archives Municipales de Lyon*. I am also grateful to the staff at the *Bibliothèque Nationale de France*, the Special Collections at the University of Chicago, the University of Minnesota Libraries, and the Special Collections at Michigan State University for helping with the reproduction of images.

I've received generous help from many scholars along the way. Jean-Clément Martin, Dan Edelstein, Sam Moyn, Rafe Blaufarb, Alex Fairfax-Cholmeley, Carolyn Purnell, and Hannah Callaway have responded kindly to various queries. Denise Davidson and Ann Larabee have read parts of the manuscript and offered invaluable critiques. Howard Brown has been especially generous in sharing his deep knowledge of the period and its archives; I am very grateful to him.

Writing a book is a solitary undertaking for the most part. One spends a lot of time in one's head. This book would not have been written without the many friends who listened patiently as I rambled on about this or that part of the project, laughed with me, worried about me, and knew when it was time to take me out for a drink. For this and much more, a big, warm thank you to Mickael Vaillant, Dani Aragon, Haviv Mizrahi, Chen Shoshani, Joseph Barash, Uzi Shamosh, Seth Kopald, Caroline Boerwinkle, Mark Shilkrut, Peter Hafford, Robert Hartle, Joie Pickett, Maya Haber, Sean Guillory, Doron Galili, Deborah Margolis, Valentina Denzel, Anne Verjus, and Lucero Radonic. Thanks to Guy Beiner for his friendship and for inspiring me to go to grad school in the first place. Dorothee Brantz has shared my interest in the bizarre and the morbid and has believed in this project from its inception. Thanks to Xuefei Ren for her support. I am very fortunate to have found Yvon le Bot and Janine Perrimond, landlords who have become dear friends. We had, and continue to have, many memorable evenings debating politics and ideas over wine in their lovely Parisian home. A special thanks to Sophie Wahnich, *historienne extraordinaire de la Révolution française*, for her friendship and inspiring scholarship. Parts of this book were written at the home of Lauren Ross and Lisa Fithian in Austin; I am grateful for their hospitality. Bette Oliver has edited the manuscript. I am very grateful to her for this and for the many years we've spent discussing the French Revolution, poetry, and cats. I have been talking about history, theory, and life with Pablo Ben for almost twenty years now: the imprint of his sharp, knowledgeable mind is all over this work.

When I first met Emily Andrew, my editor at Cornell University Press, I remember thinking "she understands what I am trying to do better than I do!" I am deeply grateful to her for guiding this project expertly to its fruition, for knowing what to say and when, and for her patience with the recurring e-mails, whose content boiled down to: "Eh, I am going to need a few more days." I am also grateful to the two anonymous readers at Cornell for their helpful suggestions.

My deepest gratitude is to those with whom I share the most intimate bonds. My mother, my father and his partner, and my brother have supported my various endeavors over the years. They may not have always understood what I have been doing, but I know they are happy it is done. Many writers know the value of a cat's companionship. Thanks to Kafka the cat for all the purrs. Finally, this book would not have been written without the love, support, and *joie de vivre* of Geneva White. Many a time, when I was especially exasperated about some part of the writing, she just smiled at me and said: "Write your book, Ronen." There, I did.

THE AFTERLIVES OF THE TERROR

Introduction

Approaching the Aftermath of the Terror

The Reign of Terror was an episode of state-sanctioned violence in the middle of the revolutionary decade in France. For a period of about eighteen months, from March 1793 to July 1794, French citizens were subjected to an escalating series of restrictive measures. Freedoms of speech and movement were curtailed severely. Special ad hoc commissions and tribunals were granted broad mandates to arrest and try people suspected of counterrevolutionary dispositions. There was an expanded application of the death penalty. Executions by guillotine became a daily spectacle in many urban centers. By the end of it all, tens of thousands of citizens had been executed, a collective death sentence was hanging over the heads of some 140,000 political refugees—the "émigrés"—and hundreds of thousands of citizens were languishing in makeshift prisons across the country.[1]

Imagine that such an event took place in our day and age: What would its aftermath look like? Among the many possible scenarios that come to mind, the following one emerges with particular force. No doubt, numerous psychiatrists would appear on the scene, ready to discuss the traumatic effects of what had just taken place. Testimonies from victims would appear in the media for months and years after the event. There would be an earnest but only partially successful attempt to hold those responsible for the violence accountable, perhaps with the help of an international tribunal. Diagnoses of post-traumatic stress disorder (PTSD) would proliferate dramatically.[2] Above all,

the people involved directly in the unfolding of the event, and just about any-
one else who might feel affected by it somehow, would be encouraged to talk,
and to talk repeatedly about what had transpired, so that the process of "working through" could begin in earnest.[3]

That this scenario suggests itself so readily to mind is a reflection of dominant trends in world politics and culture since the end of World War II. The
twentieth century is often presented as a period of unprecedented bloodshed,
but it was also a period that saw the emergence of a wide array of responses
to atrocity and mass violence.[4] Over the last seventy years or so, states and
societies in different parts of the world have experimented with novel institutional and legal measures aimed at dealing with the legacies of collective brutality. International tribunals, truth commissions, bureaucratic purges, the
opening up of archives, restitution of stolen land and cultural artifacts, reparations for loss of life and property, formal apologies delivered by heads of
state, sometimes decades and even centuries after the events in question—all
have been and continue to be employed in various configurations and with
varying degrees of success around the world.[5] At the same time, a whole new
language has emerged around injury and healing.[6] Individuals and groups making claims on the body politic identify themselves increasingly as victims of
historical injustice, demanding that the harm done to them be acknowledged
and remedied in some way.[7] The concept of trauma in particular has emerged
as a powerful trope for contemporary attitudes toward the past. Originating
as a rather specific psychiatric category, it has come to stand for a whole range
of experiences and their effects on individuals and societies. Thus, we talk of
traumatized nations, traumatized histories, and cultures of trauma.[8] Before
the modern period, the past was seen and taught as a source of emulation and
inspiration. It is now seen to a large extent as something one must recover from
or overcome. In the words of sociologist John Torpey: "The concern in contemporary politics and intellectual life with 'coming to terms with the past'
has become pervasive."[9]

This book applies that set of concerns to the time of the French Revolution. It asks how contemporaries of the revolutionary era grappled with the
legacies left in the wake of the Reign of Terror. What legal, political, intellectual, cultural, and even therapeutic models were available to them in order
to address the effects of mass violence on self and society? How did they think
and talk about traumatic events before the advent of modern trauma-talk? The
chapters of the book follow revolutionary leaders, relatives of victims, and ordinary citizens as they struggled to bring those whom they saw as responsible
for the Terror to justice, provide some sort of relief to those who suffered the
brunt of its repressive measures, and commemorate loved ones in a political

and social context that favored forgetting. This introduction discusses how the book approaches the aftermath of the Terror. First, however, we turn to a man who was closer to the events at hand and who had insight into the issues that also stand at the heart of this book.

Quinet's Insight

"The Terror was a first calamity; a second one, which defeated the Republic, was putting the Terror on trial."[10] Thus wrote the historian Edgar Quinet in his magnum opus, *La Révolution*, which was published in 1865. He was talking about a series of trials of key functionaries involved in the apparatus of the Terror, which took place after the fall of Maximilien Robespierre. But more generally, he was lamenting the tendency of the French, and especially of the revolutionary leaders, to talk incessantly about the violence of the Terror in its aftermath. Quinet contrasted this with the conduct of Lucius Cornelius Sulla, the Roman dictator who carried out a brutal purge of the city's notables in 81 BC, abdicated, and took to walking the streets of Rome without the protection of guards, ready to explain how his actions had served the interests of the Republic. Not so with the National Convention after the Reign of Terror. "Once it has committed barbarities, it denounces them itself; once they have been denounced, they must be expiated. . . . This is why the Convention does not enter history in the manner of the tyrants of antiquity: it did not know how to impose silence on posterity."[11]

Quinet's complaint sounds strange to modern ears. We are much more likely, in our day and age, to be highly critical of governments that try to "impose silence on posterity." Scholars in the social sciences and the humanities tend to view silence and silencing as problems to be studied, not as solutions.[12] If one could boil down to a maxim the myriad ways of dealing with the legacies of mass violence in modern times, it would be "talk about it." But Quinet's point was not really to endorse silence as the appropriate response to the terrible things that have happened in the past. Rather, his point was that terror was fundamentally incompatible with the democratic impulses of the French Revolution.

Quinet saw terror as a tool of the Old Regime. Kings and princes, tyrants and dictators—those were the rulers who had regular recourse to violence, repression, and intimidation as means to political ends. They could afford to do so, because their rule did not rely on the consent of those whom they ruled. The source of their power came from elsewhere, from God or perhaps from tradition, not from the people they governed. The French revolutionaries, in contrast, tried to create a political order based on popular sovereignty. The source of political power in the new order was not God, but the people.[13] This does not mean, of course, that all French citizens took an active role in politics overnight. Studies of electoral behavior during the French Revolution show that relatively few chose to do so, even when they had the opportunity.[14] It does mean, however, that the French embarked on a long process of transformation from subjects to citizens.[15] The day-to-day work of governing was carried out by a relatively small group of elected officials, but as the Revolution evolved, more and more segments of the population could express their wills in a variety of ways and venues. As Lynn Hunt has argued: "The French Revolution enormously increased the points from which power could be exercised, and multiplied the strategies and tactics for wielding that power."[16] Terror was incompatible with this democratic trajectory. The new political order required the consent of a large enough part of the population in order to function, and the repressive measures that the revolutionary government adopted in 1793–1794 eroded this support. In a nutshell, the Terror damaged the legitimacy of the Republic. In Quinet's words, "Terror cannot succeed in a democracy, because a democracy must have justice, whereas an aristocracy or a monarchy can do without it."[17] The Reign of Terror, according to Quinet, was the Old Regime rearing its head in the middle of France's attempt to catapult itself into the modern age, and that is why it was bound to fail.

One need not agree with Quinet's interpretation in order to appreciate his insight. His understanding of the French Revolution was political and ideological through and through. At the time of writing, he was in self-imposed exile in Switzerland, having left France after Louis-Napoleon's coup of 1851. Here was a man of the "French generation of 1820," an intellectual and political milieu born during or immediately after the Revolution.[18] Like many of his generation, Quinet was dismayed at the country's tumultuous swing from one regime to another. From monarchy to Republic, from Republic to a Napoleonic Empire, from Napoleon to a restored monarchy, from a restored monarchy to the Second Republic, and from the Second Republic to another Napoleonic coup d'état. To many at the time, it must have seemed as if France was stuck in a cyclical pattern it could neither control nor understand. Quinet was also a Protestant in a country that was by and large Catholic. His interpretation of the Revolution did not sit comfortably with any of the political or ideological camps of the time. Religious without being Catholic, republican without being radical, Quinet's book pleased few and upset many. His analysis of the Terror, in particular, gave rise to a very public dispute with other historians on the left.[19]

The conduct of the revolutionaries after the fall of Robespierre marked something new in history. Earlier regimes did not reckon with their own historical records in the same way, especially when those records were tainted by brutality. The democratizing dynamic unleashed by the Revolution transformed the way French society struggled with its own difficult past. In his discussion of the aftermath of the Terror, Quinet brought up numerous historical examples: the assassinations that the nobles of Venice practiced on each other; the role of the house of Valois in instigating the Saint Bartholomew's Day Massacre; the machinations of Richelieu; Louis XIV's persecution of French Huguenots following the revocation of the Edict of Nantes in 1685—all had been shrouded by the same silence. "What would have become of the Spanish Monarchy," Quinet asked rhetorically, "were it to condemn all those who had massacred the Indians of America on its own orders, and publicize their deeds? The Spanish Monarchy would have been dishonored by its own hands."[20] Kings, Quinet implied, know how to institute amnesia. This was something that the French Republic could not do. The Republic could neither decree amnesia nor control memory because of the democratizing thrust of the Revolution. There were simply too many competing voices in the public arena for any single entity to enforce silence after the Terror.

The Indeterminacy of the Terror

The Terror is the best-studied episode of the French Revolution, but it remains a subject of much controversy. Historians disagree on its chronology, nature, geographic incidence, and the number of its victims. They disagree vehemently on its origins.[21] A few years ago, the former director of the Institut d'histoire de la Révolution française at the Sorbonne (The Institute for the History of the French Revolution at the Sorbonne), Jean-Clément Martin, suggested that we should stop talking about it altogether. Instead of an organized campaign of political repression, as the name connotes, Martin argued that what actually took place was a bumbling, chaotic series of actions that were more anarchic than systematic, and that were given the appearance of a unified phenomenon after the fact.[22]

There are two main reasons for the difficulty of talking clearly about the Terror. The first has to do with the moral and political stakes of revolutionary historiography. The second has to do with the nature of the Terror as an event. For better or worse, the French Revolution functions as the founding myth of the modern age, at least in the West. By myth, I mean a story of origins that endows a given period or culture with its central values and identity.[23] If the Revolution is a founding myth of modernity, the Terror is the scandal at its heart. The Revolution gave the world the *Declaration of the Rights of Man and Citizen*, but also the guillotine. What then are the fundamental values of this modern age? Are they embodied in the idea of human rights, in the guillotine, or in both? More troubling, is the guillotine necessary in order to realize the emancipatory promise of the Revolution? To take a position on these questions is to take a position on the foundations of the modern age.

Consider the two main interpretations of the Terror. According to the first, the Reign of Terror was an unfortunate but necessary response to a series of threats facing the young Republic in 1793. These threats included foreign war, civil war, counterrevolution, and a subsistence crisis. From this perspective, the Terror was a temporary aberration from the revolutionary struggle, an unfortunate means to a laudable end.[24] According to the second interpretation, terror and violence were inevitable features of the Revolution. The political culture of the Revolution, so the argument goes, owed much to the Enlightenment, especially to the ideas of Jean-Jacques Rousseau. Rousseau argued that the proper use of reason should lead all members of a political community to desire the same things for the benefit of all. He called this principle the General Will. The problem with this idea is that it left no room for dissent. From this vantage point, it was a short step to see differing opinions as treason, and to react to them with repressive measures.[25] The first interpretation justifies revolutionary violence implicitly, whether it intends to or not. The second interpretation condemns it, and sometimes quite explicitly.[26]

Indeed, violence is a polarizing subject.[27] It is difficult to write about it without defending or condemning it in some way. This much was apparent already in the revolutionary era. "The violence of the Revolution caused much harm, but it also brought about its success," wrote the French diplomat Adrien de Lezay-Marnésia in 1797.[28] The Irish statesman John Wilson Croker was much less forgiving. He wrote in 1843 that "the whole French Revolution, from the taking of the Bastille to the overthrow of the Empire, was one long Reign of Terror."[29] One would think that the passage of time would make the ideological implications of interpretations of the Terror less relevant, but this has not been the case. The historian Timothy Tackett ended the introduction to his recent book on the origins of the Terror by stating his "personal reticence toward condemning outright the men and women of the French Revolution for their acts of violence, even for their obvious moral crimes, without attempting to understand and contextualize why they did what they did." Asking ourselves how we would have acted in their place is, according to Tackett,

among the "most important questions posed for people living through perilous political times."[30] Therefore, the first reason for the difficulty of writing
about the Terror is that the stakes of doing so have long gone beyond the mere
establishment of facts: they cannot be separated neatly from one's political and
moral worldviews.

The second reason is that the revolutionary decade in France saw many instances of mass violence. It is quite difficult to determine which among them
formed part of the Terror and which belonged to other, distinct yet related
processes of contention. Take, for example, the September Massacres of 1792.
A crowd of Parisian militants, incensed by rumors of an imminent Prussian
invasion, descended on the prisons of the Capital and began killing inmates
out of fear that they would join the Prussians and wreak vengeance on the
city. According to most estimates, some 1,300 prisoners were killed, while the
authorities proved powerless to stop the massacre.[31] Should this be seen as part
of the Reign of Terror? According to some historians, this incident did indeed
signal a revolutionary turn to violence and intimidation. According to others,
the Reign of Terror was instituted precisely in order to take violence out of
the hands of the people and establish the state's monopoly over the use of
force.[32] Furthermore, while violence stands at the heart of the Terror, the Terror cannot be reduced to violence. The same regime that passed repressive
laws and made liberal use of the death penalty also abolished slavery throughout the French Empire and experimented with radical forms of social welfare, such as annual pensions to widows, and free public education.

So, the Reign of Terror is a fuzzy concept. On the one hand, it was an
intense, visceral experience for many French women and men in the 1790s.
Thousands of people were executed, hundreds of thousands arrested, and an
untold number of citizens lived in daily fear, worrying that they or their loved
ones might be next. "It was a time when the claims of the rights of man and
the mournful voice of nature found no echo in sensible hearts."[33] This was
how Louis-Sébastien Mercier, the indefatigable chronicler of Parisian daily life
during the Revolution, described this period. On the other hand, most certain-
ties about the Terror dissolve when one looks closely at the details. Its violence was not arbitrary, but neither was it as systematic and organized as it
may seem. Some interpretations isolate the Terror from other instances of
mass violence in the Revolution, while other interpretations see it as one point,
albeit one of exceptional significance, along a broader "continuum of destruction," leading from the storming of the Bastille to the exterminatory campaigns in the Vendée.[34] The Reign of Terror had a real impact on those who
lived through it, but its contours as an event are blurry. It resists a neat, con-
cise description.

This book will not offer one. On the contrary, this book is in many ways about how difficult it was for those who experienced the Terror to tell its story. The French Revolution constituted "a deep rupture in remembered experience."[35] Those who were affected by it were well aware that they were witnessing something momentous, yet had difficulties describing what was happening. "It is impossible to express," is a phrase repeated again and again in testimonies from the time.[36] Events followed each other at such speed that they seemed to outpace the ability of contemporaries to narrate them. The German philosopher Wilhelm Traugott Krug distinguished in 1796 between "new history" and "newest history, that is, the history of the day."[37] He saw the latter as characterized by uncertainty and analogous to myth. In the context of the revolutionary maelstrom, it became harder to record the history of one's own time.

The men and women who lived through the violence of the Terror struggled in its aftermath to transform a series of chaotic experiences into a narrative that made sense. Theirs was the time of memory, of fragments, when cause and effect, the why and the how, were still unclear. In 1816, when the surviving members of the National Convention who had voted for the regicide of Louis XVI were exiled, many of them went to Brussels, and there, as old men, they passed the time writing their memoirs.[38] Fifteen years later, the first serious histories of the Revolution would begin to appear.[39] This book tries to capture this liminal time between memory and history, between lived experience and retrospective narration.

The Aftermath of the Terror

How should we approach this twilight zone between experience and narration? How should we think about the aftermath of the Terror? The vast historiography of the Revolution has refrained for the most part from posing these questions. It has been more focused on the origins and evolution of revolutionary violence than on its consequences. The work of the historian Bronislaw Baczko is the exception to this norm. In a pathbreaking study, published at the time of the bicentennial of the Revolution, Baczko launched an inquiry into the process of ending the Terror. "Ending the Terror," Baczko pointed out, "was not an act but a process, tense and with an uncertain issue. The Terror was not brought to an end by the fall of Robespierre; it was a road to be discovered and travelled."[40]

That road turned out to be long and winding. The first step was dismantling the institutional apparatus of the Terror. This was done rather swiftly in the weeks after the fall of Robespierre. The Convention repealed repressive laws, reformed the organs of revolutionary justice, purged the personnel that enforced its decrees in the provinces, and began releasing prisoners. Changing the political culture, however, proved to be a much more daunting task. The revolutionaries had to face difficult questions about the path that led them from the promise of 1789 to the violence of 1793. The trials of public officials who were involved in the Terror incensed public opinion with revelations about the extent of the brutality, especially in the provinces. The revolutionaries, and French society more generally, had to work out what kind of political and institutional arenas were necessary and even possible after the Terror. As the *conventionnel* Merlin de Thionville put it several weeks after 9 Thermidor, the problems facing the Republic required a clear answer to the following questions: "Where have we come from? Where are we? Where are we going?"[41] If the goal was to regain stability, and bring the Revolution to an end, the French had to imagine new ways of resolving their political and ideological disputes. Baczko's study showed that there was considerable continuity between the Terror and the political culture that rose in reaction to it. The Thermidorian counterimagination crystallized "within a framework . . . that was born of the Terror and modeled by it."[42]

Baczko's work has had a significant impact on the historiography of the Revolution. It has led to a reevaluation of the Thermidorian Reaction and to a renewed interest in the period between the fall of Robespierre and the rise of Napoleon.[43] Howard Brown has taken this inquiry forward by examining how the Thermidorian Reaction and the Directory struggled to bring the Revolution to an end by quelling various forms of civil violence. Brown's research has shown how the regimes that followed each other at a dizzying pace between 1794 and 1804 employed repressive measures that were similar to the measures employed by the Jacobins in Year II. The combination of the democratic culture of the Revolution with a heavy-handed security apparatus led to a hybrid state, which Brown called "liberal authoritarianism."[44]

Two conclusions that emerge from the recent wave of research about the aftermath of the Terror are especially important for this book. First, the Thermidorian Reaction can no longer be seen exclusively as the triumph of the bourgeoisie and the defeat of the popular movement. Rather than a "drab interlude" between the fall of Robespierre and the rise of Napoleon, it has come to be seen as a distinct moment in the Revolution with a specific set of problems.[45] The Thermidorians, according to Baczko, "did not possess a political strategy."[46] Rather, they faced a unique and largely unprecedented set of challenges that had to do, in one way or another, with regaining stability and reestablishing order.

Second, one of the main questions that occupied contemporaries of the revolutionary era after 9 Thermidor was what to do about the past. As the chapters of this book show, revolutionary leaders and ordinary citizens, whose lives had been impacted by the violence of Year II, engaged in a broad process of reckoning with the legacies left in the wake of the Terror.[47] This process began by constructing the events of 1793–1794 as a difficult past, which is the subject of chapter 1. Chapter 2 analyzes the trials of public officials for their role in the Terror. The trials gave rise to debates about accountability, and they enabled victims to face perpetrators in front of packed courtrooms. Chapter 3 discusses the effort of widows of victims to get their husbands exonerated posthumously, and to regain possession of the property that had been confiscated from them. Many revolutionaries who took an active part in the repression lost their positions in the administration and were shunned or persecuted by their communities. Family members and friends of the victims fought to bring their loved ones to proper burial. Chapter 4 examines how they tried to find space for commemoration in a political context that was changing constantly, often in radical ways. Indeed, when one considers those whose lives had been rent by the Terror, one wonders what it means to speak of its end at all. Surely, for them and for many others, the events of 9 Thermidor were not really a denouement, but rather the beginning of a long process of coming to terms with what they had been through. For this reason, chapter 5 focuses on haunting, bringing together a variety of iterations that illustrate the ghostly presence of the Terror in the postrevolutionary landscape. The aftermath of the Terror emerges here as a retrospective moment; it invites us to consider how contemporaries of the revolutionary era faced a "difficult past" in the context of a movement oriented toward the future.[48]

Transitional Justice, Trauma, and the French *Vergangenheitsbewältigung*

The approach to the aftermath of the Terror in this book is rooted in concerns and themes that dominated the political and cultural life of the late twentieth century, especially as those pertain to the long shadow cast by the Holocaust. In a recent essay on the historical consciousness of our time, the historian Alon Confino argued that certain events constitute "foundational pasts." He meant by this "an event that represents an age because it embodies a historical novum that serves as a moral and historical yardstick, as a measure of things human."[49] Foundational pasts mark a rupture in historical time. They generate fundamental questions of politics, culture, and values that define an entire era. Confino argued that the French Revolution constituted the foundational past of the West from 1789, but it was replaced around the 1970s by the Holocaust, which has come to serve as "the actual emblem" of our historical epoch.[50]

If Confino is right—and I think that he is basically right—this means that the emblematic atrocities of the twentieth century are the dominant prism through which historians, and not only historians, view the past. As Jan Goldstein noted, while reflecting on the state of French history in the new millennium, the optimistic questions that made the study of the French Revolution so attractive for much of the twentieth century have given way to a more somber reflection on the horrors of the past: "The defining event of modernity now seems to be the Holocaust."[51] The tragic horizon that dominates contemporary attitudes to the past has not been lost on historians of the Revolution. Jean-Clément Martin has noted recently that "the history of the French Revolution occupies without a doubt a place that is similar to that of the destruction of the Jews. . . . The stakes of the debate have long surpassed the mere establishment of facts."[52] Hunt observed that the genocides in Rwanda and Bosnia, respectively, have reshaped the views of historians on the violence of the French Revolution in powerful ways.[53]

Transitional justice and trauma are two concepts that have proven particularly salient for elaborating the challenges that individuals and societies face in the aftermath of mass violence. Transitional justice is a fairly recent term. It emerged in the 1990s to describe the global wave of transitions from authoritarian to liberal regimes in South Africa, Latin America, and Eastern Europe. Its precise definition is a matter of debate, but at its broadest, it refers to "those mechanisms, judicial and non-judicial, employed by communities, states, and the international community in order to deal with a legacy of systematic human rights abuse and authoritarianism."[54] These mechanisms range from formal ones such as criminal trials, truth commissions, and reparations to less formal ones such as commemorative monuments, art, and therapy. A helpful way of thinking about these various measures is to situate them on a spectrum "between vengeance and forgiveness," as defined by legal scholar Martha Minow.[55]

The concept of trauma is, of course, more widely known.[56] It first emerged in the 1860s to account for a particular pathology, which was known as "railway spine."[57] In modern psychiatry, trauma designates a mental and physiological response to events that are so extreme—usually events involving a close encounter with violence, death, and the threat of bodily harm—that they cannot be processed through the normal mechanisms of memory and cognition.[58] They become split off in the brain, giving rise to a host of symptoms that take on a life of their own, disconnected from the original event. Essentially, trauma is a phenomenon of mental dissociation.[59] But in the course of the twentieth century, and especially after PTSD has been adopted as a formal clinical diagnosis by the medical profession in the United States, trauma has come to denote a much broader range of phenomena that have to do with the persistence of "difficult pasts" in the present. As Didier Fassin and Richard Rechtman have argued recently, it has become "one of the dominant modes of representing our relationship with the past."[60]

The concepts of transitional justice and trauma, respectively, are invaluable for thinking about the aftermath of the Terror in revolutionary France.[61] Transitional justice calls our attention to the series of dilemmas that the revolutionaries faced after the fall of Robespierre. The revolutionaries, and French society more generally, had to negotiate a treacherous path between justice and stability, peace and truth, memory and amnesia, vengeance and forgiveness. Someone had to be held accountable for the excesses of Year II, but who? And what if doing so risked plunging the Republic anew into a cycle of reprisals and recriminations? Victims needed to be compensated for the harm done to them, but what if doing so meant in effect destroying many of the social and economic achievements of the Revolution? Could a revolutionary movement, focused as it is on the future, afford a reckoning with its own past? These questions have no definite answers, but the revolutionaries faced them without a blueprint, without a script or a set of measures they could draw on from experience.

The concept of trauma, in turn, helps us see how the Terror continued to figure in the social and cultural life of postrevolutionary France. Physicians writing in the late 1790s and early 1800s wondered about the effects of revolutionary violence on public health. Debates about the death penalty became occasions for reflecting on the imprint that the guillotine left on the psyche of an entire generation. Multimedia shows that took place after 9 Thermidor, and that made use of innovative visual technology, featured images of ghosts rising from the dead. These were different iterations of the notion that revolutionary violence may have been over, but it was not gone; it continued to figure in the present in uncanny, disruptive, and often intangible ways.[62] To paraphrase social theorist Avery Gordon, the concept of trauma calls on us to confront the ghostly aspects of the Terror's aftermath.[63]

The approach of this book to its subject, and the kinds of questions it sets out to answer, have been shaped heavily by a constellation of issues that arose in reaction to the catastrophic death toll of the twentieth century. There is a word in German that captures this constellation of issues particularly well: *Vergangenheitsbewältigung*. It is composed of the word *Vergangen*, meaning "past," and the word *Bewältigung*, meaning "to wrestle with or tame." It can thus be translated as "mastering or coming to terms with the past." Initially, it referred to the particular set of challenges that German society struggled with in the aftermath of the Third Reich, most notably around the process of denazification. It has since come to denote a broader preoccupation with the Nazi past in various arenas: film, literature, monuments, and even the writing of history.[64] In a sense, this book describes a French *Vergangenheitsbewältigung* in the late eighteenth and early nineteenth centuries.

This might lead some readers to deduce that this book draws an analogy between the Reign of Terror and the massive democides of the twentieth century.[65] This is not my intention. The revolutionary state in eighteenth-century France had neither the ability nor the design to carry out devastation and surveillance on the scale of modern totalitarian regimes. Whatever else it may have been, the Reign of Terror was not a modern atrocity in the twentieth-century sense of the term. The questions that this book poses are rooted in the epistemological and existential anxieties of the twentieth century, but this does not imply an analogy between the events in question. The concepts I employ in order to analyze how men and women in the late eighteenth century struggled to come to terms with the Terror may be recent, but the difficulties they address are not. In drawing on them, this book shows how contemporaries of the revolutionary era grappled with similar issues to those that arose in the aftermath of more recent cases of state terror, but on their own terms, with the concepts and frameworks available to them at the time.

Argument and Structure

In the aftermath of the Terror, revolutionary leaders, relatives of victims, and ordinary citizens, in and beyond France, struggled to come to terms with the catastrophic violence of Year II. The first steps in this process were judicial or institutional in nature, and they combined retributive justice with restorative justice. Some public officials were put on trial after 9 Thermidor, beginning with Jean-Baptiste Carrier, who had been the *représentant en mission* in Nantes during the Terror, and culminating with Joseph Le Bon, whose case is the subject of chapter 2. Other people who had been identified with the regime of Year II were dealt with more summarily and less legally. Several hundred Jacobins and so-called *terroristes* were rounded up and lynched during the White Terror, a wave of more or less spontaneous killings that spread through the south of France in the winter of 1795.[66] Vengeance, wrote Baczko, was a "Thermidorian passion."[67] But alongside revenge, there was also redress.

A partial restoration of the property, which had been confiscated from victims of the Terror, was under way by the summer of 1795. The founders of a new civic religion, Théophilanthropie, stated that one of its goals had been to "heal the wounds of the Revolution . . . by preaching mutual forgiveness and the forgetting of all wrongs."[68] In its last session as the legislative assembly of France, the National Convention adopted a sweeping amnesty decree; changed the name of Place de la Révolution to Place de la Concorde; and discussed proposals to abolish to death penalty and burn the guillotine publicly. These measures were meant to close the books on the most painful episode of the Revolution.

Yet, as this book tries to show, the Reign of Terror had a long afterlife. Relatives of victims struggled to locate an appropriate space for the commemoration of their loved ones throughout the first decades of the nineteenth century. In many cases, they constructed expiatory monuments on, or near, the mass graves where the victims of the Terror had been buried. At times these projects were carried out with the support of the authorities and at times they were suppressed. As late as the 1840s, departmental and municipal councils in various parts of the country were still dealing with conflicts around monuments to victims of the Terror. The notion that those who had lived through the violence of the Revolution were doomed to live with its emotional consequences for some time to come found expression in a variety of arenas, long before the emergence of modern trauma-talk. One such arena was the Gothic, which, according to literary historian Joseph Crawford, could easily have remained a marginal part of British literature "had it not been seized upon by writers eager to find new vocabularies of evil in the years following the revolutionary Terror."[69] Debates on the abolition of the death penalty in the 1830s drew on the fear that public executions might recall the specter of 1793. Children of *conventionnels* changed their last name, so as not to be identified with the men who had voted for the death of Louis XVI and sanctioned the Law of Suspects.[70]

The argument of this book is that the distinct difficulties around coming to terms with the Terror, and the particular debates that this process gave rise to, were derived from the political and social transformations of the Revolution. Popular sovereignty led to debates about accountability after the fall of Robespierre, for if the citizens were the source of power in the Republic, they shared in the responsibility for its actions. How, then, were individuals to be held accountable for mass violence? The revolutionary politics of property made it extraordinarily difficult to consider restitution after 9 Thermidor because restoring possessions, even to those who, ostensibly, had been victims of historical injustice, threatened to undo many of the social and economic achievements of the Revolution. How far back, then, should the state go in trying to undo the damage caused by its own actions? The politicization of memory and of death during the Revolution gave rise to particular difficulties around the commemoration of victims of the Terror. How was one to commemorate a contentious past without reawakening civil strife? These dilemmas around retribution, redress, and remembrance derived from the democratizing dynamic of the Revolution; they would have been unthinkable under the Old Regime. In this sense, the modern question of what to do with difficult pasts is one of the unpredictable consequences of the French Revolution.

Of course, not all these changes began in 1789. Secularization and the emergence of the public sphere had transformed the attitudes of Europeans toward events of mass violence, including natural disasters, long before the Revolution. Accountability had been emerging as a central principle of European statecraft since the Renaissance. The new links forged between the ownership of private property and civic participation—indeed, the very definition of private property—were part and parcel of the expansion of capitalism. The cult of the dead had been changing in Europe since the Middle Ages in ways that invested burial sites with new meanings and tied their fate to moments of radical, political change.

Nevertheless, the French Revolution, and the revolutionary era more generally, accelerated and inflected these changes, thus rendering them visible in a dramatic fashion. It was in the decades leading up to the Revolution, according to Keith Baker, that society was invented "as the symbolic representation of collective human existence and . . . as the essential domain of human practice."[71] In the context of the Revolution, society emerged not only as an object of rational analysis and reflection, but also as a subject capable of reflecting upon itself.[72] The dilemmas explored in this book, and indeed the very notion that society must somehow come to terms with the violence of its past, were rooted in this revolutionary institution of social reflexivity. According to Hunt, the Revolution marked the invasion of politics into the everyday. "Because revolutionary rhetoric insisted on a complete break with the past . . . every nook and cranny of everyday life . . . had to be examined for the corruption of the Old Regime and swept up in preparation for the new."[73] This desire for total transformation was enshrined most vividly in the project of the Republican calendar, which had the audacity to begin time itself anew. In this book I argue that the same radicalizing dynamic, which was predicated on a complete break with the past, also made it very difficult, and perhaps even impossible, to leave certain pasts behind.

The chapters of the book focus for the most part on the period from the 1790s to the 1830s. French society experienced multiple regime changes during these years, but it is my contention that the process of coming to terms with the Terror continued throughout these transformations—underneath the surface, as it were, of the political upheavals of the time. The chronological arc of the book corresponds roughly to the lifespan of the generation that experienced firsthand the events in question. The themes of the chapters—naming, retribution, redress, remembrance, and haunting—advance from more concrete responses to the Terror to ones that are more amorphous, harder to pin down. One could visualize the structure of the book as a series of expanding, concentric circles. The process of facing the legacies of mass violence in postrevolutionary France is presented here as a ripple effect: the farther one moves from the original event, the more opaque the circles in the water become, but also all the more encompassing.

CHAPTER 1

Nomenclature

Naming a Difficult Past after 9 Thermidor

On August 28, 1794, precisely one month after the execution of Robespierre, the Thermidorian leader Jean-Lambert Tallien delivered a seminal speech in the National Convention on the future of the revolutionary government in France. There had been much uncertainty since the events of 9 Thermidor. On the one hand, there was little doubt that the repression, which had characterized the previous months, was being relaxed. In the time that had passed since those events, the revolutionary government abolished repressive laws, relaxed censorship, and began the mass release of prisoners. According to the journalist Jean-Joseph Dussault, the gates of the prisons were not so much opened as "torn off their hinges."[1] The playwright Georges Duval described in his memoirs the revival of Parisian night life after a year of Jacobin austerity: "From every corner of the Capital, the joyous sounds of the clarinet, the violin, the tambourine, and the flute call on passersby to the dance halls."[2] On the other hand, it was far from clear that the dangers of the Terror were over.[3] Two days before Tallien delivered his speech, his former secretary, Méhée de la Touche, published a pamphlet titled *La queue de Robespierre*.[4] The pamphlet was a diatribe against the Montagnards, but its title became a popular catchphrase of the period, warning readers that they must remain vigilant against "Robespierre's Tail," that is, those who would revive the Terror.[5] Officially, the government was still revolutionary, and the

Republic was in a state of emergency. It was time then, declared Tallien, to put an end to "this state of oscillation we have been living in for a month now."[6]

To end the instability, one had to define the present moment, and to define the present moment, one had to define the Reign of Terror. The Terror, according to Tallien, was a political system based on the principle of fear. "The art of Terror," he said, "consists in setting a trap for every step, a spy in every home, a traitor in every family." The regime must know how to use the public death of the few to terrify the many. Executions had to be spectacular, even theatrical, in order to make a lasting impression on the spectators. The goal was not to eliminate the enemies of the Revolution but to break their will to resist. To be effective, the Terror had to be unpredictable and self-expanding. "One achieves nothing by having cut off twenty heads yesterday if one is not prepared to cut off thirty heads today, and sixty tomorrow." This method of governing, according to Tallien, split society in two: "those who are afraid, and those who make others afraid." So unique was this system of power, that Tallien used a new word—*terrorisme*—to describe it.[7]

This was the birth of the modern definition of terrorism.[8] Historians of political violence point routinely to the French Revolution as the first time that terror was used systematically and deliberately to create a new and better social order.[9] Scholars, philosophers, and revolutionaries have been arguing since the late eighteenth century about the relationship between the violent overthrow of the Old Regime and the emergence of the new one.[10] The terms used during the Revolution to describe these forms of political violence— *terreur, système de terreur, système de la terreur, terrorisme,* and the derivative *terroriste*—meant many different things, but as Annie Jourdan has argued recently, they constituted, first and foremost, "a rhetorical strategy for intimidating or delegitimating an adversary."[11]

But the Reign of Terror was something else as well: a difficult past. Tallien introduced this problem early in his address. "The shadow of Robespierre," he said, "still hovers over the Republic; the minds that have been divided for so long and agitated so violently . . . have not yet been reconciled." The Terror, in other words, may have ended, but its effects were present. Tallien described these effects explicitly in his speech. "The Terror," he stated, "produced a habitual trembling; an external trembling that affects the most hidden fibers, that degrades man and likens him to a beast." The experience of Terror had a negative impact on the physical, psychological, and mental well-being of those who went through it, resulting in "a real disorganization of the mind. . . . An extreme affliction." These effects were not limited to individual psyches; they were collective as well. The Terror, Tallien exclaimed, "de-fraternizes, de-moralizes, and de-socializes."[12] In a language that traversed the domains of political analysis and medical diagnosis, and that brings to mind modern definitions of PTSD, Tallien named the Terror a difficult past; that is, a destructive episode that was over, but not gone.[13]

This chapter is about the construction of the Terror as a difficult past after 9 Thermidor. The narratives about the Terror that emerged after the fall of Robespierre are usually seen as part of the Thermidorian Reaction; that is, as a political tactic designed to delegitimize the previous regime and to legitimize the current one. This is undoubtedly true, but as this chapter tries to show, there is more to it than that. Representations of revolutionary violence that were produced after 9 Thermidor were not only part of a political reaction but also the result of much broader processes. Secularization and the rise of the public sphere—developments that predate the Revolution—transformed European attitudes to cataclysmic events. Natural disasters and mass violence came to be seen less as manifestations of divine will and more as social and political problems. The Revolution accelerated and inflected these changes. Specifically, the Revolution opened up a debate about the relationship between violence and the social order. Violence came to be seen as the guarantor of the new world the revolutionaries were trying to create, and, at the same time, as its very undoing. Representations of the Terror after the fall of Robespierre displayed a telling ambivalence. On the one hand, revolutionary leaders, writers, and ordinary citizens proclaimed repeatedly that the Terror had ended, and that the violence of Year II was a thing of the past. On the other hand, the texts that they produced often included the acknowledgment, sometimes explicit and sometimes implicit, that this was a past that could not be laid to rest so easily; that its traces were all around, in the landscape and in the minds of people. This chapter situates these iterations in the context of changing attitudes to catastrophic events, as well as in the new understandings of the relationship between violence and the social order that emerged from the Revolution. Ultimately, it argues that the construction of the Terror as a difficult past after 9 Thermidor was rooted in a semiotic crisis created by the Revolution; that is, the increasing difficulty of reading and interpreting the social world in the context of the tumultuous events that unfolded from the storming of the Bastille.

Attitudes to Cataclysmic Events on the Eve of the French Revolution

Massacres, atrocities, disasters, wars, famine, and political upheaval: this litany of calamities was part and parcel of the collective memory of European men and women on the eve of the French Revolution. Historians of Europe have shown that there was a steady decline in the incidence of violence in everyday life between the early modern and modern periods.[14] The agricultural revolution of the eighteenth century, the beginnings of industrialization, and the ongoing imposition of judicial order by ever stronger centralized states meant that increasing numbers of people had access to more and better food and fewer chances of meeting a violent death. Life, generally speaking, was becoming safer.[15] Yet Europeans did not need to look far for reminders that dangers abounded. The Thirty Years War (1618–1648) had left an imprint of death and destruction on European culture.[16] The Enlightenment emerged, at least in part, as a reaction to the religious violence of the preceding century. Incessant warfare continued throughout the period, from the War of the Spanish Succession at the beginning of the century (1701–1713) to the War of the Austrian Succession in its middle (1740–1748.) The Seven Years War alone (1756–1763) left over a million combatants dead, although most of them lay buried across the Atlantic.[17] Apart from war, the eighteenth century was also a period of extensive natural disasters.[18] The Lisbon Earthquake (1755) in particular left a lasting impression on Europeans, though the number of people killed in it was much lower than the number of people killed as a result of war. The eighteenth century, writes the philosopher Susan Neiman, "used the word *Lisbon* much as we use the word *Auschwitz* today."[19]

Collective attitudes toward cataclysmic events changed in the transition from the early modern to the modern period mainly because of two developments: secularization, and the emergence of the public sphere. Secularization is a controversial concept. In its classic formulation, it refers to the growing rationalization and declining religiosity of the modern world. One of the major results of the Enlightenment, according to this view, was the gradual replacement of belief with scientific understanding. The sociologist Max Weber referred to this transition to modernity as the "disenchantment" of the world.[20] This view of secularization has come under increasing criticism in recent decades. Religion, scholars point out, has not faded from modern life. The relationship between science and faith, Enlightenment and religion, was never as antagonistic as the narrative of secularization would have it. Instead, what has emerged is a more complex set of accommodations, whereby church and secular society adapt to each other.[21]

In the case of French history, the critique of secularization has yielded a more nuanced understanding of the changing place of religion in everyday life. The Enlightenment had its religious dimensions, and most of the *philosophes* that were identified with it held on to religious belief.[22] A majority of the population clung to Catholic rituals even after the aggressive dechristianizing campaigns of the French Revolution. *Laïcité*, the French version of secularization, emerged in the nineteenth century in an effort to codify the relationship between state and church, but that does not mean that religious faith was disappearing from the lives of French men and women.[23] Nevertheless, it remains clear that the transition from the early modern to the modern periods entailed a profound transformation of the place of religion in everyday life. Perhaps it is best to understand secularization as a change in the degree to which people possess a sense of existential security, "that is, the feeling that survival is secure enough that it can be taken for granted."[24]

What does all this have to do with changing attitudes to cataclysmic events in the period leading up to the French Revolution? As life in Europe became increasingly safer, religious explanations for massive destruction became less common or less appealing. Narratives written in the aftermath of the Saint Bartholomew's Day Massacre (1572) show that people at the time made sense of the carnage mostly by referring to divine will. Most interpretations of the event situated it in the context of the great cataclysms mentioned in the Bible: the deluge, Sodom and Gomorrah, the Babylonian exile—all evidence of God's anger.[25] In contrast, authorities turned to science in order to make sense of disaster after the Lisbon Earthquake. The Portuguese secretary of state, the marquis of Pombal, distributed a questionnaire to the parish priests of the country in 1756, but, tellingly, the questions were mostly scientific in nature, marking a "repudiation of those who viewed the earthquake primarily as an act of God."[26]

Although some French writers did interpret the violence of the Revolution from a religious perspective, theological explanations were becoming less and less persuasive by the late eighteenth century.[27] This "secularization of catastrophe" matters for the aftermath of the Terror because it means that those who sought to make sense of revolutionary violence after 9 Thermidor had to look less in the realm of divine will and more in the realm of human action.[28] In this context, the bloodshed of the Revolution became a political rather than a theological problem. This politicization of cataclysmic events would have all kinds of implications for questions of retribution, redress, and memory; implications that will be explored more fully in the following chapters.

The second development that transformed how Europeans approached cataclysmic events was the emergence of the public sphere. Here too there is considerable disagreement on what this term means and what it implies for our understanding of the past. It was coined by the German theorist Jürgen Habermas, who used it to describe a new kind of collectivity that came into being in eighteenth-century Europe. The public sphere marked an area of social life where literate individuals, mostly bourgeois men, entered into critical debate with each other, relying only on their reason. At first the debates were mostly about literature. But as they turned from aesthetics to politics, the public sphere became an area of opposition to the state, an autonomous region, separate from the court or the home, where the status quo could be questioned in relative freedom. Habermas argued that the public sphere took shape through various social institutions, such as the literary salons of eighteenth-century Paris, the coffeehouses of eighteenth-century London, and "everywhere," thanks to the printing press. In France, according to Habermas, the public sphere assumed its full political function after the publication of the state budget by the minister of finance, Jacques Necker, in 1781. The publication of the *Compte Rendu*, which made the dire fiscal situation of the monarchy clear, caused such a stir that, from that moment on, "the public sphere in the political realm . . . could no longer be effectively put out of commission."[29]

Habermas's concept of the public sphere has had a tremendous impact on the historiography of the French Revolution. From literary salons to courtroom dramas, from medical advertisements to restaurants, historians have used it to illuminate the emergence of new arenas of contestation in Old Regime France, where notions of self, society, and the relationship between them were refashioned, sometimes in radical ways.[30] The concept and its historiographical uses have also been criticized roundly as a fantasy of egalitarian, democratic, and rational communication; a fantasy that, needless to say, never had its corollary on the ground.[31] Perhaps the public sphere is best understood as a metaphor, which brings together several processes in one iconic image: the rise of literacy, the expansion of the press, the growth of capitalism, and the emergence of a new social imaginary.[32]

These processes changed how Europeans experienced cataclysmic events. The early modern press circulated stories of violence, crime, and disasters in a variety of ways. Criminal tribunals in the seventeenth and eighteenth centuries published detailed accounts of the cases they were trying, usually in the form of posters or broadsheets. Sensationalized accounts, featuring glorified outlaws and smugglers, captured the imagination of French men and women in the *bibliothèque bleue*, a series of cheap pamphlets and books that were sold in villages and towns by traveling peddlers of literature, the *colporteurs*.[33] News spread faster and to more readers, creating a sense of contemporaneity; that is, the perception shared by more and more people of experiencing a particular event at the same time, even from a great distance.[34] Rates of literacy were not an impediment to the dissemination of printed content. In seventeenth-century France, about 29 percent of men and 14 percent of women were able to sign their names on official documents. By the late eighteenth century, this figure rose to 48 percent for men and 27 percent for women.[35] But even those who could not read had access to printed information. Literate members of rural communities would read the news to others while working in the field. In Paris, people could pay to have the news read out loud to them.[36] The circulation of crime stories created a sense that danger was all around, even though the actual incidence of everyday violence was declining.[37]

The rise of the public sphere, with its intimate ties to reading and writing, changed the relationship between representation and reality, words and things.[38] As visual and verbal representations circulated through society in growing numbers and frequencies, so the awareness of their power to shape public perceptions grew among those who produced them and, among those who consumed them, an increasing concern over their ability to manipulate people. An anonymous pamphlet published at the outbreak of the French Revolution illustrates the point. The pamphlet, titled *On the Means to Communicate Immediately with the People*, proposed a variety of machines that would make it possible to share the deliberations of the newly formed National Assembly with a large population. These included a giant megaphone or a mobile sonic projector for transmitting information.[39] That the anonymous author could imagine the means to communicate to a mass audience long before the technological capabilities to do so existed attests to what Lynn Hunt has referred to as the increasing visibility of society at the time of the Revolution.[40] More than 1,300 newspapers came into being between 1789 and 1799. The historian Jeremy Popkin described this prodigious output as "the collective creation of a society searching for new ways to govern itself."[41]

Secularization and the rise of the public sphere thus changed how Europeans processed and responded to cataclysmic events. As the place of religion in everyday life was transformed, so debates about the roots and consequences of massive destruction had less to do with divine will and more to do with human action. The emergence of the public as an arena of contestation led to a growing recognition of the power of words to incite discord, but also to end it. Violence and its effects on society became subjects of public debate.

The Debate on Violence and Society during the French Revolution

The French Revolution is inseparable from violence. From the storming of the Bastille in 1789 to Napoleon's rise to power in the late 1790s, most of its defining moments featured riots, insurrections, military exploits, massacres, executions, or assassinations. The seizure of the Bastille was a violent affair that left more than a hundred people dead. It was only after this that the press began to define what was happening in France as a revolution.[42] The assassination of Jean-Paul Marat in July 1793 was a major catalyst for the Terror.[43] This does not mean, however, that we have to endorse Simon Schama's damning verdict that "in some depressingly, unavoidable sense, violence *was* the Revolution itself."[44] As Micah Alpaugh has shown in a recent study of political demonstrations in Paris during the Revolution, only 7 percent of these gatherings became violent. For the most part, Parisians engaged in politics nonviolently, even taking special care to avoid escalation.[45] The Revolution was not violent alone, but violence was inherent to it, an essential feature that made it what it was. Following it, the adjectives "memorable and violent" appeared in the *Dictionnaire de l'Académie française*'s definition of the word *révolution*.[46] All along the revolutionary decade, violence was "both a reality and a topic of passionate discussion."[47]

Much of this discussion focused on popular violence. The journalist Elysée Loustalot left memorable descriptions of several instances early on in the Revolution, when lynch mobs killed noblemen and paraded their severed heads around Paris. Describing the fate of Bertier de Sauvigny, the royal *intendant* of Paris, Loustalot wrote how the crowd tore his "heart from its palpitating entrails."[48] Edmund Burke described how the Palace of Versailles had been left "swimming in blood, polluted by massacre, and strewed with scattered limbs and mutilated carcasses" after the October Days.[49] Graphic descriptions of this sort were often hyperbolic. The October Days, for example, were violent, but they hardly left the palace "strewed with scattered limbs." All told, the crowd killed two guardsmen. Yet this hyperbole was indicative of changing sensibilities. According to Alain Corbin, scenes of cruelty and carnage were associated with religious ritual and the sacred in the early modern period, but this association was severed in the eighteenth century, and consequently, massacre became intolerable, an outrage against public decency. It became a mark of social distinction to express horror in the face of such violence. During the Revolution, "murder and desecration by angry mobs horrified sensitive souls desperate to make sense of the sudden outbreak of blind, anonymous violence in a society suddenly deprived of its key symbols."[50]

The instances of lynching early in the Revolution gave rise to debates about the relationship between popular violence and the creation of a new social order. On the one hand, the violence of the crowd was seen as legitimate. It was an expression of the popular will. As such, it had a constructive, even foundational, capacity. The people's fury could cleanse the nascent Republic of impure elements. Defending the lynching of Bertier, the otherwise moderate deputy of the Third Estate Antoine Barnave wondered aloud whether the blood that had just been spilled was so pure.[51] Following the September Massacres, Tallien wrote that these were horrific events—a sentiment shared by the majority of revolutionaries—but that "in a time of revolution and disturbance, it is necessary to throw a veil" over them.[52] Popular violence in short was justified as part of the collateral damage of the Revolution and as a necessary element in the regeneration of the French people. On the other hand, popular violence was unpredictable, uncontrollable, sliding all too easily into outright criminality. In this sense, it had a destructive capacity that threatened to rip the delicate fabric of society apart. Faced with popular violence, the revolutionaries found themselves in a bind. They knew that the crowd's spontaneous action had often served their cause, but they also knew it could end in a bloody cycle that would engulf the entire revolutionary project.[53]

The ambivalence of the revolutionaries toward popular violence was also a matter of temperament. Most revolutionary leaders, after all, were bourgeois men. They spoke of *le peuple* incessantly, but they were repulsed by what they saw as its ignorance, its lack of refinement. Jérôme Pétion, the future mayor of Paris, acknowledged the usefulness of popular riots in 1791. "There are insurrections," he wrote, "that I cannot condemn, for they are useful to public safety, or they are ones where the people shows itself in all its majesty." "But," he continued, "calm energy suits me better. . . . I abhor excess. Turmoil and disorder dishonor the people and show it to be unfit for liberty."[54] This attitude expressed itself also in how revolutionary legislators viewed the participation of women in urban riots. Women took an active part in many of the revolutionary *journées*. They did not shy away from violence, whether in the form of the *bagarre*—street brawls—or as leaders of the crowd, as was the case in the October Days.[55] Revolutionary leaders tended to extoll the republican virtues of these women, but at the same time they were uncomfortable with the implications of such participation for the traditional role of women in the family.[56] Revolutionary leaders praised the spontaneous actions of the people and of the women among them, but at the same time they were terrified of the inherent uncontrollability of both groups, their inability to be governed.

The revolutionaries did not argue only about popular violence, but also about the state's right to execute its citizens. In 1791, the National Assembly spent several days debating the abolition of the death penalty. Those who argued that the death penalty should be maintained believed that the state had both the right and the duty to sentence certain people to death. A citizen who has taken the life of another, so the argument went, excluded himself or herself from the social contract. He or she had to pay with their own life to maintain the stability of the social order. "The death penalty is the fundamental basis of all political aggregation," argued the deputy Jean-Antelme Brillat-Savarin, who would go on to win fame as a pioneer of modern gastronomy.[57] Executions had to be dramatic and spectacular so as to deter future criminals. "It is extremely important," claimed the deputy Joseph Golvan Thouault de la Boverie, "that a man, exposed to all the passions of humanity, returns home after an execution with his heart penetrated by terror and dread."[58]

Those who argued for the abolition of the death penalty maintained that it was both inhumane and ineffectual. Drawing on the ideas of the Italian *philosophe* Cesare Beccaria, whose *Treatise on Crime and Punishments* (1764) had a tremendous impact on judicial reform in Europe, the deputy and magistrate Adrien Duport argued that there was a general tendency to overestimate the influence of the law on human behavior.[59] Education, the inculcation of proper values and sentiments, was a better way of preventing future crimes. "The sight of spilled blood," Duport added, "encourages crime."[60] Maximilien Robespierre delivered one of the most eloquent arguments against the death penalty. He claimed that society had neither right nor reason to condemn an individual to death. Once the person in question had been detained, and no longer presented a threat to society, what reason could there be to kill him, except for vengeance? Robespierre believed that shame would be a much more useful deterrent. Executions were nothing but "juridical murder," and an affront to public decency. The primary duty of legislators was to shape public mores, but violent spectacles corrupt them. If the law enables "cruel scenes and corpses murdered by torture before the eyes of the people . . . it will distort notions of justice and injustice in the hearts of the citizens."[61]

The death penalty was maintained eventually, but this debate illustrates to what extent the Revolution opened up fundamental questions about the relationship between violence and the social order. According to the historian Paul Friedland, the debate on the death penalty was a laboratory of sorts, where different conceptions of society and politics were brought to light and into conflict with each other. In this debate, Friedland wrote, "we can witness radical historical shifts in a kind of slow motion, as individuals struggled to balance their desire for change with long-held preconceptions about the nature of punishment."[62] The revolutionary attitude toward violence was ambivalent at its core. On the one hand, violence and force were necessary to implement laws. And popular violence often saved the revolutionaries from their own faintheartedness. On the other hand, violence unleashed a dynamic that was unpredictable and uncontrollable. The sight of spilled blood had a barbarizing effect on the mores of the people. Revolutionary violence was both necessary and unwelcome, both the guarantor of the new social order the revolutionaries were trying to create and its very undoing.

From the Foundation of a New Society to a Difficult Past

The attitudes of Europeans toward mass violence and natural disasters changed in the decades before the French Revolution. Much of this change had to do with sensibilities. To be horrified by massacre became a sign of a sensitive soul and a mark of social distinction. The Revolution opened up a debate about the relationship between violence and the social order. The revolutionaries were horrified by popular violence and at the same time they viewed it as necessary, hence legitimate. The construction of the Terror as a difficult past after 9 Thermidor was rooted in these broader developments. As Alain Corbin put it, "After Thermidor, the new sensibility began to take hold. In retrospect, people began to describe the violent mobs of years past as 'cannibals.' Tales of bloodthirsty violence began to appear in the summer of 1794." The outpouring of these tales, according to Corbin, "would leave indelible traces on the national memory."[63]

The construction of the Terror as a difficult past entailed a transformation in its meaning from a means to create a new order to an event of mass violence that one had to come to terms with. It is difficult to talk of a unitary concept of terror during the French Revolution. The term meant different things to different people, and it was used for various purposes. In June 1793, for example, Louis Antoine de Saint-Just, who would go on to become Robespierre's right-hand man in the Committee of Public Safety, accused the Girondins of having created a "system of terror" to encourage the hatred of Paris in the provinces.[64] After the assassination of Jean-Paul Marat, whose famous newspaper *L'ami du peuple* became the most influential platform for the sansculottes, numerous popular societies demanded that the government turn to terror in order to vanquish the enemies of the Revolution. Thus, a day after the assassination, a political club in Paris assured the Convention that "our calm and the force of our union will terrorize tyrants." The editors of another periodical warned their readers that "it is only by striking the soul of traitors with terror that you will have assured the independence of the fatherland."[65] But the clearest articulation of the concept of revolutionary Terror, or at least the most famous one, was delivered by Robespierre in February 1794, when the repression was well under way. Terror, according to Robespierre, was necessary in order to create a republic of virtue. The violence employed by the revolutionary government was necessary not only in order to break the will of counterrevolutionaries, but also in order to create a new moral order. Robespierre described this moral order as a utopia: "We want to substitute . . .

morality for egoism, probity for honor, principles for custom, duty for propriety, the empire of reason for the tyranny of fashion. . . . The greatness of man for the pettiness of the great."[66] The Terror, as described by Robespierre, was a transformative experience. It was terrible, to be sure, but the French people would emerge the better for it. Before 9 Thermidor, the Terror was defined in terms of the future it would bring about.[67]

After 9 Thermidor, however, the Terror was defined in terms of its negative impact on the Republic. On 14 Thermidor, Betrand Barère, who had been one of the "twelve who ruled" alongside Robespierre, claimed that the measures employed by the revolutionary government before 9 Thermidor amounted to a "system" that robbed patriots of their "liberty and their trust" in the political project of the Revolution.[68] He compared Robespierre to Caligula, arguing that the former encouraged the centralization of power "in order to usurp it," and called on the Convention to "substitute inflexible justice for stupid Terror."[69] The Convention heeded the call, at least in part, for in the same session it abrogated the Law of 22 Prairial that had led to a dramatic increase in the rate of executions during the summer of 1794—the so-called Great Terror.[70] It also decreed the reorganization of the revolutionary tribunal, ordered that an indictment be prepared against its chief prosecutor, Fouquier-Tinville, and began the reform of the revolutionary government, most notably by deciding that from then on four members of the Committee of Public Safety would rotate monthly, a measure that was aimed at ensuring that this body would not be able to assume dictatorial powers again.

The basic elements in the Thermidorian rhetoric about the Reign of Terror were already articulated in these early statements. First, the Terror constituted a system of oppression. It was a mass crime perpetrated intentionally and meticulously against the French people. Lexicometric studies have found a marked increase in the usage of the phrases "the system of Terror" and "the system of the Terror" after 9 Thermidor.[71] Second, the main culprit behind this system of oppression was Robespierre. There was no end to the aspersions cast on *l'incorruptible* in this moment of the Revolution: Nero, ferocious tiger, bloodthirsty tyrant, monster, Caligula, Catiline.[72] An advertisement for a new book on Oliver Cromwell noted that "in reading about his life, one would find the same system of oppression operating in the same manner; one would believe oneself to be traversing a history of the present day."[73] According to Bronislaw Baczko, the impression created by the newspapers, parliamentary records, and pamphlets of the time is that "all of France awoke on 10 Thermidor anti-Robespierrist."[74] Consequently—this is the third element in the Thermidorian rhetoric about the Terror—the oppression came to an end with the fall of Robespierre. The government remained revolutionary, but the Thermidorians drew a clear distinction between the regime that had been in place before 9 Thermidor and the regime that came into power since then. The former was identified with vice, crime, and despotism, while the latter was identified with virtue, justice, and liberty. The speech by Tallien, which opened this chapter, ended by declaring that "terror . . . is the most powerful weapon of tyranny, and that justice . . . alone should be the order of the day," thus establishing an inverse symmetry with the famous call from September 1793 to "make terror the order of the day."[75]

Of course, this conception of the Terror did not correspond to the realities of Year II. Revolutionary violence was neither as systematic nor as controlled as the Thermidorians would have it. As Jean-Clément Martin pointed out, there was little ideological or political unity in the Reign of Terror.[76] Nor did the repressive measures employed by the Jacobins cease with the downfall of Robespierre. Mette Harder has shown recently that the legislative purge, which had led to the arrest and execution of many members of the Convention, continued well beyond 9 Thermidor.[77] To paraphrase Annie Jourdan, if the perception of the Terror that most people still hold today is something of a myth, it was the Thermidorians who invented it.[78]

They did so for good reasons. Many of the leaders who shaped the Thermidorian rhetoric about the Terror were themselves implicated in the political repression of Year II. The revolutionary career of Jean-Lambert Tallien is a case in point. As a *représentant en mission*, he oversaw the repression of the federalist revolt in Bordeaux in 1793. As the Terror radicalized, and after his common-law wife Thérésia Cabarrus was arrested, he turned against Robespierre. He was probably among the organizers of the coup on 9 Thermidor, and, subsequently, he reinvented himself as the persecutor of *terroristes*. By the time he delivered his famous address in August 1794, he was fast emerging as a key leader of the Reaction, "an idol of the Convention."[79] Tallien and other revolutionary leaders had good reasons to describe the Terror in a way that would minimize their role in it.[80]

The image of the Terror that emerged from Tallien's address was completely different from the image that emerged from Robespierre's address several months earlier. In Robespierre's address, the Terror was defined by the future; in Tallien's reformulation, it was described as receding into the past. Robespierre's articulation of the Terror was remarkably abstract. It was theoretically astute, groundbreaking even, but it was devoid of any references to the guillotine, to cadavers, and to prisons; devoid, in short, of any references to the sensory realities of the repression. In contrast, Tallien's discussion of the Terror was intensely corporeal. It resounded with the smells, sights, and sounds of massive violence: "Death has to be rendered atrocious in order to spread fear," he claimed. "At first the idea of hemlock suffices to terrify the imagination; soon it has to be followed by . . . the sight of spilled blood; then the victim must be surrounded by other victims. . . . A man must watch the death of fifty others before he is killed."[81] Finally, the Thermidorian transformation of the meaning of the Terror entailed redefining its relationship to the social order. Tallien implied that all governments rely on fear and violence to a certain extent, or at least on the threat of violence, but whereas legitimate governments target people because of what they do, the Reign of Terror targeted people because of what they are. The actions of legitimate governments produce "potential fear," which is the consequence of one's actions, whereas the measures employed by a system of terror result in "incessant torment . . . which establishes itself in the mind in spite of one's innocence."[82] If Robespierre's discussion of the Terror focused on its political goals—in a word, regeneration—Tallien's definition of Terror focused on its emotional effects.[83]

The Problem of Representing the Violence of the Terror

How could those who had lived through the Terror describe its effects on themselves and on others? How could language capture the physiological and psychological experience of mass violence? This problem was not unique, of course, to the revolutionary era. Violence and language have an uneasy relationship. As Paul Ricoeur argued, they mark each other's limits; indeed, they are opposites.[84] This is captured well in what parents say to children who have been acting out violently: use your words. Periods of political violence are often accompanied by semiotic destabilization. Repressive regimes impact not only people's lives, but also the social production of meaning. They invent new words that mask the gruesome realities they create, while victims often find themselves in a linguistic crisis of sorts, unable to narrate what they had been through.[85]

The concern over the instability of language was explicit in the aftermath of the Terror. In September 1794, Michel-Edme Petit, a relatively moderate member of the Convention, argued that those who had been responsible for the violence of Year II "have introduced a great number of new words into language, classifications that they have chosen at their own discretion for men and things, to be hated or loved by a people that has been led astray."[86] Petit proposed to outlaw certain words, such as "Jacobin," "Montagnard," or "Muscadin," because of their propensity to incite discord. The royalist journalist Jean-Gabriel Peltier wrote in 1797 that "when one looks back at all the names of parties and factions . . . one doubts whether language itself could ever be forgiven for the crimes it had committed."[87] To quote the historian Sophia Rosenfeld, after 9 Thermidor the revolutionaries were concerned with "ending the logomachy."[88]

These misgivings about the precise meaning of words had a direct bearing on the construction of the Terror as a difficult past. Dealing with a difficult past begins by naming it; that is, by transforming a series of chaotic experiences into a narrative that makes sense. This is often a painful process, but it was especially challenging in the context of the revolutionary decade. It was challenging because the Revolution had given rise to a crisis of representation by instituting a new relation to the social world.[89] Society, so to speak, became the ground of meaning instead of religion.[90] The substitution of the social for the divine as the ultimate frame of reference made the process of transforming the experiences of the Terror into a coherent narrative especially difficult because it rendered the meaning of words and of names unstable and uncertain. The Revolution, in other words, constituted a rupture in the symbolic order; that is, the web of customs, institutions, mores, rules, norms, practices, rituals, and traditions within which human beings interpret the world around them.[91] The crisis of meaning that the Revolution engendered made it especially difficult to find the right terms, indeed the right language, to describe the effects of the Terror on self and society.

Consider the following letter, which was sent in February 1795 by an ordinary citizen named Pindray to the Committee of Public Education. The subject of the letter was grammar. Specifically, Pindray had written to complain about some new words that have been introduced during the Revolution. He mentioned two words in particular: *burocratie*, spelled thus in the original letter, and *sanguinocratie*. The first word was coined in 1791 to refer to the power of state officials. The second word was coined at some point in 1793 or 1794 to refer to the Reign of Terror. Pindray's problem was that these compound words mixed stems from two different linguistic origins. The word *burocratie* was derived from the French word *bureau*, meaning "desk or office," and the Greek suffix *-kratia*, meaning "the power of." It could thus be translated as "office-power," or more precisely, "the power of administration." The second word was derived from the French adjective *sanguin*, meaning bloody, and the same suffix, *-kratia*. It could thus be translated as "the power of blood" or, if one prefers, "bloody power." In both cases, the stems of these words mixed French (from Latin) and Greek origins. This rendered them linguistically incorrect. Indeed, citizen Pindray found them to be "absolutely barbaric." If one wanted a new word to designate what he referred to as the "despotism of commissaries," it should be *graphocratie*, from the Greek word *grafeio*, meaning "desk or office." As for *sanguinocratie*, the correct word for "the power of blood" would be *aimatocratie*, from the Greek word for blood, *aíma*.[92]

Pindray's letter is interesting for what it tells us about the difficulty of naming the Terror in its immediate aftermath. There is something misplaced about his linguistic pedantry seven months or so after the fall of Robespierre. It seems wrong to be worried about grammar when the country was reeling from fifteen months of political repression. But the more interesting aspect of the letter is the tension between the two neologisms. The English form of the first word, "bureaucracy," has become a permanent fixture in our vocabulary. It connotes rules, regularity, predictability, and paperwork: the quiet world of the office that Max Weber identified as the linchpin of modern rationality.[93] The second word has all but disappeared from language. There is some evidence that it was fairly familiar at the time of the Revolution: Louis-Sebastien Mercier has an entry on the *sanguinocrates* in his ethnographic compendium *Paris pendant la Révolution*.[94] The word brings to mind rivers of blood, torn limbs, and the shrieks of the dying; images reminiscent of Phlegethon, the river of boiling souls in Dante's *Inferno*.[95] Weber's rationality and Dante's hell; paperwork and the guillotine; the predictability of office routine and the unpredictability of violence unleashed—the two poles of modern state power.[96] Pindray put his finger here, probably without being aware of it, on the crisis of meaning that made it difficult to find terms for the new forms of power that the Revolution hurled onto the surface of social life.

One man who took it upon himself to do just that was the revolutionary journalist Louis-Marie Prudhomme. Prudhomme was the founder of the successful newspaper *Révolutions de Paris*. As a republican, he was an enthusiastic supporter of the Revolution in its early days, but like so many others who had held similar political views, he grew disillusioned as it became more radical and more violent. He was arrested briefly in June 1793. By early 1794 he had had enough: he closed down his paper in February and left Paris with his family. Having kept a low profile for several years, he returned to the capital during the early days of the Directory and tried to revive his journalistic career. It was in that context that he conceived of a new project: an exhaustive catalogue of the Revolution's crimes. It was a perilous enterprise, or at least it was important for Prudhomme to present it as such. "I am the first," he stated, "to employ his iron quill with courage in order to trace the deplorable repertoire of all the offenses human perversity is capable of."[97] In an introductory historical essay titled *On the Necessity to Make the Crimes of Tyrants Known during Their Reign*, Prudhomme provided a long list of regimes that, throughout history, have persecuted, repressed, and killed their own people. These included the "religious tyranny of Moses" and the mass executions ordered by Charlemagne, the St. Bartholomew's Day Massacre, and the expulsion of the Protestants from France.[98] Prudhomme claimed that no one has ever dared to hold those in power accountable for their wrongdoing. "Terror has engulfed the universe. . . . And no one dares reproach the executioners of the human species."[99] Against this background of silence throughout history, Prudhomme presented his project as speaking truth to power: an epigraph on the frontispiece of the third volume reads simply "I have dared!"

Prudhomme's project consisted, in its final form, of six volumes and more than five thousand pages. Published as a serial in 1796–1797, it was titled *A General and Impartial History of the Errors, Offenses, and Crimes Committed during the French Revolution*. It contained a dictionary of the dead, which was a list of the people who had been condemned to death by revolutionary tribunals, including such details as their age, place of residence, occupation, and the nature of the charges against them. The following is a representative entry: "Perrier, widow of Hilaire, age 62, born in Clermont, department of Puy-de-Dome, residing there, a cart-woman condemned to death on 25 Messidor, Year II, as an enemy of the people, for having said that she has been ruined ever since France came to be governed by the race of buggers."[100] The *General History* also included Prudhomme's interpretation of the Revolution, and reports on atrocities, crimes, and various instances of brutality committed between 1787 and 1795. These reports formed the bulk of the project, and they were organized according to the political chronology of the Revolution. So, for example, volume 3 lists crimes that occurred under the Constituent Assembly, whereas volumes 5 and 6 are devoted to crimes that were committed when the National Convention was in power. Prudhomme collected these stories of violence and excess from readers all over the country, and he seems to have published them all, with little to no editorial discretion.

The result is monumental and chaotic; the work is exhaustive and fragmentary at the same time. Historical analysis is interspersed with accounts of graphic violence. Mourning, commemoration, shock, a desire to make sense of a chain of events that seemed to defy reason, and a tinge of self-aggrandizing all operate side by side in Prudhomme's text. Perhaps because of this, historians of the Revolution have not made much use of it. According to Mona Ozouf, all the basic explanations for the Terror have already been laid out *in nuce* during the Thermidorian Reaction. The more graphic tales of violence published in the same period are of little use to historians, because their main goal was to scandalize the public, not to explain what had taken place.[101] Ozouf is right that the goal of the more graphic accounts of revolutionary violence was to provoke an emotional response. Prudhomme, for example, stated that he would "set frightening portraits of butchery . . . [before] the reader's distraught soul."[102] But it is unfortunate that the style of the *General History* and other similar texts has led historians to dismiss it. It is precisely this odd combination of the horrific and the analytic, the commemorative and the titillating, the comprehensive and the fragmentary that makes Prudhomme's text valuable as a historical source. As Joseph Zizek has argued, Prudhomme's project illuminates a post-Thermidorian dilemma: "What kind of 'history' was possible after the Terror?"[103]

Prudhomme certainly believed that his project marked a new way of writing history. He was especially proud of the inclusion of numerous lists in the *General History*: lists of legislators and of laws, of *départements* and communes, of civil and military courts, nomenclatures, chronological tables, and statistical data. Prudhomme believed that the inclusion of "objective" facts—today, this kind of information would be called raw data—rendered his history scientific.[104] It was also part of his mission as he saw it: to be the voice of a society that had been torn apart by revolutionary violence. "The orphans of a nation that has been buried in a coffin raise their eyes to the heavens and ask, 'where is the man who would be courageous enough to describe the secret and public crimes of our tyrants'. . . . Well, I shall be that man."[105] Throughout the book, Prudhomme engaged in numerous instances of naming and shaming public officials for their excess, corruption, and cruelty.

The *General History* also included many images. One of them is an etching that appears in some editions of the work on the cover of the second volume.[106] At the center of the image is a man striking a dramatic pose, his hands stretched, his head turned to his left. He is looking at a group of women and children. The women seem to be weeping, and the children are on their knees in a posture that suggests they are begging or imploring. To his right is a bust with a seated figure holding a spear, and above it another figure that is hovering in the air while lifting some sort of curtain. Some human bodies are lying on the ground, perhaps dead. There seems to be a severed head. A group of men, their arms raised, is fading into the background. Demonic figures of some sort seem to be emerging from, or retreating into, dark clouds. A paragraph on the following page explains the curious image: "Time is lifting the veil of Error, which has covered the statue of Liberty. . . . Terror disappears in a chasm; the relatives of Victims demand justice from Posterity; it is promised to them by . . . a friend of Humanity."[107]

This vignette can be read as a visual representation of a difficult past. It captures the intersection of themes involved in coming to terms with mass violence: history and memory, truth and justice, loss and mourning.[108] It suggests that contemporaries were aware on some level that the Terror had not ended on 9 Thermidor, or at least that its ending was not a simple matter. Allegories

FIGURE 1.   Frontispiece to Prudhomme's *Histoire Générale*, 1796–1797. Credit: University of Chicago Special Collections.

of time, error, and liberty; the Terror fading, becoming part of the past; the victims turning to posterity, that is, to the future, demanding justice; the figure of the man, presumably Prudhomme himself, promising to deliver this to them through his project of listing and naming, calculating, and narrating. Prudhomme's image represents the notion that although the repression of Year II was over, its repercussions were still being felt all around.

The lists and tables in the *General History* also shed light on the difficulty of representing revolutionary violence after 9 Thermidor. In spite of Prudhomme's claim that the inclusion of all these lists marked an "absolutely new way" of writing history, there were actually numerous lists published during the Terror.[109] The journalist François-Barnabé Tisset published a list of the cases that were tried in front of the Revolutionary Tribunal in Paris. He titled it *Compte rendu aux sans-culottes* and prefaced it with a sardonic essay in which "Madam Guillotine" herself provides details about those "whom I have so amorously held in my arms and dispatched to the world beyond."[110] Lists with the names and addresses of legislators were published by the revolutionary government. The Office of the National Estate published lists with the names of those who had been convicted by revolutionary tribunals and whose property now belonged to the nation, including tables enumerating the confiscated possessions and their value. During and after the Terror there were numerous lists of victims published outside of France, especially in London, where there had been a significant presence of émigrés.[111] The publication and circulation of such lists in Year II attests to the democratic impulses behind the Terror. Even at the height of the repression, there was a commitment to render the workings of the revolutionary government transparent and accessible to all citizens.[112]

Prudhomme's fondness for lists was rooted in the political culture of Year II, but by the time the *General History* was published the context had changed, and with it the meaning of such catalogs. Before 9 Thermidor these various lists reflected the importance of transparency in the political culture of the Revolution. After 9 Thermidor, lists, catalogs, and nomenclatures were used in order to assess the effects of revolutionary violence, and especially the Terror, on society. The Swiss political economist François d'Ivernois, for example, used various mathematical methods to evaluate "the physical and moral depopulation of France" as a result of the revolutionary wars. D'Ivernois estimated that approximately three million people had died as a direct result of the Revolution and noted the "profound impression" made by the "daily executions" during the Terror.[113]

Prudhomme, too, was preoccupied with a general assessment of the damage caused by the violence of the Revolution. In the sixth volume of the *General History* he inserted a broadsheet titled "A General Table of the Disasters of the French Revolution." The broadsheet included the number of people who had been killed or who emigrated during the Revolution; the number of towns, villages, and castles destroyed; the number of laws passed; and a numerical assessment of the spoils of the revolutionary wars. According to Prudhomme, the French armies seized 8,900 cannons from enemy hands, as well as 268 thousand shotguns, more than four million pounds of gunpowder, and 334 flags. The broadsheet also listed the number of casualties in the colonies, broken down by race, and "the number of individuals who have committed suicide by hanging, drowning, or throwing themselves out of the window as a result of the Terror," as well as the number of women who died giving birth prematurely, and the number of individuals "driven mad by the Revolution."[114] Overall, Prudhomme estimated that more than two million lives had been lost as a direct result of the Revolution, and that the various legislative assemblies had passed about fifteen thousand new laws.

It is difficult, if not downright impossible, to verify Prudhomme's numbers. He did not provide the sources for his tally, and in any case his project was conceived and carried out in the immediate aftermath of the Terror, when the iron was hot, and outrage took precedence over the cool-headed verification

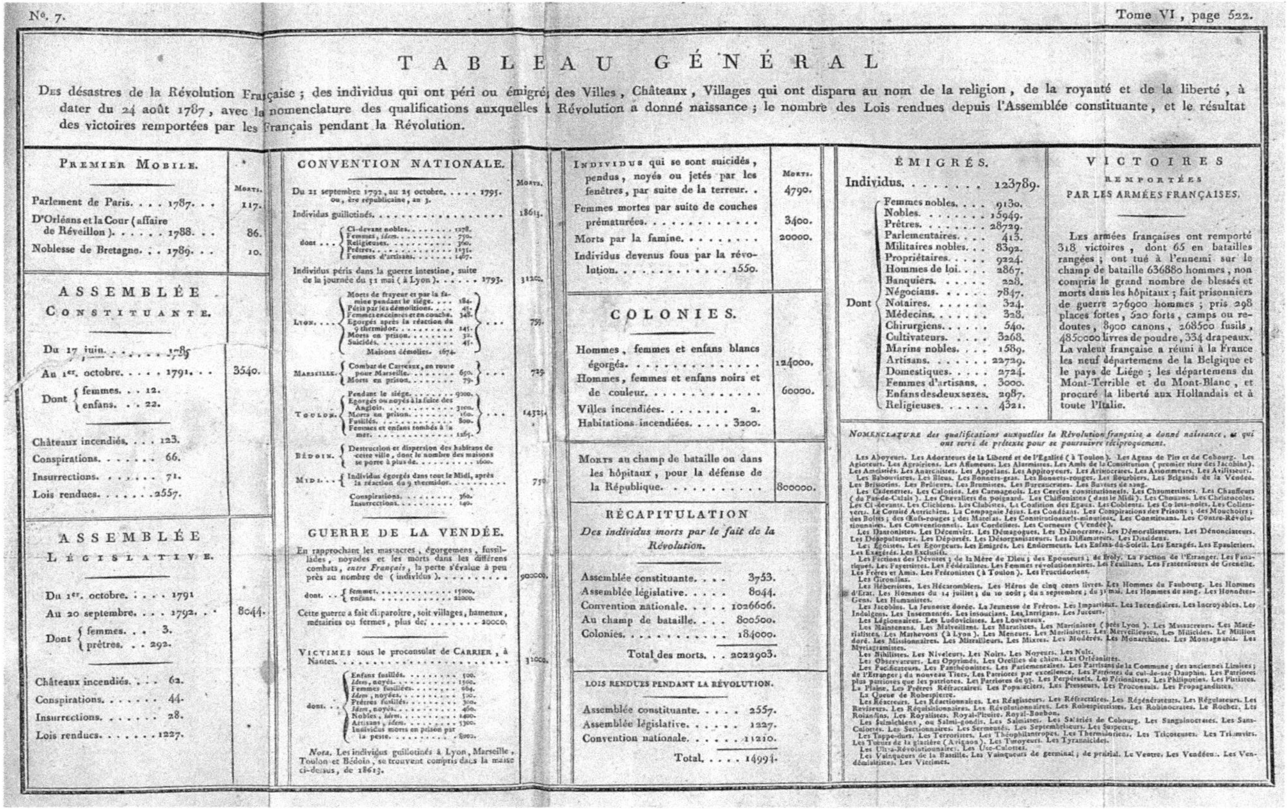

N°. 7. Tome VI, page 522.

TABLEAU GÉNÉRAL

Des désastres de la Révolution Française ; des individus qui ont péri ou émigré ; des Villes, Châteaux, Villages qui ont disparu au nom de la religion, de la royauté et de la liberté, à dater du 24 août 1787, avec la nomenclature des qualifications auxquelles la Révolution a donné naissance ; le nombre des Lois rendues depuis l'Assemblée constituante, et le résultat des victoires remportées par les Français pendant la Révolution.

Premier Mobile.

	Morts.
Parlement de Paris. . . . 1787. . .	117.
D'Orléans et la Cour (affaire de Réveillon). . . . . . 1788. . .	86.
Noblesse de Bretagne. . . 1789. . .	10.

Assemblée Constituante.

Du 17 juin. 1789	
Au 1er. octobre. . . . . . 1791. . .	3540.
Dont { femmes. . . 12. enfans. . . 22.	

Châteaux incendiés. . . . 123.
Conspirations. . . . . . . 66.
Insurrections. . . . . . . 71.
Lois rendues. . . . . . . 2557.

Assemblée Législative.

Du 1er. octobre. 1791	
Au 20 septembre. . . . 1792. .	8044.
Dont { femmes. . . 3. prêtres. . . 292.	

Châteaux incendiés. . . . 62.
Conspirations. . . . . . . 44.
Insurrections. . . . . . . 28.
Lois rendues. . . . . . . 1227.

Convention Nationale.

	Morts.
Du 21 septembre 1792, au 25 octobre. . . . . 1795. ou, ère républicaine, an 3.	
Individus guillotinés.	18613.
dont . . . { Ci-devant nobles. . . . 1278. Femmes, *idem*. . . . 750. Religieuses. . . . 350. Prêtres. . . . 1135. Femmes d'artisans. . . . 1467.	
Individus péris dans la guerre intestine, suite de la journée du 31 mai (à Lyon). . . . . 1793.	31200.
Lyon. . . . { Morts de frayeur et par la famine pendant le siége. . . . 184. Péris par les démolitions. . . . 45. Femmes enceintes et en couche. 348. Egorgés après la réaction du 9 thermidor. . . . 145. Morts en prison. . . . 32. Suicidés. . . . 45. Maisons démolies. 1674. } . . .	799.
Marseille. { Combat de Carreaux, en route pour Marseille. . . . 650. Morts en prison. . . . 79. } . . .	729.
Toulon. { Pendant le siége. . . . 9000. Egorgés ou noyés à la suite des Anglois. . . . 3100. Morts en prison. . . . 160. Fusillés. . . . 800. Femmes et enfans tombés à la mer. . . . 1265. } . . .	14325.
Bédoin. { Destruction et dispersion des habitans de cette ville, dont le nombre des maisons se porte à plus de. . . . 1600.	
Midi. . . { Individus égorgés dans tout le Midi, après la réaction du 9 thermidor. . . .	750
Conspirations. . . . 360. Insurrections. . . . 140.	

Guerre de la Vendée.

En rapprochant les massacres, égorgemens, fussillades, noyades et les morts dans les différens combats, *entre Français*, la perte s'évalue à peu près au nombre de (individus).	900000.
dont. . . { femmes. . . . 15000. enfans. . . . 22000.	
Cette guerre a fait disparoître, soit villages, hameaux, métairies ou fermes, plus de. . . . 20000.	
Victimes sous le proconsulat de Carrier, à Nantes.	32000.
dont. . . { Enfans fusillés. . . . 500. *Idem*, noyés. . . . 1500. Femmes fusillées. . . . 264. *Idem*, noyées. . . . 500. Prêtres fusillés. . . . 300. *Idem*, noyés. . . . 460. Nobles, *idem*. . . . 1400. Artisans, *idem*. . . . 5300. Individus morts en prison par la peste. . . . 3000.	

Nota. Les individus guillotinés à Lyon, Marseille, Toulon et Bédoin, se trouvent compris dans la masse ci-dessus, de 18613.

	Morts.
Individus qui se sont suicidés, pendus, noyés ou jetés par les fenêtres, par suite de la terreur. .	4790.
Femmes mortes par suite de couches prématurées.	3400.
Morts par la famine.	20000.
Individus devenus fous par la révolution. . . . . . 1550.	

Colonies.

Hommes, femmes et enfans blancs égorgés.	124000.
Hommes, femmes et enfans noirs et de couleur.	60000.
Villes incendiées. . . . . . 2.	
Habitations incendiées. . . . . 3200.	

Morts au champ de bataille ou dans les hôpitaux, pour la défense de la République.	800000.

Récapitulation

Des individus morts par le fait de la Révolution.

Assemblée constituante. . . .	3753.
Assemblée législative. . . .	8044.
Convention nationale. . . .	1026606.
Au champ de bataille. . . .	800500.
Colonies.	184000.
Total des morts. . .	2022903.

Lois rendues pendant la Révolution.

Assemblée constituante.	2557.
Assemblée législative.	1227.
Convention nationale.	11210.
Total. . . .	14994.

Émigrés.

Individus.		123789.
Dont	Femmes nobles. . . .	9130.
	Nobles. . . .	15949.
	Prêtres. . . .	28729.
	Parlementaires. . . .	413.
	Militaires nobles. . .	8392.
	Propriétaires. . . .	9224.
	Hommes de loi. . . .	2867.
	Banquiers. . . .	228.
	Négocians. . . .	7847.
	Notaires. . . .	324.
	Médecins. . . .	328.
	Chirurgiens. . . .	540.
	Cultivateurs. . . .	3268.
	Marins nobles. . . .	1589.
	Artisans. . . .	22729.
	Domestiques. . . .	2724.
	Femmes d'artisans. .	3000.
	Enfans des deux sexes.	2987.
	Religieuses. . . .	4321.

Victoires remportées par les armées françaises.

Les armées françaises ont remporté 318 victoires, dont 65 en batailles rangées ; ont tué à l'ennemi sur le champ de bataille 636880 hommes, non compris le grand nombre de blessés et morts dans les hôpitaux ; fait prisonniers de guerre 276900 hommes ; pris 298 places fortes, 520 forts, camps ou redoutes, 8900 canons, 268500 fusils, 485000 livres de poudre, 334 drapeaux. La valeur française a réuni à la France les neuf départemens de la Belgique et le pays de Liége ; les départemens du Mont-Terrible et du Mont-Blanc, et procuré la liberté aux Hollandais et à toute l'Italie.

Nomenclature des qualifications auxquelles la Révolution française a donné naissance, et qui ont servi de prétexte pour se poursuivre réciproquement.

Les Aboyeurs. Les Adorateurs de la Liberté et de l'Egalité (à Toulon). Les Agens de Pitt et de Cobourg. Les Agioteurs. Les Agrairiens. Les Affameurs. Les Alarmistes. Les Amis de la Constitution (premier titre des Jacobins). Les Amnistiés. Les Anarchistes. Les Appelans. Les Apitoyeurs. Les Aristocrates. Les Assommeurs. Les Avilisseurs.

Les Babouvistes. Les Bleus. Les Bonnets-gras. Les Bonnets-rouges. Les Bourbiers. Les Brigands de la Vendée. Les Brissotins. Les Brûleurs. Les Brumistes. Les Bureaucrates. Les Buveurs de sang.

Les Cadenettes. Les Calotins. Les Carmagnols. Les Cercles constitutionnels. Les Chaumettistes. Les Chauffeurs (du Pas-de-Calais). Les Chevaliers du poignard. Les Chiffonistes (dans le Midi). Les Chouans. Les Christocoles. Les Ci-devants. Les Clichiens. Les Clubistes. La Coalition des Egaux. Les Coblentz. Les Collets-noirs. Les Collets-verts. Le Comité Autrichien. La Compagnie Jésus. Les Condéans. Les Conspirations des Prisons ; des Mouchoirs ; des Boîtes ; des Œufs-rouges ; des Matelas. Les Constitutionnels-minutieux. Les Constituans. Les Contre-Révolutionnaires. Les Conventionnels. Les Cordeliers. Les Corneurs (Vendée).

Les Dantonistes. Les Décemvirs. Les Démagogues. Les Démocrates. Les Démoralisateurs. Les Dénonciateurs. Les Dépopulateurs. Les Déportés. Les Désorganisateurs. Les Diffamateurs. Les Dissidens.

Les Egoïstes. Les Egorgeurs. Les Emigrés. Les Endormeurs. Les Enfans-du-Soleil. Les Enragés. Les Epauletiers. Les Exagérés. Les Exclusifs.

Les Factions des Dévotes ; de la Mère de Dieu ; des Epouseurs ; de Broly. La Faction de l'Etranger. Les Fanatiques. Les Fayettistes. Les Fédéralistes. Les Femmes révolutionnaires. Les Feuillans. Les Fraterniseurs de Grenelle. Les Frères et Amis. Les Fréronistes (à Toulon). Les Fructidoriens.

Les Girondins.

Les Hébertistes. Les Hécatombiers. Les Héros de cinq cents livres. Les Hommes du Faubourg. Les Hommes d'Etat. Les Hommes du 14 juillet ; du 10 août ; du 2 septembre ; du 31 mai. Les Hommes de sang. Les Honnêtes-Gens. Les Humanistes.

Les Jacobins. La Jeunesse dorée. La Jeunesse de Fréron. Les Impartiaux. Les Incendiaires. Les Incroyables. Les Indulgens. Les Insermentés. Les insoucians. Les Intrigans. Les Jureurs.

Les Légionnaires. Les Ludovicistes. Les Louveteaux.

Les Maintenans. Les Malveillans. Les Maratistes. Les Martinistes (près Lyon). Les Massacreurs. Les Matérialistes. Les Mathevons (à Lyon). Les Meneurs. Les Merlinistes. Les Merveilleuses. Les Milicides. Le Million doré. Les Missionnaires. Les Mitrailleurs. Les Mixtes. Les Modérés. Les Monarchistes. Les Montagnards. Les Myriagramistes.

Les Nihilistes. Les Niveleurs. Les Noirs. Les Noyeurs. Les Nuls.

Les Observateurs. Les Opprimés. Les Oreilles de chien. Les Orléanistes.

Les Pacificateurs. Les Panthéonistes. Les Parlementaires. Les Partisans de la Commune ; des anciennes Limites ; de l'Etranger ; du nouveau Tiers. Les Patriotes par excellence. Les Patriotes du cul-de-sac Dauphin. Les Patriotes plus patriotes que les patriotes. Les Patriotes de 93. Les Perpétuels. Les Pétionistes. Les Philipotins. Les Pittistes. La Plaine. Les Prêtres Réfractaires. Les Populaciers. Les Presseurs. Les Proconsuls. Les Propagandistes.

La Queue de Robespierre.

Les Réacteurs. Les Réactionnaires. Les Régisseurs. Les Réfractaires. Les Régénérateurs. Les Régulateurs. Les Reviseurs. Les Réquisitionnaires. Les Révolutionnaires. Les Robespierristes. Les Robinocrates. Le Rocher. Les Rolandins. Les Royalistes. Royal-Pituite. Royal-Bonbon.

Les Salmichiens, ou Salmi-gondis. Les Salmistes. Les Salariés de Cobourg. Les Sanguinocrates. Les Sans-Culottes. Les Sectionnaires. Les Sermentés. Les Septembriseurs. Les Suspects.

Les Tappe-durs. Les Terroristes. Les Théophilantropes. Les Thermidoriens. Les Tricoteuses. Les Triumvirs. Les Tueurs de la glacière (Avignon). Les Tutoyeurs. Les Tyrannicides.

Les Ultra-Révolutionnaires. Les Use-Culottes.

Les Vainqueurs de la Bastille. Les Vainqueurs de germinal ; de prairial. Le Ventre. Les Vendéens. Les Vendémiairistes. Les Victimes.

FIGURE 2. Prudhomme's "General Table of the Disasters of the French Revolution," 1796–1797. Credit: Michigan State University Special Collections Library.

of facts. But the accuracy of Prudhomme's figures is beside the point. The point, rather, is the particular way he went about classifying and enumerating the consequences of the Terror. In the right-hand bottom section of the broadsheet, in tiny print, there is a list of names. It is titled "A nomenclature of the identifiers to which the French Revolution has given birth, and which have served as an excuse for people to persecute each other." It is a political taxonomy, listing the names of various groups and factions that appeared and disappeared during the Revolution. Some of these names remain well known today, such as Girondins, Montagnards, or Enragés. Others have faded into obscurity, such as the Démagogues, "the Knights of the Dagger," or "the Conspiracy of the Red Eggs."[115] The following sequence is especially delightful: "the Patriots; the Patriots par Excellence; the Patriots of the Dauphin Cul-de-Sac; the Patriots more Patriotic than the Patriots."[116] All told, Prudhomme listed 211 names in his political nomenclature.

Prudhomme's broadsheet makes for a strange set of juxtapositions: the number of suicides alongside the number of seized cannons; the number of women who have died giving birth prematurely alongside the number of chateaus that were burnt down; the number of people of color who were killed in the colonies alongside an exhaustive nomenclature of political factions. It brings to mind the *Celestial Emporium of Benevolent Knowledge*, the fictitious Chinese encyclopedia created by Jorge Luis Borges, which Michel Foucault quoted as the inspiration for his critique of modern systems of classification, *The Order of Things*.[117] In Borges's fabricated encyclopedia, animals are classified in a way that baffles the modern reader. They are categorized as "a) belonging to the Emperor, b) embalmed, c) tame, d) suckling pigs, e) mermaids, f) fabulous," and so on.[118] Foucault noted that the striking thing about Borges's encyclopedia was the impossibility of understanding its logic of classification. It was impossible to understand this logic because the common ground, which made it possible to juxtapose fabulous animals with animals that have been "drawn with a very fine camelhair brush," has been destroyed, and can only be accessed through excavation.[119] For us, the question that arises out of Prudhomme's table is: Do these things belong together? What is a political nomenclature doing alongside the number of people who have been driven mad by the events of the Revolution? Classification, of course, is not just a representation, or a way of organizing reality; it also constructs the reality it purports to describe. Prudhomme's project sheds light on the construction of the Terror as a difficult past because its fragmentary nature and the strange system of classification he seems to have employed suggest a social world that has become, in a sense, illegible.

What's in a Name?

One of the processes that shaped the social world, and at the same time made it difficult to read it during the Revolution, was naming. The revolutionaries named and renamed everything repeatedly and obsessively from the very beginning of the Revolution: people, places, and events. The representatives of the Third Estate in the meeting of the Estates-General renamed themselves the National Assembly in June 1789, thereby claiming their right to speak for all French men and women. The map of France was divided into departments, symmetrical administrative units that were named after rivers or mountains in their respective geographic regions. The concern with nomenclature became more apparent as the Revolution radicalized. Time and space were stamped with a whole new vocabulary. The Republican calendar, adopted in 1793, renamed the days and the months: *primidi*, *duodi*, and *tridi* became the first, second, and third days of the week, respectively. The months of winter were renamed *Brumaire* (October 22 to November 22), from the French *brume* meaning "fog," and *Nivôse* (December 21 to January 21), from the Latin adjective *nivosus* meaning "snowy." Three thousand towns and villages changed their name in Year II.[120] The city of Lyon, after being bombed into submission by revolutionary forces, was renamed Ville Affranchie (Liberated City). People renamed themselves or were renamed by others, sometimes against their will. Louis XVI was renamed Louis Capet after his failed attempt to flee France in 1791, signaling that he was to be treated from now on as an ordinary citizen. Numerous children received names drawn from the revolutionary nomenclature: *liberté*, *loi*, *fraternité*. A baby girl born in Épernay two weeks after the Convention adopted the Constitution of 1793 was named Victorine Constitution Liberté Égalité.[121]

Several factors drove the revolutionary preoccupation with names. It was an attempt to impose revolutionary values on the consciousness of contemporaries. The names of the months in the Republican calendar derived from the central place nature held in the political culture of the Revolution.[122] The symmetric division of the map of France inscribed the values of reason and rational planning on the spatial imagination of French citizens. Naming was also driven by ideology. Names that brought to mind the Old Regime were replaced with names that reflected the new political landscape. Thus, Montmartre became Mont-Marat and boys called Louis were renamed Brutus or Spartacus.[123] But names are not just expressions of values or ideological loyalties. They are also coordinates of the social world. They serve to orient oneself in the intricate web of identities, symbols, practices, and spaces that constitute daily interaction.[124] During the Revolution, this web was being rewoven repeatedly. As Denise Davidson argued, the aftermath of the Revolution saw "conscious and unconscious . . . efforts to find more reliable and stable ways to order and read society."[125] The emergence of a new nomenclature marked an effort to stabilize a social reality that was fluctuating in the most extreme ways.

After 9 Thermidor, there was widespread concern with changing or modifying names that reminded one too explicitly of the Terror. A functionary in the National Treasury by the name of Aïgoin sent a petition to the Convention several days after 9 Thermidor. He was asking to change his son's name. Apparently, he had named his son Robespierre while in the throes of revolutionary enthusiasm, but now, in the new political landscape, he wanted to spare him the burden of being named after "the most frightful, the most dangerous conspirator."[126] Children who were born during the Terror and were given names that reflected the ideological preferences of the moment rushed as adults to have their names changed. Thus, Julien Fructidor Brossard had his middle name removed by a formal act, and one "L'aurore de la liberté Dufour" changed his name to the rather more modest Louis Dufour.[127]

In 1797, Jean-Baptist Dauchez, member of the Council of Five Hundred, presented a special report "concerning the deletion of revolutionary first names given to children whose birth was recorded during the Reign of Terror."[128] Dauchez was a lawyer from Arras, a man of royalist leanings. He had been arrested briefly during the Terror. He was elected to represent Pas-de-Calais in the Council of Five Hundred in 1797 but was removed from office after the coup of 18 Fructidor on account of his royalist sympathies. His interest in the subject of name changes thus had something to do with his politics, but it was also part of a broader concern with nomenclature after 9 Thermidor.

Dauchez recommended that the government authorize parents to change the first name of their children if these names "bring upsetting memories to mind." He did not specify which names exactly would fit this criterion. It was, he admitted, "a delicate question." He did, however, specify that this authorization would apply only to children who were born between May 31, 1793, and September 22, 1794. It is an interesting chronology. Dauchez conceded that Terror had been spreading through France before this date but argued that it was only with the purge of the Girondins in May–June 1793 that the Convention itself was "enslaved," and that the "empire of crime and brigandage" emerged victorious. As for the closing date, he claimed that there was no reason for children born after this date—the first day of Year III—to bear names reminiscent of the times before the fall of Robespierre.[129]

Dauchez's report implied that the Terror persisted somehow in the names of these children. The report included two stipulations that are especially interesting in this regard. The first stipulation concerned children who had died in the meantime. Dauchez recommended the authorization of posthumous name changes, so as to spare their families the burden of being associated with these difficult memories. The second stipulation concerned parents who did not want to change the names of their children because they remained attached to the political or ideological motivations behind them. In these "interesting cases," which involved "blind or fanatic revolutionaries," Dauchez recommended that the children themselves be allowed to apply for a name change, even though some of them were about five or six years old at the time.[130]

This concern at the highest levels of government to change the first names of children born during the Terror can be read in several ways. It was an act of erasure, aimed at suppressing the memory of the most radical phase of the Revolution. It was a purge, an act of purification, as if the very existence of children whose names were associated with the Terror polluted somehow the social and political environment. It was also a way of coming to terms with a difficult past. After all, "coming to terms" is a phrase that denotes an act of containment; that is, the effort to leave the past behind by, among other things, naming it.[131] The concern with naming and renaming after the Terror was an essential part of ending it, but, by the same token, it implied an acknowledgment that this was an elusive ending, one whose reverberations were bound to be felt for some time to come in the postrevolutionary landscape.

Conclusion

The literary critic Maurice Blanchot wrote once that "the disaster always takes place after having taken place."[132] He meant by this that a series of occurrences take on the meaning of a catastrophe only after the fact, when they have been named and narrated as such.[133] This, in a sense, is what this chapter has tried to show. The iterations proclaiming the end of the Terror after 9 Thermidor smacked of the lady doth protest too much. On the one hand, the repression of Year II had been relaxed, and the narrative marking the fall of Robespierre as a dramatic turning point—the end of the Terror—crystallized rather swiftly, thanks in no small measure to the efforts of the Thermidorians themselves.[134] On the other hand, the texts from this period that have been examined in this chapter also show an awareness that this was a past that could not so easily be left behind. If Thermidor marked the "ending of the Terror" rather than the end of the Terror—that is, a process rather than an event—it was to be an elusive ending.[135]

This chapter situated this understanding of the Terror as a difficult past in a broad context, beyond the politics of the Thermidorian Reaction. Collective attitudes to mass violence and cataclysmic events have been changing in the transition from the early modern to the modern period. Secularization and the rise of the public sphere, among other processes of change, led to a view of catastrophes as political and social, rather than theological, events, and created new arenas of debate and contestation, where the effects of such events on the social order, as well as on individual psyches, could be discussed in relative freedom from the imposition of the state or the church. For its part, the French Revolution generated debates on the relationship between violence and the social order. The views of violence that emerged from these debates were ambivalent. Violence was seen as necessary for the creation of a new order, and at the same time, as having the potential to be its very undoing. After 9 Thermidor, this ambivalence rendered representations of the violence of the Terror problematic. Prudhomme's work was an attempt to create an immediate history of this violence, but the textual topography of his book—its fragmentary nature—and the preoccupation with lists and classification, also suggested an inherent difficulty to read the social reality he purported to describe. The naming of the Terror as a difficult past would have profound implications on questions of accountability, redress, and remembrance in postrevolutionary France.

CHAPTER 2

Accountability

The Case of Joseph Le Bon

The name Joseph Le Bon probably rings very few bells today.[1] During the Thermidorian Reaction, however, this name was synonymous with some of the worst excesses of the Reign of Terror. As the *représentant en mission* in the departments of Pas-de-Calais and the Nord, Le Bon was responsible for carrying out the orders of the Committee of Public Safety in the north of France. Under his jurisdiction, a revolutionary tribunal was set up in the town of Arras—Robespierre's hometown—and hundreds of people were sentenced to death.[2] After 9 Thermidor, Le Bon was recalled to Paris and placed under arrest. He spent more than a year in prison awaiting trial and writing pamphlets that justified his conduct as a public official. His trial took place eventually in August–September 1795 before the criminal tribunal in Amiens, department of the Somme. The court heard 122 witnesses. Le Bon acted as his own counsel. He was found guilty and sentenced to death. Le Bon was executed in Amiens on October 15, 1795, just days before the National Convention, in its last session as the legislative assembly, adopted a sweeping amnesty decree for "all acts related purely to the Revolution."[3] This case offers a unique perspective on the thorny problem of justice after the fall of Robespierre because Le Bon was the last person to be held accountable for his actions during the Terror.[4]

For a long time, historians have seen the trials of Le Bon and other officials like him as reactionary in essence. Albert Mathiez argued that the criminal sanction of *représentants en mission* after the fall of Robespierre served to delegitimize the Revolution. It is here, writes Mathiez in his classic interpretation of Thermidor, that "the red specter, the memory of which was so often to check the march of progress, begins to loom up in our story."[5] According to Albert Soboul, the persecution of "terrorists" in Year III went hand in hand with the suppression of the sansculottes.[6] Even François Furet and Denis Richet argue in their revisionist narrative of the Revolution that the attacks against individuals who were identified with the Reign of Terror stemmed from a combination of "popular resentments and bourgeois vengeance."[7]

In recent years, historians have been advancing a more nuanced understanding of justice after the fall of Robespierre. Bronislaw Baczko and Corinne Gomez-Le Chevanton individually argue that the trials of Year III served as crucial sites for the construction of a particular memory of the Terror—a Thermidorian counterimagination—as well as for the cultivation of a republican pedagogy.[8] Howard Brown, in particular, has argued that the view of the Thermidorians as social reactionaries and political opportunists is grossly simplistic. In the aftermath of the Terror, revolutionary leaders and ordinary citizens faced an impossible situation. The demands of abstract morality— perpetrators must be punished; victims must receive recompense—clashed with the muddy waters of political compromise. The Thermidorians may have failed in their effort to establish an effective form of justice after the fall of Robespierre, but, argues Brown, this should not blind us to their pioneering efforts in this area.[9]

This chapter examines the trials of public officials after the Terror through the prism of transitional justice. It argues that the trials of Le Bon and other functionaries in the apparatus of the Terror were not so much a reaction against the French Revolution as a logical consequence of some of the Revolution's most enduring political and social innovations. The Revolution established accountability as a fundamental principle of the new political order. Men of power increasingly had to answer for their actions. Ordinary citizens took part in this process by, among other things, denouncing the unjust or unlawful conduct of public officials. After 9 Thermidor, the new standards of accountability ushered in by the Revolution gave rise to an unpredictable dilemma, namely, how to establish individual accountability in the aftermath of mass crime. The trial of Le Bon was a central site for negotiating this difficulty. On the one hand, the public officials who were put on trial after the fall of Robespierre were scapegoats. Their punishment served to exculpate the revolutionary leadership, which was heavily implicated in the repression. On the other hand, there was strong public pressure to hold officials like Le Bon accountable for their actions. Moreover, Le Bon himself took full responsibil ity for his part in the repression, claiming that it served the interests of the Republic. Le Bon's trial and punishment may not have held up under close scrutiny, but they emerged nonetheless from the same democratizing impulses that motivated him and many other political actors from the outset of the Revolution.

Accountability and Transitional Justice in the Early French Revolution

The establishment of mechanisms that are aimed at ensuring accountability is a hallmark of transitional justice.[10] The early French Revolution offers a striking example in this regard. Two hundred and ninety-seven of the *cahiers de doléances* (lists of grievances) that were collected in preparation for the meeting of the Estates-General included demands for some form of ministerial accountability.[11] Efforts to define the nature of ministerial accountability took place consistently yet sporadically between the Estates-General and the drafting of the Constitution of 1791. In December 1791, Hérault de Séchelles, a prominent member of the Legislative Assembly and a close friend of Georges Danton, articulated three kinds of ministerial responsibility. These included capital responsibility, "which is related to accusations"; pecuniary responsibility, "which is virtually impracticable"; and moral responsibility, which, "by a condition remarkable all the more as it is the least real, is the most common and is alone capable of producing an effect at any moment among free governments that conduct themselves by mores."[12] Early on then, revolutionary leaders tied the establishment of accountability to the French concept of *moeurs*, that is, the moral habits of a people.[13] For its part, the Constituent Assembly elaborated no less than six kinds of ministerial responsibility: general responsibility, which was related to all offenses against the security of the state and the constitution; particular responsibility, which related to damage caused to the property and liberty of private citizens as a result of ministerial decisions; criminal or penal responsibility, which related to alleged crimes; civil responsibility, which related to all matters of public finance; positive responsibility, "for all that he [the minister] might do"; and negative responsibility, "for all that he might neglect to do."[14]

These standards of accountability must be seen in a wider context. In the literature on transitional justice, accountability is mainly a political and moral concept. It refers to the need to bring agents of mass atrocity and the governments that support them to justice. Without such a reckoning, so the argument goes, societies emerging from episodes of mass violence and repression would not be able to build a new political order based on the rule of law and respect for human rights.[15] But the origins of accountability were fiscal, not moral or legal. Accountability emerged as a central principle in modern European states out of earlier innovations in the management of financial records. Specifically, double-entry bookkeeping, which was invented in Northern Italy around 1300, had enormous implications for the nature of political power. By representing the workings of government as a series of numbers—expenditures and revenues, gains and losses—double-entry bookkeeping rendered it less sacred and more transparent.[16] This story had distinct European aspects, but it was not only European. Moral accountability, that is, the idea that rulers are responsible in some way to their subjects, had long been an important notion in countries influenced by Chinese Confucianism.[17] But formal accountability, that is, the establishment of mechanisms that check the power of government and even, in some cases, allow the citizens to replace it, gained special prominence in early modern Europe. By the late eighteenth century, accountability, which first emerged as a fiscal innovation, had become a central moral and political feature of European states.

France on the eve of the Revolution is a good illustration of this process. In 1781, Jacques Necker, then director general of French Finances, published the *Compte Rendu*, an explanation of the Crown's management of money. The report, which sold hundreds of thousands of copies and was translated into several languages, included precise figures on the expenses and revenues of the French state. The revelations in it caused a public outcry. It turned out that the king had spent many more millions on the maintenance of the court and other noble households than he did on roads, bridges, and the Paris police. Of course, people had known this for some time, but the *Compte Rendu* made this truth visible in hard numbers. It was a major blow to the legitimacy of the monarchy and an important step on the path leading to 1789. The practical implications of accountability were visible in other countries as well. Revelations of corruption and abuses of power led to the impeachment of Warren Hastings, the British governor-general of India, in 1787. The lengthy trial that followed featured a passionate indictment of Hastings's conduct by Edmund Burke, who would go on to become one of the most influential critics of the French Revolution.[18] But as Jacob Soll argued, it was in France that "a political language of public accounting and accountability emerged more forcefully."[19]

The establishment of formal mechanisms of accountability was evident also in the judicial reforms that were launched early in the Revolution.[20] The courts of the Old Regime tended to conduct their hearings behind closed doors, considering written depositions in the absence of the defendants or any counsel on their behalf. Indeed, the royal ordinance of 1670, which defined the juridical principles of the monarchy, denied the right to such counsel because it was believed that lawyers hindered the quest for truth.[21] Moreover, the king could order the arrest of any subject of the realm on unspecified charges and for an undefined period by issuing a *lettre de cachet*, a sealed letter, which was a royal prerogative that attracted much ire from the *philosophes* and represented for them the arbitrary nature of justice under the monarchy.

The revolutionaries began reforming these judicial practices early in the Revolution. Their innovations focused especially on criminal justice and on the rights of defendants. Six articles in the *Declaration of the Rights of Man and Citizen* dealt with such matters as presumption of innocence and defense from arbitrary arrest. The new criminal code, which the revolutionaries adopted in 1791, stipulated that trials were to be conducted orally and publicly, and defendants would have the right to legal counsel. The linchpin of revolutionary judicial reform was the introduction of trial by jury. Twelve jurors were to be selected from lists furnished by local authorities across the country, and a majority of seven was needed to obtain a conviction. According to Howard Brown, these judicial reforms stood at the heart of the political order the revolutionaries were trying to create. The practice of trial by jury reflected the belief that the people, using their common sense and civic virtue, were better qualified than professional magistrates to decide on matters of justice.[22] The judicial reforms that were launched early in the Revolution were thus part of a process that had begun centuries earlier and had led to the establishment of accountability as a major principle in French politics and culture.

Indeed, the English words "responsibility" and "accountability" may have derived from the French language. "Accountability" may be an English translation of the French word *comptabilité*, which first appeared in dictionaries in the late eighteenth century. As for "responsibility," it was defined for the first time in the *Dictionnaire de l'Académie française* in 1798 as "a legal obligation to answer for one's actions; to be the guarantor of something. . . . It applies especially to ministers, to men in public affairs."[23] It seems, however, that it was mentioned in a text written several years earlier by Necker, who wrote that the government was responsible for guaranteeing the validity of property titles.[24] The term responsibility emerged then in relation to the demand that rulers be answerable to those whom they rule, and to the claim that it was the government's duty to guarantee basic economic transactions.

The most dramatic moment in the story of accountability during the French Revolution was the regicide of Louis XVI.[25] It was not so much the killing of the king that endowed this moment with its extraordinary significance. After all, kings had been killed throughout history, only to be replaced by others who claimed the throne. Rather, it was the trial of the king before the National

Convention that proved transformative. As Michael Walzer put it: "Public reg-icide is an absolutely decisive way of breaking with the myths of the old re-gime, and it is for this very reason, the founding act of the new."[26] The revolutionaries faced a legal-theoretical conundrum when they decided to put Louis on trial. The Constitution of 1791 defined the person of the king as "sa-cred and inviolable."[27] If the king was inviolable, then how could he be held accountable? Defining the king as inviolable meant, in effect, sovereign immu-nity. It was a modern version of the Roman principle *rex non potest peccare*, the king can do no wrong. In this sense, inviolability was the ultimate form of unaccountability.[28] By deciding to go ahead with the trial, the revolutionaries signaled that no one would be above the law in the Republic. In other words, they enshrined accountability as a fundamental principle of the new order.

It is perhaps in this spirit that one should read François Furet's statement: "The Convention did pass terrorist laws, but it also founded modern civil so-ciety."[29] Such an endorsement of the Terror is quite surprising, coming as it does from the historian most identified with the revisionist interpretation of the Revolution. But it is consistent with Furet's overarching project, namely, to situate the French Revolution in a broad narrative of democratization.[30] The establishment of mechanisms for ensuring accountability from 1789 to 1793 attests to the democratizing impulses of the early Revolution. Indeed, account-ability derived from popular sovereignty. It is noted often that the Revolution entailed the transfer of sovereignty from the monarchy to the nation.[31] It is noted less often that popular sovereignty implies a democratization of respon-sibility. If the members of a nation are the source of its power, then they share in the responsibility for its actions, at least in some measure. As the Na-tional Convention wrote in May 1793, in a decree concerning the authority of the *représentants en mission*: "They must envision that a great responsibility is the inevitable consequence of great power."[32]

The Dilemma of Accountability after the Terror

The democratization of responsibility in the early French Revolution led to an unpredictable and very modern dilemma after the fall of Robespierre: how to establish individual accountability in the aftermath of mass crime.[33] Crim-inal prosecution presupposes individual accountability.[34] Yet the mechanisms of mass crime—Hannah Arendt referred to this as "administrative massacre"—dilute the very possibility of attributing such precise levels of accountability and responsibility to a specific individual.[35] If the *représentants en mission* rep-resented the Convention, and the Convention embodied the sovereignty of the French people, how could one hold public officials accountable for the Terror without, ipso facto, implicating the entire chain in the crime? Where precisely did responsibility for the Terror lie?[36] This dilemma derived from the democratizing thrust of the French Revolution; it would have been unthinkable under absolutism.

The Thermidorians faced this conundrum when they first considered prosecuting public officials for their role in the Terror. The subject came up in August 1794, when the *conventionnel* Laurent Lecointre delivered an extensive denunciation against the members of the committees of the revolutionary government who were in power before 9 Thermidor. Lecointre directed his allegations against seven individuals in particular: three from the Committee of Public Safety and four from the Committee of General Security. But his extensive indictment mentioned Le Bon as well.[37] The Convention, for its part, rejected Lecointre's motion by an overwhelming majority. Nevertheless, the debate that ensued from Lecointre's denunciation shows the problematic implications of criminalizing the Terror.

The *conventionnel* Goujon argued that in denouncing public officials for their role in the repression "it is actually the Convention that is being accused; it is the French people that are being put on trial for having tolerated the tyranny of the infamous Robespierre."[38] The relatively moderate deputy Jean-Baptiste Matthieu declared that "this is not about submitting several individuals to judgment, but about the Revolution in its entirety."[39] Louis Legendre, a close friend of Danton, added another layer of complexity to the matter by pointing out that "it is written in the code of nations that when a people look back after having carried out a revolution, it never achieves its goals. . . . I ask you, for example, if we should pursue today those who have burnt down the castles at the beginning of the Revolution."[40] The Reign of Terror occurred under a representative government. Accusing elected representatives of criminal conduct was tantamount to accusing those whom they represented. The implication here is that responsibility for state actions in a representative system of government cannot be individuated completely. On some level, it must be shared by all members of the polity. Moreover, the process of placing blame for the crimes of the Revolution on the shoulders of individuals risked turning into a snowball effect, as suggested by the reference to peasants burning down *chateaux* during the Great Fear of 1789. Revolutionaries, implied Legendre in his comments, cannot afford an accounting of their past.

Yet others in the Convention pointed out that an accounting of one's own past follows logically and necessarily from the Revolution's political principles. Thus, Tallien argued that by rejecting the criminal sanction of its own members, the Convention would be "surrounding itself with a space of inviolability. . . . It

would then be said that you are stifling the truths that the people are presenting to you."[41] The sudden appearance of this term—inviolability—is most re-
vealing here. It harkened back to the definition of the king as inviolable in the
Constitution of 1791 and to the debates that preceded the king's trial. Tallien
was implying that the Convention would be regressing to the Old Regime by
refusing to hold public officials accountable for their role in the Terror. It
would be like saying that the state can do no wrong.

Fairly soon after the fall of Robespierre then, the dilemma of accountability that emerged from the democratizing thrust of the Revolution was quite
apparent. On the one hand, the establishment of mechanisms for ensuring accountability in the early stages of the French Revolution meant that criminal
sanction in the aftermath of the Terror was unavoidable. On the other hand,
the democratization of responsibility meant that individual accountability,
which is a precondition for criminal trials, was in a sense impossible. What was
to be done?

In the initial weeks after the fall of Robespierre, it looked as though the
Convention was progressing rapidly toward retribution. It dismantled the institutional apparatus of the Terror and began the mass release of prisoners.[42]
Joseph Le Bon was removed from office a day after 9 Thermidor, and arrested
five days later, alongside Antoine Fouquier-Tinville, the chief prosecutor of
the revolutionary tribunal in Paris.[43] The Convention also recalled about
60 percent of the *représentants en mission* from the provinces and replaced them
with more moderate men.[44]

But then, after this initial bout of activity, the Convention stalled, unsure
what to do. By the end of Year II, it seemed poised to choose impunity over
accountability. A report delivered by Robert Lindet in the name of the revolutionary government on September 20, 1794—the last day of Year II in the Republican calendar—urged the French to leave the bitter legacies of the Terror
behind. The revolutionaries, Lindet declared, should not reproach themselves
for the mistakes they have made. "We have all been thrown pell-mell into the
same galloping race. . . . The Revolution has left victims in its wake. . . . Are
you now going to authorize inquiries into each specific case? Reason, the welfare of the fatherland, does not allow you to look back on the ruins that you
have left behind."[45] The metaphor of the revolution as a galloping horse race
depicted the violence of the preceding period as part of a collective dynamic
that no one could control or predict. It was not the fault of identifiable actors.
Moreover, it was dangerous to hold the actions of revolutionary leaders during Year II to a close legal scrutiny because it risked undoing many of the real
achievements of the Revolution. The revolutionary gaze, implied Lindet, must
remain fixed resolutely on the future, on the social and political order that is

yet to come, and not on the past. The position of the revolutionary government at the end of Year II was that it would be best to let bygones be bygones.

The Retributive Turn

If there is anything that the aftermath of the Terror shows clearly, it is that bygones do not remain gone. They come back, and often from several directions at once. In spite of the revolutionary government's desire to leave Year II behind, denunciations of public officials came pouring in from across the country. A petition from Arles, published at the Convention's expense, told of what had transpired in the town during the Terror. The petitioners accused the local representatives of the revolutionary government of having emptied the granaries of the city, which were traditionally kept to aid the poor during bad harvests, and of ordering that the bodies of two suspects who had been guillotined—"two poor workers: Jacques Blain, a porter, and Gravat, aka Cabanon"—be dragged through the streets.[46] Providing graphic details, and naming perpetrators and victims, the authors of the petition stated that "the time has come perhaps when the perpetrators of so many atrocities will regret not having interred the witnesses in the same grave as the victims."[47] The citizens of Avignon applauded the Convention for removing Robespierre from power but added that "now you must learn of the actions of the agents of his cruelty and deliver them to justice."[48] An assembly of citizens from Arras described what they had experienced during Le Bon's mission in their city as a "long and terrible dream" that they could not recall "without horror," and asked the deputies in the Convention, whose "energy had saved France from a tyrant," not to let "any of his accomplices escape punishment."[49] Two citizens from Cambrai appeared in person before the Convention to denounce Le Bon, who, they said, came to a meeting of the Revolutionary Society in town and "presented himself as a despot, putting on the airs of a buffoon, stomping his feet, drawing his sword, spreading terror and fear everywhere."[50]

It is difficult to determine how much truth there was in such allegations, but, in a way, this is beside the point. They were part of a denunciatory genre that flooded the literary marketplace after the fall of Robespierre and that made vengeance a "Thermidorian passion."[51] These texts usually included detailed stories of excess and they usually ended with calls to bring those responsible to justice. The language in these denunciations was continuous with the rhetoric of Year II, and the practice of denunciation was deeply embedded in revolutionary political culture. Denunciations sought to unmask the sinister intentions behind seemingly laudable actions, instituting politics as a "spectacle of transparency."[52] In this sense, public pressure to hold officials accountable for their roles in the repression illustrates Baczko's argument that the process of emerging from the Terror unfolded "within a framework—political and symbolic, institutional and social—that was born of the Terror and modeled by it."[53] Stories and revelations about the brutalities of Jacobin repression were popular after 9 Thermidor, perhaps because they struck a chord with the widespread sentiment that the Reign of Terror was an outrage, a massive atrocity that called for some kind of reckoning.

By the winter of 1795, this reckoning was in full swing. The Jacobin clubs were shut down in November 1794. Bands of Muscadins—dandyish young men wearing musk perfume, whence the name—began roaming the streets of Paris, attacking Jacobins with cudgels.[54] In December 1794, the Girondin deputies, who had been expelled by Jacobins in June 1793, returned to the Convention. In February 1795, Jean-Paul Marat's body was removed from the Pantheon. Through the winter and spring of 1795, a wave of largely spontaneous acts of revenge, which came to be known as the White Terror, spread throughout the south of France. Jacobins and former so-called *terroristes* were hunted down in the streets, massacred in prisons, or murdered at home. In Tarascon they were rounded up and thrown off the roof of the medieval castle in the town.[55] Most of these acts constituted a very local settling of scores: many assailants knew their victims personally.[56]

There were several reasons for this retributive turn. Internal politics played a part. The return of the Girondins signaled a reckoning with former colleagues in the Convention. The public pressure generated by petitions and testimonies about the extent of the repression was also a factor, but the decisive moment was probably the trial of Jean-Baptiste Carrier. This was the greatest cause célèbre of the Thermidorian period, but it began well before the fall of Robespierre. In August 1793, Carrier had been sent on mission to the Vendée, a region that had been in open rebellion against the authority of the Convention since March. He arrived in Nantes with a mandate to do what was needed to pacify the area. The campaign to crush the rebels in the Vendée was brutal. The Convention took measures aimed at "the extermination of the Vendéens."[57] The Infernal Columns of the revolutionary army, led by General Louis Marie Turreau, adopted a scorched-earth policy, burning down villages and killing inhabitants to cut local support for the rebels. Carrier's mission then unfolded in an area that saw some of the worst internal fighting of the revolutionary period. In October 1793, Carrier drew up a list of 132 notable citizens and businessmen in Nantes and had them all arrested on the charge that they had been involved in a federalist plot. They were sent to Paris to stand trial before the revolutionary tribunal. Thirty-five of them died during the journey to the capital, which took place in midwinter, on foot. Three more died in prison. The remaining ninety-four were dispersed in various prisons, awaiting trial. The trial opened eventually in September 1794, more than a month after Robespierre's death. Of course, the political atmosphere in the capital was dramatically different now. The trial of the notables of Nantes turned quickly into a trial of Carrier's mission in the west. The jury acquitted all ninety-four defendants and the accused became accusers as the Convention ordered the arrest of Carrier and other members of the revolutionary committee in Nantes.[58]

Carrier's trial became a watershed moment. The public followed the details emanating from the courtroom avidly. It learned of the Drownings at Nantes, where hundreds of suspects were tied together on boats or barges and drowned. It learned of "republican marriages," a euphemism used allegedly by Carrier and his acolytes to refer to the practice of tying together priests and naked young women before drowning them. The image of the Loire River, reddened by the blood of victims, was seared into the collective imagery of the time. "It was like an immense poem by Dante, which made France descend into the circles of hell, unknown even to those who had just traversed them" is how the historian Jules Michelet described the effects of Carrier's trial on the public.[59] The Jacobin *conventionnel* Pierre-Joseph Cambon accused Carrier of committing atrocities "against humanity," a phrase surprising in its modernity.[60] Gracchus Babeuf, relying on the records of the trial, published a lengthy indictment of the revolutionary government, which, he argued, created "the system of depopulation" in the Vendée.[61] In short, Carrier's trial furnished an opportunity for a public discussion of the violence of Year II, and it did much to establish an official narrative of the Terror as a massive atrocity perpetrated by a revolutionary leadership that had become corrupted by its own power.

Carrier's trial was followed by other cases of retribution against public officials for their roles in the Terror. In May 1795, Fouquier-Tinville was condemned to death along with fifteen other members of the revolutionary tribunal of Paris after a trial that lasted more than a month.[62] In June it was the turn of the members of the Popular Commission of Orange. At the height of the Terror, this body had sentenced to death hundreds of residents in the city of Orange, including thirty-two nuns. Its members had been on the run since 9 Thermidor, but most were caught by the spring. Their trial opened in Avignon on June 2, 1795. There were ten defendants in the dock, including Jean Fauvety, who had been the president of the Popular Commission of Orange, and Viot, who was its chief prosecutor. They all had to defend themselves after the defense attorneys appointed by the court failed to show up. All ten were found guilty, but only six were sentenced to death. The judgment described the trial as a drama of cosmic significance. "Ever since men have been reunited in a society, justice did not have to decide on the fate of guiltier men than Viot and Fauvety."[63] The executions took place in Avignon on June 26 before a big crowd. Fauvety, Viot, and the other four condemned men were led to the guillotine dressed in the red shirt that was reserved for common criminals. After the execution, their bodies were snatched by the spectators and thrown unceremoniously into the Rhône River.[64]

Le Bon's Revolutionary Career and His Mission in the North

Le Bon's trial took place in this atmosphere. To understand why he was one of the few public officials to be held accountable before a court of law after 9 Thermidor, it is necessary to examine his revolutionary career and his mission in the north more closely. There was little in Le Bon's early life to suggest the role he would go on to play in the French Revolution. Born in 1765 in Arras, he was the second child of nine, only four of whom would survive to adulthood. The family lived in an insalubrious part of the town, close to the river. Le Bon was a sickly child, perhaps because of the odors emanating constantly from the nearby abattoirs. Academically, however, he distinguished himself early in life. At age sixteen he was admitted to the prestigious Collège des Oratoriens, and was immediately elected to preside over its literary society. Destined for a career in the priesthood, Le Bon was appointed as a professor of rhetoric in the seminary at Beaune, in the region of Burgundy. He seems to have spent more time discussing the ideas of the Enlightenment than scripture. He was especially attracted to Rousseau's writings, a relationship that would last throughout his life. He seems to have been much loved by his students. Several of them would testify on his behalf during his trial, and one of them would go on to adopt Le Bon's son after his death.[65]

At the outbreak of the Revolution, Le Bon was still in Beaune, teaching in the seminary and experimenting with hot air balloons.[66] That same year he was ordained to the priesthood by Talleyrand, who was then bishop of Autun and who would later become one of the most influential diplomats of the period, serving as Napoleon's foreign minister. Le Bon's career in the church was to be short lived. Swept up in the enthusiastic winds blowing from Paris, he joined the Society of Friends of the Constitution and was immediately removed from his teaching post. At the Society he made the acquaintance of men like Robespierre's brother Augustin and Armand Guffroy, who would go on to serve in the Convention alongside Le Bon and would later become his chief detractor. In 1791, Le Bon took the ecclesiastical oath of the clergy, a decision which seems to have upset his mother greatly. He was moving away from his clerical vocation, but this does not mean he was losing his faith. As Timothy Tackett has shown, many priests saw the revolutionary reforms of the church as a return to, rather than a departure from, the true message of Christianity. "The reforms had returned to the spirit of the religion of Jesus; they had brought back the primitive purity of the Church, so long debased by time and by acts of avarice."[67] Le Bon seems to have remained particularly attached to the church's traditional role of poor relief. He spoke of this issue often, and brought it up as part of the defense during his trial. His first public speech in the National Convention was a call to "wipe out mendacity."[68] The Ventôse Decrees, which the revolutionary government passed in the winter of 1794 and which stipulated that the property confiscated from the émigrés and other enemies of the people would be distributed to the needy, seem to have been especially dear to his heart. He implemented them rigorously during his time as a *représentant en mission*.[69] In effect then, Le Bon renounced the priesthood after the outbreak of the Revolution, but he was and would remain profoundly religious throughout his life.

It was perhaps this religious outlook that explains, at least in part, Le Bon's zealous implementation of repressive measures in the north. Having served as the mayor of Arras in 1792, he was elected to the National Convention in June 1793 and was sent on mission to Pas-de-Calais in November. In December his jurisdiction was extended to the department of the Nord. As a *représentant en mission* reporting directly to the Committee of Public Safety, he enjoyed considerable but not unlimited power. In theory, the representatives sent by the revolutionary government to the provinces were, as Colin Lucas put it, "repositories of the will of the people. . . . To resist a *représentant en mission* was to resist the will of the people."[70] In practice however, their authority was dynamic, waxing and waning according to the revolutionary chain of events, and in any case a subject of frequent debates.[71] Be that as it may, the *représentants en mission* became identified with the Terror in the provinces, and as such they were the main targets of popular anger after the fall of Robespierre.

This was even truer in the case of Le Bon, whose mission in the north ended up being particularly repressive. Part of the reason had to do with his personality. From an early age, he seems to have had a knack for making enemies and for getting involved in personal, local, and protracted feuds.[72] But to a great extent, the nature of his mission was determined by the proximity of the area under his jurisdiction to the English border. The geographic incidence of the Terror shows that the patterns of repression ebbed and flowed according to the war. Repressive measures were harsher in border regions or in areas that had a strong federalist presence and softer in regions that were less affected by the war.[73]

Le Bon's ideological commitment to the revolutionary cause was clear from the beginning. Within days of his arrival in Arras he attended a performance of Voltaire's play *Brutus* in the local theater. He addressed the actors on stage during the intermission, reminding them that "you are now public instructors" and exhorting them to "make yourself worthy of revolutionary beneficence."[74] One of his first acts in Pas-de-Calais was to centralize power. A decree issued a day after the beginning of his mission observed that it was impossible to find "seven decent republicans who are free from the influence of the rich and the big farmers" in the surrounding rural areas and that, therefore, all the surveillance duties, which had been carried out by local bodies, would be carried out from now on by the surveillance committee in Arras, under his close supervision.[75] In January 1794, Le Bon established a revolutionary tribunal in Arras, modeled on the one that had been operating in Paris since March 1793. Soon after that, he established another one in Cambrai. These were two of a handful of revolutionary tribunals in France during the Terror, and Le Bon seems to have been involved deeply in their day-to-day operations, approving lists of jurors and attending social functions with the magistrates. Thousands of citizens were sent to prison. Le Bon's orders provided each detainee with basic necessities, including "one mattress and one cover, two sheets, six shirts, six handkerchiefs, six pairs of underwear."[76] By July 1794, more than five hundred people had been sent to the guillotine by Le Bon's tribunals. Of these, about 430 were men and the rest women.[77] Whether due to his choices as a representative or to circumstances beyond his control, the repressive nature of Le Bon's mission in the north made him a likely target for retribution after 9 Thermidor.

The Case against Le Bon

The indictment against Le Bon was presented to the Convention in June 1795. It was prepared by a committee of twenty-one deputies, the Commission of Twenty-One, according to the procedure established for the case of Carrier several months earlier.[78] The charges in the indictment were divided into four categories: juridical assassination, which meant the use of legal institutions in order to commit murder; mass repression of citizens, which referred to the alleged system of tyranny, arbitrary justice, and intimidation that Le Bon had instituted in the north through the unlawful delegation of powers; the abuse of powers vested in him in order to carry out personal vendettas; and finally, theft, corruption, and the squandering of public funds.[79]

While presenting the indictment, the *rapporteur* recounted the following story. One day, two women, one citizen Davigne and her daughter, were sitting on one of the ramparts that encircled the town of Arras, reading leisurely in the novel *Clarissa* by Samuel Richardson. They were suddenly accosted by Le Bon and two of his subordinates. First, Le Bon drew out his pistol and fired a shot in the air, just to scare them. Then, he tried to grab the book they were reading. According to the story, the young girl held on to the book defiantly, telling her mother that "there is nothing suspect about it." This comment seems to have infuriated Le Bon, who knocked the girl down with a fist. He then demanded that the two women hand over their possessions, including their purses, and proceeded to strip-search them "with the most indecent brutality." Le Bon then dragged the girl and her mother to prison, but released them the next day. The report in *Le Moniteur* included an engraving of this incident, depicting Le Bon and his acolytes in a way that suggested their monstrosity, with the title "The Cruelties of Joseph Le Bon in Arras."[80]

Obviously, this anecdote was meant to illustrate how Le Bon abused the powers vested in him, but here is the puzzling detail: Why mention the specific novel that the two women were reading? And this was not the only reference to this curious detail. In the opening statement at Le Bon's trial in Amiens, in August 1795, the chief prosecutor reiterated the same story: "Reasons of health have led the *citoyenne* Davigne and her mother to the ramparts of Arras, there to take in some air, and to read the story of Clarissa Harlowe."[81] How was the fact that the two *citoyennes* were reading the story of Clarissa Harlowe relevant to the indictment against Le Bon?

Let us recall briefly the plot of Richardson's novel, published in 1751.[82] Clarissa Harlowe comes from a family of the English gentry. She is very beautiful, witty, and, most importantly, has a tidy sum to her name. She is also somewhat obsessed with her virtue, so when her family decides to marry her off to an unrefined old aristocrat as a means of climbing up the social ladder, she recoils in horror. She runs away with a young, charming gentleman named, of all things, Lovelace. Lovelace turns out to be something of a sinister libertine, in spite of his charming looks, manners, and seemingly sincere love for Clarissa. For the next few months he shuttles her from one depraved lodging to another, including a stint at a brothel. Lovelace plans to seduce Clarissa, so as to make her and her fortune his, but she manages to resist his ever more explicit advances. Eventually, unable to control himself, Lovelace drugs and rapes Clarissa with the help of the madam who runs the brothel. Her virtue thus lost, Clarissa manages to escape from the brothel and from Lovelace, but

FIGURE 3.   "The Cruelties of Joseph Le Bon in Arras," *Moniteur*, 1795. Credit: Regenstein Library, University of Chicago.

becomes terribly ill on account of all her woes, and ends up dying miserably. Clarissa Harlowe then is a story of virtue betrayed and outraged.

The theme of virtue betrayed was central to the case against Le Bon. The campaign against him began to unfold well before the end of the Terror, when groups of disgruntled citizens from Arras and Cambrai denounced Le Bon's mission in the north and suggested that he should be recalled to Paris.[83] This in itself was not unusual. Complaints about the *représentants en mission* in the provinces were frequent enough before 9 Thermidor.[84] However, Le Bon had a powerful enemy in the Convention, the deputy Armand Guffroy, who also hailed from Arras. During the Terror, Guffroy published a newspaper, *Le rougyff*—the second word an anagram of his name—whose crude rhetoric surpassed even the notorious *Père Duchesne* and would lead eventually to his exclusion from the Jacobin club.[85] Guffroy retained, however, the printing press that he owned and made frequent use of it in order to attack Le Bon, both before and after 9 Thermidor. Most of the printed material in this *affaire* bears the imprint of his shop. In one of these pamphlets, written before the fall of Robespierre, Guffroy addressed himself to the citizens of Arras, to the Convention, and to public opinion, while announcing that "it is with the hard organ of virtuous austerity that I forge the political dagger with which I shall strike you down, Joseph Le Bon."[86] Note the interplay of sexual overtones, violent tropes, and the theme of virtue—hard organ, political dagger, virtuous austerity.

It seems that Guffroy's campaign against Le Bon had some success, for there was an attempt to recall him to Paris in early July 1794. At this stage, however, Le Bon had his own powerful protectors in the Convention. Bertrand Barère, member of the Committee of Public Safety, stepped up to defend Le Bon, attributing to him a decisive role in the success of the revolutionary armies in the north, most notably in the Battle of Fleurus in June 1794. Barère admitted that Le Bon's methods may have been "somewhat acerbic," but he had "saved Cambrai from treason."[87] Besides, Barère continued, it was not a good idea to look too closely into the actions of the representatives in the provinces. They were harsh but also necessary, and it would be better to surround them with a certain respectful silence because, as Barère put it, "liberty is like a virgin": one should be cautious when lifting her skirt.[88]

Nine Thermidor signaled an immediate reversal of Le Bon's fortunes. On 10 Thermidor, he was recalled from Cambrai to Paris by orders of the Committee of Public Safety.[89] Five days later, he was already under arrest. Le Bon's downfall provoked a flood of denunciatory petitions from those who had suffered the brunt of his repressive measures in the north. The widow Lallart, for instance, from an Artois family of merchants, had a pamphlet printed at Guffroy's store, in which she wrote that "death encircles me and I am surrounded by coffins; the remains of fifteen of my relatives, victims of the furies of this traitor, form a funerary procession that is constantly before my eyes."[90] An address from the popular society in the rural district of Béthune exclaimed: "All that is most repelling in vice, knavery, perversity, and barbarism was put to work by Le Bon, in order to realize his sinister goals. . . . He has tampered with crime in order to oppress virtue."[91]

Recent studies highlight the significance of virtue in the political culture of Thermidor. The concept of virtue had been tainted deeply by its association with the Terror, yet it remained central as a republican value.[92] Andrew Jainchill has shown how the pedagogic projects of the Convention in Year III were meant to establish a new "cultural infrastructure for the nation," centered on the cultivation of civic virtue.[93] Sergio Luzzatto has explained how the political discourse of Thermidor replaced the opposition between crime and virtue with a distinction between crime and error.[94] This allowed the Thermidorians to describe the conduct of some representatives during the Terror as misguided yet committed to republican virtue, and the conduct of other representatives as intentionally criminal and, in this sense, opposed to the ideals of the Revolution. Depicting Le Bon's actions as an attack on virtue implied that his mission in the north was, in effect, counterrevolutionary.

Moreover, the theme of virtue betrayed resonated with influential cultural tropes in the eighteenth century. This was so particularly with melodrama, a literary and theatrical genre that flourished in the late 1790s and early 1800s. The main themes of melodrama were moral polarization, a Manichaean worldview, the indulgence of strong emotions, hyperbolic rhetoric, and a sharp yet elusive distinction between virtue and vice.[95] Melodramatic overtones could be heard all across the unfolding of the *affaire Le Bon*. Indeed, the case was the subject of several theatrical plays. In one of them, the author, "fearless Jean," promised the audience that "the absolute victory of virtue over crime . . . leaves no doubt that Joseph Le Bon and his acolytes will soon expiate their wrongdoings."[96] A song celebrating the anniversary of Le Bon's execution quipped that "crime has its partisans / intrigue has its artisans / this I find discouraging / by using its might / virtue will establish new rights / this I find encouraging."[97] Representing the case of Le Bon within the aesthetic framework of melodrama allowed the Thermidorians to describe the Reign of Terror as the persecution of virtue and 9 Thermidor as virtue's deliverance.

Consider here the central place of sexual violence in the allegations against Le Bon. A book recounting the horrors of the prison in Arras under Le Bon's jurisdiction told of indecent body searches.

> If a female citizen was arrested . . . just for having found herself in the street at the same time as Le Bon and his acolytes . . . she was led to the surveillance committee; there, she was forced to undress, and when she remained with nothing on but an undershirt, public officials would take corruption to such a degree so as to shove their hands . . . saying, *you are well capable of sticking papers even there.*[98]

Fréron's *L'orateur du peuple* ran a story about a woman in Arras who came to beg Le Bon for her husband's life. Le Bon, so the story goes, demanded sexual favors in return, but after the woman agreed, changed his mind and tried to buy her off. The woman, humiliated and enraged, tried to attack Le Bon, but was immediately detained and led to the guillotine with her husband. "This," wrote Fréron, "is how Le Bon made it impossible to establish the Republic on the basis of virtue."[99]

It is impossible to ascertain today whether these allegations of sexual violence against Le Bon were true. None of them appeared in the official transcript of his trial. The important point here is the role they played in the criminalization of the Terror. Describing Le Bon's mission in the north through allegations of sexual transgression dissociated it from its political and legal context. Public officials did have to undertake drastic measures sometimes in order to defend the Republic. Sometimes such actions were misguided. But sexual violence was beyond the pale because there was no way to justify it in terms of serving the interests of the people. To criminalize the Terror in this way was to sever its association with virtue, an association made by the Jacobins. Furthermore, it was to reclaim civic virtue as a central part of the Thermidorian project.

According to Michel Biard, claims about the unbridled sexuality of *représentants en mission* were a recurring motif after 9 Thermidor, constituting a discourse on the corrupting effects of absolute power.[100] A report by the committee that was charged with examining Robespierre's papers after his execution called the attention of the Convention to "the atrocious Joseph Le Bon, who, surrounded by the objects of his lecherous fury, in his homicidal embraces, could have said with more accuracy than Caligula: *That beautiful head of yours will be cut off in an instance upon my orders.*"[101] The reference to Caligula served to depict Le Bon's mission in the north not merely as an attack on virtue, but specifically on female virtue, constituting an allegory of power out of control.

Le Bon's Defense

The allegations of sexual aggression finally caused Le Bon to break his silence. Having spent the last five months in prison, Le Bon launched his campaign of self-defense within days after the publication of the Convention's report on Robespierre's papers. Addressing himself to E. B. Courtois, the author of this report, Le Bon challenged the Convention to furnish any evidence for "the lecherous furies, the homicidal embraces, the orgies with courtesans, and the caresses à la Caligula, of which you accuse me."[102] Le Bon's defense consisted for the most part in letters, which he wrote in prison to justify his mission in the north and refute the accusations against him. In the first of these *lettres justificatives*, Le Bon complained bitterly: "Calumny haunts me . . . and chief among these monstrous imputations is the depiction of barbarism, lechery, perfidy, and profound wickedness described in *L'orateur du peuple.*"[103]

Calumny, as Charles Walton has shown, was a major concern for public figures during the Revolution.[104] Yet Le Bon was an unrepentant terrorist. Unlike many of his colleagues, he did not repudiate Robespierre or disavow the repressive measures of Year II. It was the accusations of sexual wantonness that proved particularly injurious to him. Why? One reason may be his ecclesiastical past. Stories about the sexual misconduct of priests were a common trope in eighteenth-century literature.[105] Certainly the newspapers were aware of this detail in Le Bon's biography when reporting on his case. Fréron's *Orateur du peuple* referred to Le Bon as "this luxurious priest" in recounting his alleged sexual exploits.[106] Allegations of sexual debauchery may have been then particularly harmful to Le Bon as a man of faith.

But there was another, more important, reason that Le Bon found the allegations of sexual violence especially outrageous, namely, that they clashed with his self-perception as a man of virtue. One of the striking things about Le Bon's defense is that far from denying the main accusation against him—namely, that he oversaw a system of repression in the north—he claimed full responsibility for it, arguing that in so doing he was fulfilling his duty toward his fellow citizens but that now, in the transformed historical circumstances of Thermidor, these same actions were being represented as crimes. Referring to the revolutionary tribunal that he founded in Arras, Le Bon wrote: "This tribunal that today is being called a tribunal of blood did not possess this odious name beforehand."[107] In his fourth justificatory letter, Le Bon observed that what was seen as enthusiasm or patriotic zeal during the Terror was now being reinterpreted as fanaticism and excess. "I will not try to justify in the light of cool reason all that circumstances and enthusiasm have led me to undertake in times that are no more. . . . The Convention itself had adopted measures that it has since disavowed."[108] Overseeing repressive measures, signing orders for the incarceration or execution of other people—all this was difficult but necessary in the context of the crisis of Year II. "There is no doubt that, as men, we cannot but be saddened by the spilt blood of even the most ardent royalist . . . but as citizens, our first tears belong by right to those who march with us on the path of the Revolution."[109]

The tension between man and citizen, and, by implication, between nature and culture, stood at the heart of Le Bon's defense. When appearing before the Convention in July 1795 to respond to the indictment against him, Le Bon referred to the story of Regulus, the Roman general who sacrificed himself to the Carthaginians in order to serve the interests of Rome. "I shed tears in reading this sublime story. . . . Regulus rejected the pleas of his wife and children. . . . What a monster to nature! But what a great man to his compatriots!"[110] This focus on the tension between man and citizen reveals Le Bon's deep engagement with the notion of virtue, particularly as Rousseau elaborated it. As Judith Shklar has argued, the main problem of modern life as defined in Rousseau's social theory was the tension between nature and culture. According to Rousseau, "All our self-created miseries stem from our mixed condition, our half natural and half social state."[111] Virtue, as Le Bon understood it, meant the effort to resolve this tension through self-mastery, the resolve to be a citizen first and foremost; that is, to give priority to one's political existence. In this sense, Le Bon's defense advanced a competing notion of virtue to the one elaborated by the Thermidorians.

Rousseau, as we have seen, was of special significance to Le Bon. He named his son, who was born while he was in prison and whom he would never see, Emile. In one of the boxes in the archives pertaining to Le Bon's case there is a leather pouch that he had with him in prison, and in it there is a crumpled note in tiny handwriting that reproduces a lengthy passage from Rousseau's *Emile*:

> Good social institutions are those that know best how to *denaturalize* man . . . to elevate the self into communal unity. . . . He who wishes to preserve the primacy of his natural sentiments in the civic order does not know what he wants. Always in contradiction with himself, always floating between his dispositions and his duties, he will be neither a man, nor a citizen. . . . He will be nothing.[112]

Virtue for Le Bon meant the masculine commitment to do one's duty, even when it contradicted one's feelings. "As for me . . . I definitely wanted to be something. . . . I resolved to be a citizen in the full sense of the term."[113] Far from being reckless, criminal, or excessive, Le Bon defended his actions in the north as the fruit of virtuous, republican self-mastery and, in this sense, political through and through.

Competing notions of virtue continued to play a decisive role in Le Bon's case all the way to the end. The presiding magistrate in his trial informed the jurors in the criminal tribunal of Amiens that, in making their decision, "you should consult nothing except the profound sentiment that nature has engraved in your hearts . . . that internal voice that is altered neither by prejudice nor by the passions, and which discerns with such wisdom between virtue and vice."[114] As for Le Bon, one might suspect that the rhetoric of virtue was part of self-posturing, a tactic that he employed in order to defend himself, but there is some evidence to suggest that this was a deeply personal issue for him. In the last letter that he sent to his wife from prison on the eve of his execution, and which was never intended for publication, Le Bon wrote:

> I have entertained . . . the most terrible notions of the situation in which a man who is condemned to death finds himself during the hours that precede the execution of his judgment. I was wrong. These moments are like all others in the life of a man whose conscience is clear. . . . I revisit the times that are no more. Rather than bringing to my mind sad souvenirs, they present to my memory nothing but a chain of virtuous actions. I speak here of my public conduct, of all that I had done for the cause of liberty. . . . It is not as your spouse that I must die; it is as a real citizen, as one of the leaders of the popular cause.[115]

Le Bon died unrepentant, convinced of the political truths embodied in his mission in the north. Yet he had no illusions that his revolutionary record would ever be vindicated. On the day of his execution, dressed in the red shirt of ordinary criminals, he told the prison guard who was leading him to the Market Square in Amiens, where the guillotine stood waiting: "No one will talk of me anymore after my death."[116] Ten years later, the grounds where he had been buried were dug up. According to local historians of Amiens, residents of the town recognized his corpse by the quantity of stones that had been thrown on it by "the indignant populace."[117] Apparently, a local surgeon took possession of Le Bon's skull and added it to his anatomical collection.

Conclusion

Looking at the trials of the Thermidorian Period from the perspective of transitional justice enables a different understanding of how the revolutionaries struggled with their own, recent past. Their efforts were flawed, messy, but also unprecedented to a large extent. They were unprecedented because they emerged from the democratizing impulses of the French Revolution. This chapter analyzed the case of Le Bon as a prism into the problem of justice after the fall of Robespierre. The trial of Le Bon and the trials of other functionaries in the apparatus of the Terror were not merely reactionary. They emerged from the consecration of accountability as a fundamental principle in the early French Revolution. This gave rise to an unpredictable dilemma after 9 Thermidor: How does one go about holding individuals accountable for a mass crime? The Convention responded to this dilemma by depicting Le Bon's actions as an attack on republican virtue. This dissociated his mission in the north from its political and legal context, thus condemning it as intentionally criminal while exculpating the leadership. Put differently, this allowed dissociating the Terror from the Revolution. For his part, Le Bon accepted full responsibility for his mission and defended his actions as serving the interests of the people, that is, as acts of republican virtue through and through. The point is not whether Le Bon was convicted justly or whether his trial holds up to close scrutiny. Of course, it does not. The point is rather that both the case against Le Bon and his own defense emerged from the political innovations of the Revolution.

CHAPTER 3

Redress

Les Biens des Condamnés

In 1819, François Antoine de Boissy d'Anglas published a book on the life of Lamoignon de Malesherbes, the royal official in charge of the book trade from 1750 to 1763, who was guillotined in 1794. During the Revolution, Boissy was a centrist and very cautious member of the National Convention. He voted against the execution of Louis XVI, distrusted Robespierre, but knew how to pay tribute to his power when it was the wise thing to do politically.[1] After 9 Thermidor, he was appointed to the Committee of Public Safety. In that capacity he was occupied mostly with matters of subsistence. His decision to ration bread during the difficult winter of 1795 earned him the nickname Boissy Famine. He presided over the Convention during the insurrection of 1 Prairial (May 20, 1795), when a crowd of Parisian sansculottes, incensed by the harsh economic conditions, invaded the hall and presented the head of the deputy Jean-Bertrand Féraud to him on a pike. As the 1790s were drawing to a close, his opinions became more openly royalist. In spite of that, he managed to avoid being exiled after the coup of 18 Fructidor (September 4, 1797), though he had to keep a low profile. He returned to political life under Napoleon, becoming a *comte de l'Empire* in 1808, and a member of the Legion of Honor in 1811. The most illustrious chapter in his parliamentary career, however, unfolded during the Restoration. Elected to the Chamber of Peers in 1815, Boissy emerged as a staunch defender of liberal principles, taking a decisive stand for freedom of the press and of

religion. He made a valiant effort to defend his former revolutionary colleagues when Louis XVIII had many of them exiled, writing numerous petitions on their behalf and intervening personally with the king. His efforts in
this matter served to rehabilitate his reputation somewhat in republican circles.[2] It was at this time in his life that Boissy sat down to write the essay on
Malesherbes.

In the preface to the book, dedicated to his children, Boissy noted that he
had written it for their edification and did not intend it for publication. But
upon completing the work, he came to realize that a tribute to a man such as
Malesherbes should not remain a private matter. After deciding to publish the
work, he added in its first pages a speech, which he had originally delivered in
March 1795 at the Convention, on the restitution of property that had been
confiscated from the victims of the Terror. Boissy wrote that he found this
speech so relevant to the "painful circumstances" he had been forced to recall
that he thought it could be read with some interest today, "now that the sad
times, which rendered it necessary, are far behind us." At the time of deliver-
ing his speech in favor of restitution, not even a year had passed since the guil-
lotining of Malesherbes and his family, and Boissy ended his preface by
expressing hope that "their spirits, which have been afflicted with so much injustice, would find some consolation" in this homage to their memory.[3]

A tribute to the memory of victims of the Terror, an acknowledgment that
those difficult times are long gone, an appeal to the souls of the dead, and the
restitution of property—haunting and closure, side by side. Boissy's text speaks
to the difficulty at the heart of trying to redress the damage done to victims
of massive devastation. For at the end of the day, the victims want one thing:
to go back to where things were before the damage had been done. They are
hurt; their lives have been torn apart; and they want to be made whole again.
The term restitution itself, as the legal means by which a state fulfills its obligation to repair the harm caused by its actions, designates the desire to reestablish, as much as possible, the situation that existed before the wrongful act
had been committed.[4] The historian Charles Maier notes that the aspiration
expressed in all these "re" words—retribution, restitution, remembrance, reconciliation—is inherently impossible. "None of these functions or roles can
turn time backward. We repair and remember because we cannot return.
What community existed has been rent. All the 're' functions are designed to
enable survivors to carry on life after the rending."[5]

This chapter is about this inherent impossibility: the compulsion to undo
the damage caused by the violence of Year II and the inescapable inability to
do so. It examines the debate about the restoration of property to the widows
and children of victims of the Terror. The issue first came up in Decem-

ber 1794, when numerous relatives of victims began sending petitions to revolutionary authorities, demanding the restitution of property and the rehabilitation of memory—*restitution des biens et réhabilitation de la mémoire*—of their loved ones. These demands gave rise to painful, complex debates within and beyond the walls of the Convention. They eventually led to a decree stipulating that the property confiscated from those who had been condemned to death by revolutionary tribunals would be returned to their surviving relatives. But the decree included such a long list of exceptions, and it made such contorted distinctions between deserving and undeserving victims, that, rather than closing the books on this matter, it ensured that it would remain open for years to come.

Les Biens des Condamnés

There is a perplexing phrase in the registers of the revolutionary Committee on Legislation: *les biens des condamnés*. It records petitions for the restitution of property, which had been confiscated from victims of the Terror. The phrase first appears in December 1794 and remains on the books until the passing of the decree ordering the restoration of property in June 1795. Thereafter, it appears less often and eventually it is supplanted by other concerns, such as the property that had been confiscated from the émigrés. But for this brief window of time, the phrase appears with alarming regularity, recording over 250 petitions on this matter.[6] It is perplexing, first, because of the contrast between the two words *biens* and *condamnés*, "goods" and "the condemned." *Biens*, of course, means possessions, but as the translation to English shows all too well, it is also associated with a normative or moral meaning, the good. And the contrast between something that is good and the fate of those who had been condemned to death by revolutionary tribunals is jarring. Furthermore, the possessions of the dead are what remain after they are gone, and as long as the status of these possessions remains unclear, so too is the status of their late owners. In this sense, *les biens des condamnés* is a phrase that denotes a past that has not passed.

The origins of this category were more prosaic. The *biens des condamnés* derived from the revolutionary institution of *biens nationaux*, or national properties.[7] The creation of national properties dates back to the early days of the Revolution. In May 1790, the Constituent Assembly adopted a law regulating the sale of church lands. The profits were to be used to pay off France's national debt. But there was more to it than that. By confiscating the lands of the church, dividing them into small plots, and selling them to private citizens, the revolutionaries were creating what Rafe Blaufarb has called "the great demarcation." By that he meant the distinction between power and property, politics and society. This distinction, so fundamental to modern life, did not exist under the Old Regime. Under the Old Regime, positions of public power in the administration, the military, and the judiciary were owned privately, and could be bequeathed to one's children or sold to someone else. Real estate was for the most part owned by multiple parties who stood in legally enforced relations of hierarchy and dependency to each other. In other words, under the Old Regime, public power was privately owned, and private property was publicly owned. Indeed, it is somewhat misleading to speak of private property at all before 1789.[8]

The revolutionaries changed all that. By divorcing private interest from public power, they were making a clear distinction between the social—the realm of private interests—and the political, the realm where these multiple, competing interests would be adjudicated to the benefit of all. The creation of national properties was thus more than a response to a fiscal crisis. It was "a theoretically informed, programmatic attempt to excise property from sovereignty and return it to society."[9] This was a measure that enjoyed widespread support from the population. Many communes had expressed similar sentiments in the *cahiers de doléances* that were collected across France in preparation for the meeting of the Estates-General. The commune of Borne in the department of Ardèche, for example, demanded in March 1789 that "those rich monks, who live in sluggishness and idleness, be brought back into society and that the profit generated by the sale of their possessions serve for the payment of the national debt."[10] The nationalization of church lands, which came to be known as *biens nationaux de premiére origine*, or first-round properties, was the first step on the path leading to the confiscation of *les biens des condamnés*.

The second, more immediate step in this direction was the seizure of the property of the émigrés. The revolutionaries adopted this measure in the context of war. On February 9, 1792, the Legislative Assembly decided to seize the possessions of the émigrés "so as to ensure that the Nation receives the indemnity that is owed to it, for the extraordinary costs occasioned by the conduct of the émigrés, and to take away from them the means to harm the fatherland."[11] The war between the young French Republic and an alliance of European monarchies would break out only two months later, but the buildup to it was well under way. In December the assembly summoned an army of volunteers to defend French borders, and on February 7, two days before the Legislative Assembly's decision concerning the property of the émigrés, Austria and Prussia signed an agreement to invade France. The revolutionaries targeted the refugees who had been fleeing France because many of them had joined the monarchical coalition that was forming across the border. Most of the refugees who joined this alliance were from the French nobility. Nobles made up only 17 percent or so of the émigrés, but it was high-ranking nobles, such as the prince of Condé, who formed royalist armies that joined Austrian and Prussian forces in an effort to restore Bourbon rule and end the Revolution.[12] The logic of the first revolutionary seizure of private property was thus fairly straightforward: make those who were responsible for the war pay for it. The seized possessions of the émigrés came to be known as *biens nationaux de deuxième origine*, or second-round properties.

Les biens des condamnés emerged as a subcategory of second-round properties. It is not entirely clear when the revolutionary government decided to seize the possessions of citizens who had been convicted as enemies of the people. The Law of Suspects, which formed the legal foundation of the Terror, did not stipulate this measure.[13] It merely stated that the papers found in the homes of detained suspects be sealed. The main issue seems to have been security, not punishment. Yet fairly soon after the adoption of this law, we find the revolutionary government dealing with the difficulties that arose from the expropriation of citizens who had been condemned to death. In November 1793, the Convention discussed the case of Magdelaine Françoise de Robec, the widow Kolly. Her husband, the tax-farmer Paul Pierre Kolly, had been executed in May 1793. Madame de Robec was sentenced to death as well, but her execution had been stayed because she was pregnant at the time. This raised a difficult question: What was to be done about the infant once the stay on her execution was lifted? The Convention decided that the young children of expropriated families "belong to the Republic," and as such they would be cared for at public expense.[14] An annual indemnity was offered to families who would take on the foster care of these children.[15]

These difficulties aside, there was considerable confusion around the property of suspected or convicted enemies of the people. Practices varied between localities. Some departments sequestered and inventoried the possessions of suspects but avoided selling them until judgment was rendered. Other departments proceeded with the sale of seized goods swiftly. In January 1794 the Convention charged its executive committees with preparing a report on the matter in an effort to standardize practices. In March and April, Antoine de Saint-Just, Robespierre's right-hand man in the Committee of Public Safety, presented the Ventôse Decrees. These decrees offered a radical solution to the problem. Saint-Just proposed to distribute the possessions of the enemies of the people to indigent patriots. "That which constitutes a Republic," he argued, "is the destruction of those who are opposed to it." The enemies of the Republic have excluded themselves from the social contract by their actions. The rights of man and citizen no longer apply to them. "The property of patriots will be inviolable and sacred," Saint-Just said, "but the possessions of conspirators are there for the poor."[16] Each commune was to draw up a list of the suspects and their seized possessions, as well as a list of destitute citizens who would be receiving the confiscated goods.

The Ventôse Decrees were never applied. They encountered resistance from both left and right.[17] The indigent patriots who were supposed to benefit from these measures were not eager to register themselves with the authorities. In the end, the property of citizens who had been condemned to death by revolutionary tribunals was not distributed to the needy, but rather sold in public auctions. The following, for example, is a poster announcing the sale of "the moveable goods that used to belong to Jean-Baptist Dubbary, *condamné*." Dubbary, a nobleman from Toulouse, was guillotined in March 1794. The goods on sale included "bed decorations of fine silk, chests of drawers with their marble top, sofas, and a billiard table" but excluded "bottles of local and imported wine, liquors and fruit brandy, linen that could be useful for hospitals, items that could prove useful for the army, as well as objects needed for the teaching of botany and the cultivation of plants and vegetables."[18] At the auctions, a candle or a torch would be lit and biddings were accepted as long as the flame was burning. We thus find in the official protocols of these sales descriptions such as "we lit the first fire" or "during the second flame."[19] The buyers were sometimes ordinary citizens, but more often they were speculators or "professional buyers" who tended to drive prices up.[20]

There are two points about *les biens des condamnés* that are important for understanding some of the issues around restitution after 9 Thermidor. The first is that the expropriation of enemies of the people emerged from the context of war, much like the expropriation of the émigrés, but it did not fit neatly within it. When it came to the seizure of the property of the émigrés, the revolutionaries could rely on ancient customs established in the *ius gentium* or Law of Nations.[21] The most influential attempt to codify the Law of Nations in the eighteenth century, and the one the revolutionaries were probably most familiar with, was *Le droit des gens*, published in 1758 by the Swiss philosopher, Emmerich de Vattel.[22] Vattel argued that, in war, every nation has the right to deprive its enemies of their property. In so doing, Vattel wrote, "besides diminishing the enemy's power, we augment our own, and obtain at least partial indemnification . . . either for what constitutes the subject of the war, or for the expenses and losses incurred in its prosecution—in a word, we do ourselves justice."[23] Since most of the émigrés ended up in countries that were at war with France, and many of them joined the armies of these countries, the revolutionaries could invoke the *ius gentium* in justifying their dispossession.

Things were less clear-cut with victims of the Terror. If we follow the revolutionary legislation on seizures of property, it is easy to see an escalating dynamic whereby more and more groups are designated enemies of the Republic and treated as such. Thus, in September 1793 there was a decree ordering the expropriation of all foreign nationals; in October, it was the turn of the rebels in Lyon; in December, the Convention ordered the dispossession of parents of émigrés.[24] The expropriation of citizens delineated an ever-expanding circle of those who were excluded from the body politic. It amounted to a form of civil death, that is, "the privation of the rights and advantages of society."[25] The dispossession of victims of the Terror did eventually fall within the same dynamic, but it had different implications because it affected French citizens who did not necessarily bear arms against the Republic. In short, *les biens des condamnés* concerned civil war rather than war. Vattel's *Droit des gens* addressed this issue by arguing that "when a nation becomes divided into two parties absolutely independent, and no longer acknowledging a common superior, the state is dissolved, and the war between the two parties stands on the same ground . . . as public war between two different nations."[26] Be that as it may, the distinction between war and civil war would lead to some contorted legal and political reasoning after 9 Thermidor, when the revolutionaries would struggle to justify the restoration of property to the families of victims, but not to the émigrés.

The second point is that there was more at stake in restitution than the question of property. Petitions for restitution after the fall of Robespierre were also an effort to be brought back into society, into the body politic. They would force the revolutionaries to make difficult decisions about who was and who was not part of the social order they were trying to create. Indeed, they would force a rethinking of that social order itself. If the expropriation of victims of the Terror amounted to civil death, the struggle for restitution constituted a resurrection of sorts.

The Voices of the Victims

One of the petitions recorded in the registers of the Committee on Legislation under the heading *biens des condamnés* concerned the case of the brothers Toebaerts, merchants from Bordeaux. The two brothers were arrested as suspects during the Terror. One of them was sentenced to death. However, the wrong brother was executed in what seems to have been a tragic case of mistaken identity. In April 1795, nine months after 9 Thermidor, the surviving brother sent a petition to the Convention that began by stating, "I am André Toebaerts, merchant from Bordeaux. . . . I exist, and yet the military commission sentenced me to death." A "certificate of life" from the authorities in Bordeaux confirmed that "André Toebaerts is actually alive and is present here before us today."[27] In a different case, a prominent citizen from Lille by the name of Joseph Pâris de l'Épinard, who had been the printer of the *Gazzette du département du Nord* until he was arrested as a suspect, published a pamphlet in the fall of 1794 titled *My Return to Life after Fifteen Months of Pain*.[28] For those affected by expropriation during the Terror, 9 Thermidor marked something of a rebirth, whether as a dramatic flourish or, as in the case of André Toebaerts, quite literally.

The story of restitution after the Terror begins with the inadvertent actions of the *représentant en mission* in Bordeaux, Claude-Alexandre Ysabeau. In the weeks after the fall of Robespierre, Ysabeau, on his own accord, formed a special commission in the city. The commission proceeded to annul the judgments passed by revolutionary tribunals in the previous year and to restore property to the families of victims. The Convention did not approve of this measure. It quickly halted all actions related to the *biens des condamnés*, dissolved the special commission in Bordeaux, and recalled Ysabeau to Paris. It did not further persecute this official, "whose good views are just, no doubt, but little thought-through."[29] It was too late, however, to stop the snowball effect of Ysabeau's actions. As family members of victims learned of events in Bordeaux, they latched on to the idea of restitution, swamping the authorities with petitions. Inadvertently, Ysabeau had opened a Pandora's box.

In December 1794, a delegation of widows and orphans of victims of the Terror appeared before the Convention in Paris. The speaker of the delegation implored the legislators to "listen today to the painful cries of wives and children whose husbands and fathers have been dragged inhumanely to the scaffold." He proceeded to describe in great detail the process of expropriation: the officials arriving to sequester the property, the inventories, families deprived of resources, the corruption and speculation that accompanied the seizure and sale of these goods. He admitted that some of those convicted by revolutionary tribunals were guilty of the charges against them, but many were not. The revolutionary government itself had been saying as much since the fall of Robespierre. The speaker concluded his address by telling the deputies in the Convention that "it is from your energy . . . that France awaits a cure for the deep wounds inflicted by the barbarity of tyrants."[30] Several months later, a seventy-year-old woman appeared before the Convention to ask for an annual pension. She was the mother of Jean-Marie Girey-Dupré, a revolutionary and the editor of the newspaper *Le Patriot français*. He had been executed alongside the Girondin faction of Brissot in the fall of 1793, and his mother now had come to ask for some sort of aid or compensation. Arguing that she had spent her life's earnings on his "republican education" and that he had been her sole source of support in her old age, she asked the legislators to "hear the grim concert of groans of so many bereaved mothers who shed their tears together with the tears of a country in mourning."[31] The deputy who happened to be presiding over the session of the National Convention that day was Marie-Joseph Chénier, whose own brother, the poet André Chénier, was one of the most celebrated victims of the Terror. Chénier bestowed honors on the bereaved mother and proposed to accord her an annual pension of 1,200 livres to the resounding applause of his colleagues, who nevertheless declined to vote on the motion and promptly referred it for further discussion in the committees.

As these recurring pleas to "listen to the painful cries" and "hear the bereaved mothers" indicate, the Thermidorian Reaction opened up space for the voices of the victims. Political and economic liberalization, and even more so the relaxation of censorship, created an atmosphere where those who had been persecuted by the Jacobin dictatorship could speak of their experiences. And often, they had a captivated audience. Prison memoirs became a short-lived sensation, as former suspects freed from prison after the fall of Robespierre rushed to publish their tales of woe and misfortune. An *Almanach des prisons*, containing anecdotes, testimonies, and poems by former suspects appeared in several editions in the second half of the 1790s.[32] The most successful of these was probably the *Mémoires d'un détenu*, published in 1795 by Honoré de Riouffe. It sold multiple editions and was translated and read outside of France.[33] The narratives in these texts often followed a certain pattern: the story of the arrest, horror tales from prison, a testament of the writer's impeccable politics called a *conduit politique*, the naming of the individuals who had been responsible for the author's troubles, a demand for some form of compensation, and, often, evidence supporting the author's claims under the heading *pièces justificatives*.[34] These narratives found a readership eager for some sort of catharsis after the Terror. Victims' stories accorded with the political agenda of the Reaction, which was anxious to bolster its own legitimacy by depicting the former regime as criminal.

The petitions examined in this chapter belong to the same world, but they are also a different kind of document. Most of them were never intended for publication. They were handwritten pleas to the authorities demanding the undoing of an alleged injustice. That is to say, they were written to obtain a specific result and, as such, should be read with attention to the strategic choices behind them. But they also afford a glimpse of how those who had been affected most directly by the violence of Year II narrated what they had been through and presented themselves as victims to the state. The petitions were part of what Suzanne Desan has described as the reconstitution of civil society after the Terror. Desan studied petitions on family matters: marriage, divorce, inheritance, and property. She found that in making their personal cases, petitioners raised much broader issues, such as the gendered, patriarchal order of the Republic and, indeed, the very foundations of society.[35] Similarly, the petitions for the restoration of *les biens des condamnés* concerned specific cases, where the circumstances of each petitioner differed in some way from the circumstances of another. But here too, petitioners ended up raising broader issues, such as the nature of the Terror as a mass crime or the moral obligation of the state toward its citizens. The story of redress after the Terror unfolds in the nexus between popular demands for justice and the attitudes of legislators.

Petitions for recompense were registered in official records under the heading "relatives of condemned persons" or, more commonly, "widow of a condemned person" (*veuve de condamné*).[36] This somewhat narrow category of victimhood obscured considerable diversity from view. The Terror cast a wide net and, consequently, petitioners came from a variety of social and economic backgrounds. Most were literate, of course, or at least had access to someone who could write on their behalf. This bears mentioning because many victims of the Terror were poor, even destitute, and their names, in general, do not appear in the registers of the Committee on Legislation. As material objects, the petitions display a wide range: some form veritable dossiers, with impeccable legal reasoning, while others are little more than scribbled notes. The petition of Marie-Anne Poirevesson, for example, whose brother, Jean-Baptist Pellegrin, a captain in the gendarmerie of Gondrecourt, department of the Meuse, was executed for collaborating with the Prussian occupation of Verdun, is touching in its simplicity. Consisting of two pages, with no date and with none of the customary salutations and greetings that accompanied official letters in the eighteenth century, it makes the case that Pellegrin could not have been guilty of the charges against him because he was a real patriot. This was evidenced by the fact that he had been among the first to display the *cocarde tricolor* on his hat in his commune. The signature at the bottom of the petition seems to be in a different handwriting, suggesting that someone else had written on behalf of the petitioner.[37]

The one generalization that can be made with confidence about the petitioners is that the vast majority of them were women and, even more specifically, widows. This fact had certain social and cultural implications. The situation of single women in the eighteenth century—whether they were never married or were recently widowed—was often precarious. If they were working, their wages were barely enough for living expenses. If they were poor, they probably had lost their only source of income. They could rely on support from a network of friends and neighbors, all equally poor, but the road to utter misery was very short. The situation of widows from the nobility was quite different. In their case, the death of a husband could be liberating. They could look forward to a life of living off the income from the property of their late husbands, freed from the tutelage of marriage with its suffocating social expectations. As Olwen Hufton put it, "the wealthy, merry widow is there in her own right. *Mutilée de guerre*, hardened by experience, or made giddy with freedom . . . her *monde* was *en rose*."[38] Here too, attention must be paid to the intersection of gender norms and social status. The difficulties facing a *veuve de condamné* from the upper classes were very different from those facing a widow of a peasant or a mildly successful artisan.

What did the petitioners want? Most petitions on the matter of *les biens des condamnés* included two demands: restitution and the rehabilitation of memory. The first of these was relatively simple. Petitioners demanded that the property that had been confiscated from their husbands be restored to them. If the property had already been sold, they expected to receive its equivalent value in money or some other form of compensation. The widow Lamotte, for example, who was in her early thirties, wrote to ask for aid because much of the property that was seized when her husband was arrested had already been sold. She was left, she said, with "three poor boys . . . the eldest of whom is barely six."[39] She implored the Convention not to deprive the children of their patrimony. The reference to the difficulties of raising children without the necessary means is a recurring motif in the petitions, since many of the petitioners were mothers. Cases involving seized property that had already been sold were more complicated because restitution would mean depriving the new owners of their property. This was especially the case when either land or real estate was involved. The widow of a farmer from the area of Lyon, for example, wrote to demand usufruct, that is, the right to enjoy the fruit of the land that had been confiscated from her husband and already sold as *biens nationaux* until the Convention decided what to do in these matters.[40]

In some cases, especially when the family in question was of modest means, petitioners wrote to ask for financial aid as compensation for the unjust execution of a husband. This was the case of the brothers Louis and Fréderic Edelmann, musicians from Strasbourg, who were guillotined in July 1794. The widow of Louis Edelmann wrote to the authorities several months after 9 Thermidor asking for an annual pension. Without such a pension, she claimed,

"I could not survive, nor could my poor children. . . . My husband had no property; he was a musician." The members of the *société populaire* of Strasbourg sent a collective petition to support her case. The petition, signed by dozens, recounted how Louis, a good republican, had been arrested on the orders of Saint-Just, "who mixed up patriots and aristocrats." The members of the society donated six hundred livres to the widow, a significant sum that they collected among themselves.[41] This grassroots, collective effort on behalf of widows of victims of the Terror may seem surprising, but it was not the only one. The members of the revolutionary Section of the Market in Paris published a collective printed petition on behalf of the widow Quatremere, whose husband, a linen merchant, had been sentenced to death by the revolutionary tribunal in January 1794. The members of the section asked that the widow be allowed to reopen the drapery shop that the couple had owned and added that the Convention should "proclaim the innocence of her husband."[42]

As this last petition indicates, there was more to restitution than property. The *Dictionnaire de l'Académie française* defines restitution as an action meant to restore that which had been taken unjustly, referring not just to material possessions but also to honor: "to restore, reestablish, to repair someone's honor."[43] Honor and property were intertwined in eighteenth-century France. Violent fights over clan honor in the countryside often concerned property transfers, where, as Robert Nye put it, "terms of dignity and reputation served as metaphors for each family's struggle to accumulate and maintain the means to survive."[44] In a society where the ability of the state to regulate and shape interpersonal relations was not yet what it would become in the course of the nineteenth century, honor and reputation were matters of survival no less than material possessions.[45]

Hence, petitioners demanded not only the restoration of property but also posthumous exoneration. This demand was captured in the evocative phrase *réhabilitation de la mémoire*. This phrase alluded to a variety of measures aimed at establishing the innocence of those who had been found guilty by revolutionary tribunals. In technical, legal terms, the demand for rehabilitation of memory could mean revision (*révision*) or annulment (*cassation, annulation*). The first of these meant reviewing the material in a given case in order to determine whether the tribunal in question had followed due process and whether it was necessary to launch a retrial. The second meant a straightforward abolition of the judgment, as if it had never existed. The distinction between the two legal measures was established in a pamphlet written on behalf of the widows and orphans of victims of the Terror by the celebrated lawyer Tronson-Ducoudray. Famous for having defended Marie-Antoinette at her trial, he was incarcerated during the Terror but released from prison after

9 Thermidor. He went on to defend the notable citizens of Nantes in the trial that led to Carrier's indictment.[46] In the pamphlet he published on behalf of the widows, Ducoudray argued that revision was impossible because trials in the revolutionary tribunal were by jury; hence, testimonies were oral rather than written. There was simply not enough written material in order to review the cases.[47] Ducoudray concluded that the only feasible recourse for the Convention was to declare an annulment en masse of all the judgments handed down by revolutionary tribunals.[48] Revision and annulment were both forms of rehabilitation, but the political and moral implications of each were different. Revision was a slow, laborious process, but it implied that some of the judgments of revolutionary tribunals were valid. Annulment, on the other hand, implied that all victims of the Terror were innocent and, in this sense, the policies of the revolutionary government in Year II and, by implication, the very foundation of the Republic, were a massive act of injustice.

The demand of victims of the Terror to undo the injustice that had been done to them was embedded in a particular view of the recent past, a certain historical narrative. The widow Hélyot from Toulouse, whose husband had been a magistrate in the city's *parlement*, or appellant court, and had been guillotined in 1794, embedded her demand for posthumous exoneration in a Thermidorian narrative of crime and redemption: "It was not under the blade of the law, but under the murderous dagger of the bloody Robespierre that he had been killed so inhumanely. . . . A few silk threads of consolation now pierce through the funerary ribbons that engulf us: the Reign of Justice has arrived. It is you, citizen representatives, that brought it back to life."[49] Some of the tropes in this petition—bloody Robespierre, the Reign of Justice—were recurring motifs in the political rhetoric of the Reaction. Perhaps there was a tinge of tailoring here, using the same tropes that emanated from the debates in the Convention in order to obtain the petitioner's desired outcome. The insistence that the victims of the Terror were murdered rather than tried and found guilty, and that their executions were "juridical assassinations," was another motif that recurred in these petitions.[50]

Posthumous exoneration was also about removing the stain of being branded a traitor—letting those who had been affected back into the folds of the social contract.[51] The widower Louis François Mayoul from Arras wrote to demand the exoneration of his wife and two daughters who were executed on the same day in May 1794. "The republic cannot bring back to life the unfortunate victims," he wrote, but at least "it would provide the most unfortunate of fathers and husbands the satisfaction of seeing their memory cleansed from the horrible accusation of having conspired against the liberty of their *patrie*."[52] Sometimes petitioners made their demands in public. This was especially the case when the petitions concerned *conventionnels* who had been executed. On April 18, 1795, the widow of Gustave Dechézeaux appeared before the Convention in Paris. She came to demand the restitution of property and the rehabilitation of memory of her husband, a deputy in the Convention, who was executed in 1794 for having protested the purge of the Girondins. The widow Dechézeaux came to make her case in person, but she was not the one who actually spoke. Her brother-in-law spoke on her behalf. "You see before you the widow of Gustave Dechézeaux," he told the deputies in the assembly. "He was sacrificed, assassinated under the appearances of judicial forms for having protested those *journées* that all of France regards today as among the cruelest, most disastrous periods in world history."[53] Another member of the Convention, one Pènières, introduced the private letters that Dechézeaux had written to his mother and wife before he was guillotined.[54] There followed an emotional, public reading. The petition of the widow Dechézeaux, and all of the supporting material in her case, were collected in a book that was published at the Convention's expense and ran to some 240 pages.[55]

The appearance of the widow Dechézeaux and of others like her before the Convention was especially painful.[56] Eighty-two members of the Convention had been executed or had died in prison during the Terror.[57] The demand of the widows to undo that, which at the end of the day could not be undone, brought the fresh memories of these internal bitter conflicts to the surface. There was something of a performance of mourning in these events: the public reading of last letters, the loss of colleagues and friends, the presence of the widow, standing there silent, a mythical figure drawn from biblical tropes of vulnerability and helplessness—widows, orphans, and the poor.[58] This placing of the revolutionary widows in the limelight stood in contrast to their actual condition, which worsened during the Thermidorian Reaction. It was actually the Jacobins who had introduced a comprehensive scheme for war widows' pensions in 1793. The Thermidorians stopped allocating funds for this project gradually, and in 1798 it was repudiated along with most policies of Year II.[59] One must mention, however, that in 1796 the Council of Five Hundred decided to accord an annual pension of 2,000 francs to the widows of the Girondin deputies who had been executed in the spring of 1793. Félicité Dupont, the widow of Jacques Pierre Brissot, was one of the women who received this pension.[60] Be that as it may, the public appearances by widows of victims of the Terror to demand the rehabilitation of their loved ones illustrates one inescapable fact: the violence of Year II may have been the doing of men, but dealing with its legacies was very much the business of women.

The Case of Emilie Prax

Before moving on to examine the response of the revolutionary government to the demands of the victims, let us take a closer look at one particular case, that of Emilie Prax, the widow of Charles Blanquet-Rouville. Her husband, a former councilor in the *parlement* of Toulouse, was executed in July 1794. Emilie Prax began petitioning for restitution and rehabilitation in May 1795. A month later, the Convention passed the law on restitution, yet the petitions in the matter of Blanquet-Rouville continued until 1797. The case was even discussed in the Council of Five Hundred. Following the unfolding of this case from its beginnings to its end, which is somewhat unclear, allows us to bring together several of the themes discussed in this chapter so far: the seizure and sale of *les biens des condamnés*, the demands for restitution, the complications that arose when the property in question had been sold to multiple buyers, the moral and political implications of posthumous exoneration, and the central role of women in the struggle for redress after the Terror.

The beginning of the case lies in the early days of the Revolution. In September 1790, the National Assembly abolished the *parlements*, which had been operating in France since the Middle Ages. In response, the *parlement* of Toulouse, second only to the one in Paris in terms of its power and prestige, issued a public protest "in the name of the King, the clergy, the nobility, and all the citizens, against the attack on the rights of the Crown, the destruction of the ancient orders, the encroachment on their properties, and the upheaval in the French monarchy."[61] Based on this, all former members of the *parlement* were arrested in the spring of 1793 but were soon released. They were arrested again in the spring of 1794 and transferred to the revolutionary tribunal in Paris, where they stood trial for conspiring against the liberty of the people. They were all sentenced to death.[62]

One of them was Charles Blanquet-Rouville, viscount of Trébons. Born in 1756 in Provence to a family that traced its noble roots back to the fifteenth century, he embarked on a brief military career before purchasing a judicial position and joining the *parlement* in Toulouse. He married Emilie de Prats de Vieux, who came from another provincial noble family. The appearance of her name in later documents as Prax, shorthand for Prats de Vieux, was meant perhaps to obscure her noble status. The couple had six children, the eldest of whom was about fifteen years old at the time of Rouville's death. The family owned land in the area of Toulouse; their most important possession was probably a chateau in the municipality of Gratens, a commune in the department of Haute-Garonne. Based on the sale of Rouville's property as *biens nationaux*, we can say that he was a man of means but not extraordinarily wealthy for someone in his position.[63]

Emilie Prax's first mention in the archival record dates to November 1793. She had appeared before the local authorities to protest the confiscation of the family's property in Gratens. It seems the property was seized because Rouville failed to comply with the law of August 1, 1793, which stipulated the removal of coats of arms from all houses, parks, and gardens.[64] The letter from the authorities refers to her as "the woman Rouville de Gratens" and notes that she had testimonies of her husband's patriotism. These testimonies, however, failed to impress their intended audience.[65] It is thus in the context of dealing with the consequences of the Terror that the widow Blanquet-Rouville acquires a voice in the archival record. Before 9 Thermidor, her presence in the archive is marginal, ephemeral. After 9 Thermidor, her role becomes central.

In May 1795, Emilie Prax sent a petition to the revolutionary government in Paris demanding the restitution of property and the rehabilitation of memory of her husband. Her main claim was that his expropriation had been illegal. Her husband, she argued, was executed without being judged. The supporting material that she submitted confirmed that his name was included neither in the list of those who were tried before the revolutionary tribunal in Paris nor in the list of those who had been sentenced to death. Since there was no judgment, she maintained, all confiscations of his property were illegal and should be declared null and void. But she had more than this in mind. "There still remains for you," Emilie Prax wrote to the Convention, "a more important duty to fulfill. It consists of conveying to posterity the regrets and remorse of the French Nation for the murders committed in front of its very eyes." She went on to demand the construction of a pillar of stone with the inscription "Charles Blanquet-Rouville was murdered, not condemned." This monument was to be located in one of the public squares in Toulouse. Its construction was to be funded from the sale of the confiscated possessions of Antoine Fouquier-Tinville, the chief prosecutor of the revolutionary tribunal in Paris who himself had been tried and executed several months earlier.[66] Redress for the widow Blanquet-Rouville, therefore, was about a great many things: the restoration of material possessions, a formal acknowledgment of the injustice done to her, a public apology, a commemorative project, an act of revenge, and maybe also a desire for closure—these were all elements in her search for rehabilitation.

In June 1795, the Convention passed a law stipulating the restitution of *les biens des condamnés*. One would think that this would have resolved Emilie Prax's problems, but this was not the case. We find her petitioning again a year later, this time for the annulment of the sales that had already taken place with regard to Rouville's estate. The land in question had been divided into small plots and sold to multiple buyers, as was often the case with national properties. The law on restitution ensured that in cases where the confiscated property had already been sold, the surviving relatives would receive monetary compensation. But the widow Blanquet-Rouville wanted the sales to be annulled and the estates themselves restored to her possession. Naming the buyers of this land, which, she wrote, was "watered with innocent blood," she implored the legislators to do her justice and expressed hope that in so doing they would "provide a salutary balm that will seal the wounds, which nothing so far could heal."[67] Legal disputes between the buyers and the original owners of national properties were fairly common well into the nineteenth century.[68] The dispute between Emilie Prax and the buyers of the Rouville estate continued under the Directory, and involved the highest echelons of the Republic. Lazare Carnot, former member of the Committee of Public Safety and now one of the five directors of the Republic, presided over a discussion that ended with a resolution to uphold the sales of the estate.[69] Several months later, Antoine Thibaudeau, former secretary of the Convention and now a member of the Council of Five Hundred, proposed an opposite motion, aimed at granting the widow Blanquet-Rouville many of her requests.[70] The final outcome of the case is unclear. The paper trail ends around 1797. By her own account, Emilie Prax did receive monetary compensation and some of the confiscated goods were restored to her, but she probably never obtained the full extent of the rehabilitative measures she had been demanding for more than four years.[71]

We learn several things from this case. First, dealing with the legacies of the Terror took very concrete forms, at least in part. Numbers, estimates of value, legal disputes: these were all an essential part of the process. Second, women were at the forefront of this reckoning. The archival record of the Terror is masculine for the most part; the majority of victims were men, as were the perpetrators. But the archival record of reckoning with the Terror is peopled with women: petitioning, appearing before the authorities, running from one administrative bureau to another, picking up the pieces. Third, for many of these women, and for many of those involved in these disputes, the Terror did not end on 9 Thermidor. Looking at the transition from the Terror to its aftermath from the perspective of someone like Emilie Prax reminds us that on the level of individual experience there were considerable continuities that are difficult to see sometimes underneath the surface of the abrupt political changes of the time. No doubt, 9 Thermidor was an important turning point. Without it, relatives of victims would not have had a chance to pursue restorative justice at all. But the effort to come to terms with the Terror, which began when the repression was under way, continued across and beyond the Thermidorian divide. Individual experience, in other words, challenges conventional historical periodization. The sociologist Andrew Abbot pointed out that whereas many of the social sciences focus on structures and their transformations, the life span of most individuals cuts across these changes, sometimes more than once. Individuals, Abbot writes, "are the prime reservoir of historical connection from past to present."[72] If the Terror constituted a difficult past, Emilie Prax was one of its bearers.

The Debate on Restitution

The various demands made by widows and relatives of victims of the Terror form part of what modern scholars refer to as restorative or reparatory justice. Unlike retribution, which focuses on perpetrators and on accountability, restorative justice focuses on the victims and the rectification of past wrongs. Its backward-looking agenda often clashes with the forward-looking gaze of the state. What should be done when the reparation of individual loss comes at the expense of public gain? And how far back should the state go in trying to undo the damage caused by its own actions?[73] Reparatory justice involves dilemmas between the retrospective and the prospective, self-interest and collective good. These dilemmas stood at the heart of the public debate occasioned by the demands for the restoration of *les biens des condamnés*.

Those who opposed restitution put forth three arguments. First, restitution would undermine the finances of the Republic, which were already fragile. Second, it was a retrogressive measure that threatened to undo much of the Revolution while trying to undo the Terror. Third, it put individual interests above the public good. The debate in the Convention started immediately after the decision to recall Ysabeau and to suspend all actions—sales or restitution—related to confiscated goods. Laurent Lecointre, famous for denouncing the seven members of the revolutionary committees, warned against the destabilizing effects of this decision on the economy. The value of the *assignats*, the paper money issued by the revolutionary government, depended greatly on the redistribution of property that had been under way since 1790.[74] Suspending the sale of *les biens des condamnés* could easily be read as a first step in a repudiation of policies in this matter, something that made both buyers and sellers very nervous. This measure, Lecointre claimed, had already resulted in a sharp depreciation of the *assignats*: "If you take one retrogressive step in this matter, what will become of public trust? What will become of our finances? If you look back even once on the matter of these possessions, you will give the government an incalculable shock."[75]

Many members of the Convention were opposed to restitution because of its retrospective nature. Reopening cases, conducting inquiries into each seizure of property, revisiting the circumstances of arrest or the denunciations that led to it—all of this could only end by delegitimizing the revolutionary project. Nicolas Raffron, who was affiliated with the Montagnards but was never really committed, argued that insofar as revolutions are like wars, there was no point in going back, trying to determine who among the dead deserved his fate. "Whatever side they have fought for, they are all buried pell-mell . . . such is the fate of war." The government, he suggested, could find other ways to compensate the families of the victims, perhaps with some sort of aid. It should "pour soothing oil on their wounds, but all other courses of action are retrogressive and are the product of the Reaction."[76]

The difficulty with restitution, and with reparatory justice more generally, was in knowing how far back to go. Jean-Baptiste Matthieu, a lawyer and a relatively moderate member of the Convention, wondered whether they were about to "lift the veil that should cover all these horrors, and to show us again the cruel spectacle of all the murders that had been committed."[77] Similar to the arguments made by Robert Lindet several months earlier, Matthieu implied that revolutions could not afford a reckoning with their own past. Their progressive nature clashed with the retrogressive implications of the victim's demands. Pierre Guyomar, a moderate member of the Convention who had tried to defend Condorcet from the Jacobins in 1793, was even more explicit: "Restoring the possessions of the condemned, this actually means a general amnesty. For, among the condemned there are émigrés, there are squanderers of public funds. Shall we restore property to the Duke of Orléans? Shall we restore to Robespierre, to Hanriot, to the conspiratorial commune of Lyon?"[78] The problem was the cumulative effect of measures like restitution. Once one started on this path, it was difficult to know when and where it would end.

The rectification of past wrongs risked undermining the revolution's most expansive vision of social justice. "I sense that you are about to restore property to those who already have," observed Guyomar.[79] The real question was how to help those who did not. Bourdon de l'Oise, a former Jacobin turned reactionary, proposed to align redress with the revolution's redistributive agenda by restoring all confiscated possessions to poor families, but only part to wealthier families.[80] At the end of the day, those who opposed restitution believed it prioritized self-interest over a broader social, perhaps even collective, vision. "The existence of society is as sacred as that of individuals. It is not for you to be generous at the expense of the people."[81]

Those who supported restitution made two arguments. First, the repressive policies of Year II were a historical injustice. As such, they had to be undone and repaired. Second, restitution was an essential element in the moral renewal of French society after the Terror. The journalist Michel Antoine Servan, whose brother Joseph had served as minister of war in 1792, published a pamphlet titled *On Assassinations and Political Theft* in 1795.[82] The repressive measures of Year II, he argued, were "juridical crimes," and the confiscation of property during the Revolution was "nothing but theft and the most tyrannical violence."[83] Situating the Reign of Terror in a *longue durée* account of spoliations and violence committed by rulers and political regimes, Servan argued that "the history of this world is nothing but a succession, a genealogy of murder and pillage." Echoing the trope of resurrection, he ended his pamphlet by writing, "Today I return, like a shadow of myself." Servan congratulated the revolutionary government for having punished the authors of these crimes but urged it not to "let the results of their most abhorrent work subsist."[84] The view that equated the confiscation of *les biens des condamnés* with theft pure and simple seems to have been rather prevalent after 9 Thermidor. The Swiss political economist François d'Ivernois analyzed what he described as the twin system of "spoliation and Terror." Referring to the guillotine as "an engine for coining money," he exclaimed that "we all know that the confiscations founded on the monstrous sentences passed by our late tyrants are robberies. . . . The ghosts of the murdered hover above this hall; they call on you to restore the property."[85]

By mentioning the duty owed to the "ghosts of the murdered," d'Ivernois may have been echoing what he heard in the speeches in favor of restitution made by members of the Convention. The most influential of these was the speech made by Boissy d'Anglas in March 1795, when he urged his colleagues to annul the judgments passed by revolutionary tribunals and to restore the confiscated possessions to the families of victims. By removing Robespierre on 9 Thermidor, Boissy told the Convention, "we have taken on before the entire universe the sacred commitment to be just, to dry the tears, to soften the pains, to cure the wounds of the unfortunate victims of tyranny. . . . We cannot bring back to life those whom crime has struck down, but at least let us console their spirits [*mânes*], which, at this very moment, surround us, follow us, press us, and roam this place." Restitution, in Boissy's words, was an act of healing, a duty of the living to the dead. But it was also a necessary measure politically and economically. Politically, it would help to rebuild the fledgling legitimacy of the revolutionary government after the Terror. "The whole of Europe has its eyes on us," Boissy told his colleagues. "It awaits in silence the decrees that are going to be pronounced by an assembly whose liberty has been restored." Economically, restitution was necessary to rebuild public trust. Against those who argued that the restoration of *les biens des condamnés* would ruin the finances of the Republic, he argued that, first, the sums involved were relatively modest and, second, a healthy republican economy could not be founded on injustice. "Good faith," Boissy exclaimed, "this is the basis of credit. . . . If we steal the property of individuals, by what right could we generate confidence in our money?"[86] Reparatory justice was morally necessary, politically wise, and economically sound.

Boissy's speech in the Convention drew extensively on the ideas of the *philosophe* the Abbé Morellet. A contributor to Diderot and d'Alembert's *Encyclopédie* and the translator of Cesare Beccaria's influential work *On Crimes and Punishments* from Italian to French, Morellet was one of the last living *philosophes* at the time of the Revolution.[87] In 1795 he intervened in the debate on *les biens des condamnés* by publishing a pamphlet titled *Le cri des familles*. By his account, it sold more than three thousand copies in two weeks.[88] In it, Morellet argued that undoing the damage done to families of victims of the Terror by restoring the confiscated possessions to them was an essential element in the moral renewal of French society. Justice, he believed, rested on two foundations: the inviolability of property and the sacredness of family ties. The expropriation of suspects during the Terror deprived children of their rightful inheritance. "This is a question of fathers and sons," he wrote. Speaking of them by using generic terms such as inheritors and relatives "hides from view the sacred relations that have guided the legislation of all peoples."[89] Restitution, Morellet was saying, was necessary for the restoration of family ties and, by implication, social ties as a whole.

The debate on *les biens des condamnés* was thus substantial. Stretching over six months, from December 1794 to June 1795, it involved the widows of victims, members of the revolutionary government, and men of letters. It raised a series of dilemmas between the backward-looking nature of reparatory justice and the forward-looking dynamic of the Revolution, between the needs of individuals and the welfare of society. At bottom, it involved a clash between two visions of the social world, one that prioritized individual rights and the other that prioritized the collective. The difficulty of closing the books on *les biens des condamnés* was the difficulty of leaving the Terror behind. Stanislas Fréron, a member of the Convention whose newspaper *L'orateur du peuple* was one of the most influential and most incendiary platforms of the Thermidorian Reaction, lambasted the buyers of property that had been confiscated from victims: "To purchase such possessions is to nourish oneself on cadavers. . . . It is to consume the innocent blood dripping from the scaffold . . . to drink the blood of the widow and the orphan."[90] Leaving aside the hyperbolic rhetoric with its mixture of Gothic imagery, associations of cannibalism, corporeal metaphors of the body politic, and Catholic motifs of the host and the blood of Christ, this passage by Fréron suggested that as long as the question of *les biens des condamnés* was unresolved, the Terror, in some sense, was not over.

The Law of Restitution

In June 1795, the Convention adopted a law regulating the restoration of property to the widows and heirs of victims of the Terror. It stipulated that the property be restored to the families of victims en masse, without the need for exoneration or revision of judgment. The law was divided into two parts. The first part specified who would benefit and who would be excluded from this measure. The second part detailed the way restitution was to be carried out, including such issues as monetary compensation in case the possessions in question had already been sold. The first article after the preamble to the law stated simply that "all confiscations of the goods, which have been ordered by revolutionary tribunals as well as revolutionary, military, or popular commissions, since 10 March 1793 and until 8 Nivôse, Year III, are considered null and void. . . . The surviving spouses and heirs will gain full possession of them, in conformity with the laws."[91]

Several things stand out in this law. The first is the decision to eschew the revision of judgments. The preamble to the law stated that there was less harm in restoring property to the families of a few people who were actually guilty of the charges against them than in holding on to the property of those who were really innocent. This decision was criticized roundly by the families of victims. A collective petition from Bordeaux declared that the rejection of demands to rehabilitate the memory of the victims "consecrates judicial assassinations . . . and condemns us to disgrace and misery."[92] Be that as it may, the decision to restore the property en masse amounted to an acknowledgment that revolutionary justice constituted a mass crime. The second detail that stands out is the period of application specified in the law. March 10, 1793, referred to the founding of the revolutionary tribunal in Paris. Eight Nivôse, Year III, referred to the reorganization of this tribunal several months after the fall of Robespierre.[93] Choosing March 1793 as the starting date meant, of course, that the seizures of property carried out before that time, such as the expropriations of the church and the émigrés, would remain in effect. But more than that, it embedded redress in a particular narrative. "Every type of response to historical injustice," writes the legal scholar Robert Gordon, is also "a narrative that stitches together the society's past and future. . . . The regime's response to injustice is a way of defining the new society's identity . . . by getting history back on track."[94] The chronological arc of the law on restitution bracketed the interval between March 1793 and the Thermidorian Reaction as the period when things went wrong.

Finally, the list of exceptions to the law is particularly telling. It included "Louis Capet" and the royal family; the Dubarry family; those who were executed or sentenced to death in relation to 9 Thermidor; the émigrés, counterfeiters, distributors of fake *assignats*, squanderers of public funds, and, more generally, conspirators.[95] It created, in effect, a distinction between deserving and undeserving victims. One reason for this had to do with the internal politics of the Convention. The families who were to benefit from redress were mostly those who had suffered as a result of the law of suspects, the repression of the federalist revolt, and the purge of the Girondins. The political economist d'Ivernois noted that it was the need to foster alliances with former federalists and returning Girondins that shaped the policies on restitution.[96] Perhaps, but in any case the result was a compromise that accepted the need to undo the Terror but was wary of undoing too much. The distinction between *les biens des condamnés* and *les biens des émigrés* was especially interesting in this regard. During the debates that preceded the adoption of the law, the *conventionnel* Jean-Baptise Louvet, who was himself a returning Girondin, used war to justify holding on to the possessions of the émigrés while restoring the property of the victims. With the émigrés, Louvet argued, "the social pact is broken. . . . Their property is the just fruit of victory." But those who were proscribed by the laws of the Terror were part of society, and "there can be no conquest among members of the same society."[97] Setting aside the legal contortions necessary to justify holding on to one category of property while restoring another, the list of exceptions to the law on restitution was telling in its attempt to limit the retrogressive implications of reparatory justice. In effect, it drew a series of boundaries between the time of justice and the time of injustice, between deserving and undeserving victims, and, most of all, between those who were party to the social contract and those excluded from it.

The list of exceptions to the law covered many of the charges that brought people before revolutionary tribunals in the first place, so that one wonders who was left to benefit from this restorative measure. Anecdotal evidence suggests that some widows and relatives did indeed get property back. The widow of Antoine Lavoisier, the renowned chemist who was executed in 1794, managed to get back his extensive mineralogical collection.[98] Paintings, such as *Belisarius Begging for Alms* by Jacques-Louis David, were returned to their original owners.[99] So many objects of science and art were returned to their original owners that a member of the Committee of Education complained about the reduction in the collections of the Depot of Natural Science caused by "the daily restitution made to the inheritors of condemned persons."[100]

Correspondence between the revolutionary government and local authorities indicates that the process of restoration was under way within weeks after the passing of the law. It also indicates that it raised various difficulties.[101] In the absence of more systematic research, the best we can say is that the law of restitution was applied, but many families of victims probably never got their property back, or at least not all of it.[102]

Conclusion

In the aftermath of the Terror, widows of victims, revolutionary leaders, and men of letters engaged in a public debate on the restitution of *les biens des condamnés*. Petitioners demanded the restitution of property and the posthumous exoneration of their loved ones. Their demands gave rise to complex debates within and beyond the circles of revolutionary leadership. These debates were about a great many things—the stability of the Republic, the depiction of the Terror as a massive act of injustice, the extent of the state's responsibility toward those who were harmed by its actions, the clash between the rights of individuals and the collective good—but at bottom, they were about the retrospective nature of redress. It proved difficult to turn backward and face the past in the context of a revolutionary movement that was focused on the future. The law on restitution that was eventually adopted in June 1795 reflected these dilemmas. It was an ambiguous compromise between the backward-looking agenda of the victims and the forward-looking gaze of the state.

Two findings of this chapter deserve to be emphasized in particular. First, the stakes of restitution after 9 Thermidor derived from the Revolution's earlier politics of property. The revolutionaries made the ownership of property one of the essential preconditions for citizenship, that is, for full participation in civil life. The seizure of the possessions of the émigrés and of suspects during the Terror was more than an economic measure, aimed at augmenting the income of the Republic by selling these confiscated goods as national properties. It was also, and perhaps foremost, a symbolic act that aimed at signaling the exclusion of enemies of the Revolution from the body politic. In other words, it was a form of civil death; the loss of rights inflicted on a person convicted of crimes against the state. Consequently, the restoration of property marked a resurrection of sorts; the regaining of one's civil rights and a reentry, as it were, into the folds of the body politic. Second, women were at the forefront of dealing with the legacies of the Terror. The violence of Year II was by and large a masculine affair, but the struggle for redress was very much the domain of women. This fact had certain implications for how the debate on redress unfolded and for what the demands of petitioners symbolized in the public arena. The reconstruction of civil society after 9 Thermidor passed through the reparation of family ties. As was the case with religion, the process of dealing with the legacies of the Terror opened up a new space for women to emerge as political actors.[103]

The restitution of *les biens des condamnés* was the first step in a broader reparatory dynamic. It was followed soon by the restoration of the property confiscated from refractory priests.[104] Some of the possessions of the émigrés and noble families were also restored in a process that stretched across the Napoleonic period, and which was often carried out through informal arrangements and under the table.[105] In 1825, Charles X distributed a billion francs as compensation for property lost during the Revolution to some twenty-five thousand returning émigrés or their heirs. The money given out in the form of annuities via this indemnity bill, which came to be known as *le millard des émigrés*, fell short of the real value of the lost property, and the actual procedure for receiving the indemnity was widely criticized for being unfair and selective. The indemnification process was partially canceled after the 1830 Revolution, but it was discussed again during the 1848 Revolution, when the radicals demanded that the funds distributed to the émigrés since 1825 be paid back to the Republic.[106]

Reparatory justice and the demands of victims of revolutionary violence thus remained subjects of political debate well into the 1840s. This much was captured in Honoré de Balzac's novella *Le colonel Chabert*, which was published in 1832. The novella tells the story of a soldier who, having risen in the ranks of the Napoleonic army, is wounded badly while fighting against the Russians in Eylau (1807) and then left for dead on the battlefield. He survives by crawling out of the mass grave that he had been thrown into by the French soldiers who believed him to be dead. After several years, he returns to Paris only to find that his wife has remarried and that his property has been liquidated. He presents himself at the office of a lawyer, Derville, and asks him to help restore his possessions and his honor. Derville's efforts on behalf of Chabert ultimately fail, and he ends up living the rest of his days in an asylum. Balzac's novella thus brings together several of the themes that have been discussed in this chapter: redress, restitution of property, survival, and haunted memory.[107] The ghostly figure of Chabert, literally coming back from the dead to reclaim his property and his life, illustrates just how much reparation remained an open subject in the decades after the fall of Robespierre.

CHAPTER 4

Remembrance

The Mass Graves of the Terror

Balzac's novella *Le colonel Chabert*, with which chapter 3 ended, opens with the eponymous protagonist presenting himself at the Paris office of the young lawyer Derville. He tells him the story of how he died and came back to life, fighting under Napoleon in 1807. Chabert, whom Balzac describes as a "dead man," recounts how two Russian soldiers attacked him simultaneously. One of them cut him across the head with a saber, causing him to fall to the ground and be trampled by French cavalrymen in the melee. His death, he says, was announced to the emperor himself, who was very fond of him. He was thrown into a mass grave with other soldiers. He has vague memories of hearing "groans coming from the pile of corpses," and a very vivid memory of "a silence that I have never experienced anywhere else, the perfect silence of the grave." Eventually he managed to dig himself out from beneath the corpses. He describes the experience of breaking through the snow and into the light as "rising from the bowels of this pit, as naked as the day I was born." Having been found and nursed back to health by a woman and her husband, both poor peasants, it took him six months to regain his memory and realize that he was, in fact, the renowned Colonel Chabert.[1]

Balzac's novella, published in 1832, presents the Restoration as a period of recovered memories, or rather, as the struggle to recover memory. Chabert is a man of the Napoleonic period, but the book's plot unfolds after the return of the Bourbons to the throne. This return has multiple forms: the return of the king, the return of the soldier, the return of the dead, and, if one can use a concept from a later period, the return of the repressed.[2] It is effected around corpses and mass graves, carried out by digging up, by moving soil and dirt out of the way, by excavating. This was not simply a matter of metaphor. In 1815, the bodies of Louis XVI and Marie-Antoinette were dug up from the mass grave in La Madeleine, where they had been interred originally, and transferred in a royal procession for reburial in Saint-Denis, the traditional final resting place of French royalty. Other cases of digging up and reburial soon followed: Lyon in 1823, Feurs in 1829, and Orange in 1832. The Restoration was both a political and an architectural moment: the return of the Bourbons to the throne, but also the struggle to restore a dilapidated structure to its former grandeur.[3] Seen from this perspective, the Restoration emerges as a period preoccupied with digging up or exhuming the past.

This chapter is about the exhumations and reburials that took place in the aftermath of the Terror. Most of the victims of revolutionary violence were buried in mass graves. After 9 Thermidor, relatives of the victims and other citizens began gathering at these burial sites. They placed commemorative plaques there, and, in some cases, they built a cenotaph. The authorities looked unfavorably on these gatherings, worried that they might disturb the peace. This kind of spontaneous, grassroots commemoration of victims of the Terror continued at the various mass graves throughout the Napoleonic period, but in a manner that avoided publicity. The return of the Bourbons to the throne in 1814 signaled a new attitude toward the revolutionary past. This new attitude manifested itself, among other ways, in a concern for the proper burial of those who had been executed in 1793–1794. In many locations, bodies of victims were exhumed and reburied, sometimes more than once. Expiatory chapels were constructed where mass graves used to be.

In spite of the passage of time and the new politics of memory that the Restoration inaugurated, the mass graves of the Terror remained sites of contestation. Every regime change in the period was accompanied by a reevaluation of its meaning and legitimacy. After the July Revolution in 1830, local authorities expressed concern over the potential of these places to "perpetuate painful memories."[4] Following the February Revolution in 1848, the expiatory monuments were defined explicitly as "counterrevolutionary," and some were demolished.[5] Troubled and troubling places that threatened to ignite civil discord while trying to bring closure to the families of victims, the mass graves of the Terror, and the corpses they contained, were powerful, protean symbols of the political and social transformations that France experienced in this period.

As anthropologist Katherine Verdery argued, dead bodies acquire a new kind of significance in moments of radical change. They "help us see political transformation as something more than a technical process. . . . The 'something more' includes meanings, feelings, the sacred, ideas of morality, the non-rational—all ingredients of 'legitimacy' or 'regime consolidation' . . . yet far broader than what analyses employing these terms usually provide."[6] By following the transformation of these burial sites into expiatory monuments, we can see how those who were invested in, or opposed to, their maintenance tried to come to terms with revolutionary violence. Mass graves and dead bodies are material remains that make the past present. They encapsulate entire worlds of meaning: moral values, social relations, cosmic notions of life and death, time and space. By following their story from 1794 to the 1830s, we gain a glimpse at how men and women struggled to reconfigure their worlds of meaning in the disorienting context of the revolutionary era.

The Politicization of Memory in the French Revolution

Much as it did with everything else, the French Revolution politicized the memory of the dead. The earliest example is probably the death of Mirabeau in 1791. Mirabeau was one of the most popular leaders of the early Revolution and the president of the National Assembly. He was relatively young at the time of his death, only forty-two years old. His age and his fame gave rise to various rumors concerning his death. One rumor was that he died after taking part in an orgy.[7] Others suspected that his death was the result of foul play. The people of Paris, concerned over the image of their hero, demanded a clear answer; a public autopsy was performed in the presence of fifty-six witnesses. It concluded that Mirabeau had died of natural causes, unblemished, as "a great soul, worthy of the apotheosis France has conferred on him."[8] A day after Mirabeau's death the National Assembly ordered that the Church of Sainte-Geneviève be turned into a mausoleum for great men, the Panthéon. Mirabeau was the first to be buried there. Other burials soon followed: Voltaire, in 1791, thirteen years after his death; the deputy Lepeletier de Saint-Fargeau in 1793, after he was assassinated by a royalist guard; Jean-Paul Marat, interred in 1793, disinterred in 1794. Dead bodies and funerals thus became emblems of political contestation, prime opportunities for the cultivation of republican pedagogy.[9] Corpses, according to Antoine de Baecque, stood "at the heart of rituals, representations, and visions during the most critical moments of the French Revolution."[10]

The revolutionary politics of death must be seen in a broader context. At-titudes toward the dead and the dying in European culture were undergoing a sea change in the eighteenth century.[11] From the Middle Ages to the Baroque period, the idea of death was associated with pain and the torments of the afterlife. Representations of corpses emphasized the corruption and ugliness of the body after death. Secularization, and even more so the Enlightenment, transformed these notions. The *philosophes* of the eighteenth century wished to replace the Catholic cult of the dead with a more rational, scientific ap-proach. "I would like to arm decent people against the specters of pain and agony of this final period of life," wrote the Chevalier de Jaucourt, one of the most prolific contributors to Diderot and d'Alembert's *Encyclopédie*. Death, he added, was simply "narcotic sweetness."[12] According to Philippe Ariès, the fo-cus of the dying shifted from the self to the other. In Catholicism, the main concern was with the salvation of the soul, so as to save oneself from the fires of hell. With secularization, the focus shifted to the separation from loved ones, especially one's family. In this context, cemeteries, which had been languish-ing through much of the early modern period, emerged again as meaningful places, where family members of the deceased gathered to grieve and to main-tain their connection to the ones they had lost. In the decades leading to the French Revolution, and even more so in the decades that followed, cemeter-ies were relocated from urban centers to surrounding areas. They were rede-signed as spaces for quiet contemplation, Elysian Fields that mediated between the pain of loss and the comfort of memory. The early 1800s saw a "restruc-turing of the geography of the relations between the living and the dead. . . . The visit to the cemetery was one of the most significant rituals of the nine-teenth century."[13]

The transformation of attitudes toward death was thus a broad process that predated and continued after the Revolution, but it was accelerated, inflected, and made dramatically visible during the revolutionary decade. There were two contradictory dynamics at play. On the one hand, there was intense po-liticization. The *vainqueurs de la Bastille*, that is, the men who were killed storm-ing the old fortress on July 14, 1789, were immediately commemorated as martyrs to patriotism. Simple men for the most part, their funerals were lav-ish public affairs of the kind usually reserved for *les grands*, the great men of society. The National Assembly accorded annual pensions to their widows. But as the Revolution progressed, revolutionary leaders were less comfortable with honoring these men. This was because the *vainqueurs* were, after all, one of the earliest manifestations of a new phenomenon, the revolutionary crowd, which terrified the leadership in its inherent uncontrollability, its penchant for lawless violence. "Patriotism cannot be this bloody," commented Gilbert

Romme, a deputy in the National Assembly, who would go on to play a central role in the creation of the republican calendar.[14] And so the *vainqueurs* were erased from commemorations of the fall of the Bastille as time went on, though they were still honored in their respective neighborhoods by their friends and family. The politicization of the dead during the Revolution thus opened up a gap between the public and private aspects of remembrance.

On the other hand, there was an effort to dissociate funerary rites from religion, reducing death to a simple, biological fact of life. A decree issued in October 1793—this was the time of the dechristianization campaign of Year II—ordered that all religious symbols and familial decorations be removed from tombs. Visitors to cemeteries were to be greeted by one simple inscription: "Death is an eternal sleep."[15] Architectural plans proposed to harness burial places to the cultivation of republican ideals. Citizens would not be allowed to decorate the tombs of loved ones as they saw fit, out of concern that excessive adornment would violate the egalitarian principles of the Revolution. Instead, cemeteries would display allegorical images that would express republican values: "filial piety, charity, heroic courage, devotion to the fatherland, humanity, arts, sciences, literature."[16]

The revolutionary cult of the dead is best described as ambivalent. On the one hand, funerary rites were to be reduced to a minimum, stripped of the pomp and circumstance that was characteristic of the religious approach to burial. Death, as conceptualized by the *philosophes* of the Enlightenment, was simply part of nature. There was loss, to be sure, and there were complicated feelings, but it was not a spiritual transition to the afterlife. Sepulchral aesthetics were to be dignified, somber, but also austere, in line with the Jacobin ethos of simplicity and equality. On the other hand, certain deaths were mobilized to serve revolutionary ideology, and certain dead bodies were so overladen with political significance as to collapse under the weight of their own semiotic value.

The exhumation of royal cadavers from the basilica of Saint-Denis is a case in point. In October 1793, the cadavers of the kings, queens, princes, and princesses of France, which had been buried in Saint-Denis since the Middle Ages, were removed from their tombs one by one. Most were mutilated and then reburied in various mass graves. Different bodies were treated differently. The body of Turenne, marshal of France under Henri IV, was treated with respect. The body of Louis XIV was taken apart and disfigured. A republican soldier jumped into the open grave of Henri IV, *le bon roi Henri*, cut off a piece of the body, and called out while displaying it, "Here! I too am a French soldier. . . . Now I am sure to defeat the enemies of France."[17] All told, some 170 bodies were exhumed from Saint-Denis.

How should we explain this event in light of the revolutionary attitude toward death? If death was simply a biological fact of life, why bother with exhuming, mutilating, and reburying these corpses? If these corpses and their treatment were expressions of certain political values, what values were these? Certainly, it is easy to explain the profanation of Saint-Denis as an expression of anti-monarchical sentiments. But if the mortal remains of royal families were so hated as to make the thought of their ongoing presence in the city intolerable, why invest them with such potency as to make a soldier try to appropriate their power? According to the psychoanalyst Paul-Laurent Assoun, there was deep ambivalence at play here: hostility toward the royal body and, at the same time, a continuing belief in its magical qualities. As Assoun put it, the exhumation of the royal cadavers from Saint-Denis amounted to an "abolition of the past."[18]

Les cimetiéres des suppliciés

The politicization of death and dead bodies manifested itself in the burial of victims of the Terror. Everybody is familiar with the image of tumbrels carrying those about to be executed to the guillotine. It has been immortalized by nineteenth-century writers such as Charles Dickens, who wrote in *A Tale of Two Cities* (1859) about these "tumbrils . . . jolting heavily, filled with the Condemned," rolling daily through the "stony streets" of Paris.[19] Fewer people probably know or think about what was done with the corpses after the executions. Usually, a cart would carry the bodies to a burial site that was relatively close to the location of the guillotine. Upon arrival, public officials would verify the names of the dead and inventory the clothes and other belongings found on them. The bodies would then be thrown unceremoniously into a common grave, which would remain open until it was filled. Quicklime was used to decrease the odor from the decomposing bodies.[20] Unlike the tumbrels immortalized in Dickens's descriptions, the burial places of victims of the Terror have not become widely familiar symbols of this period of the Revolution. At the time of the events in question, however, they were quite familiar to Parisians and to the residents of many other towns in France. The burial places of victims of the Terror became known as *les cimetières des suppliciés*, the cemeteries of the punished.

There were multiple sites of this kind across France. In Paris, there were three: La Madeleine, Monceaux, and Picpus. La Madeleine, at the center of Paris, was the designated site of a church, which was incomplete when the Revolution broke out. It had a previous history of mass burial: in 1770, hundreds of people who had been trampled to death in a stampede following an illumination in honor of the Dauphin's marriage to Marie-Antoinette were buried there.[21] The main reason for the choice of La Madeleine as a burial site during the Terror was probably its proximity to the guillotine, which, since the beginning of 1793, stood at the Place de la Révolution, today's Place de la Concorde. Louis XVI, Marie-Antoinette, and many Girondins were buried in the mass grave at La Madeleine.[22] The second *cimetière des suppliciés* in Paris, in the Monceaux district—today's Parc Monceau—was opened in March 1793 as an ordinary cemetery called Errancis. It replaced the Madeleine as the burial place for victims of the Terror after the latter was closed down.[23] Georges Danton and Camille Desmoulins, who were both executed in April 1794 for their opposition to the continuation of the Terror, were buried there. So were Robespierre and Saint-Just. The location of the third site in the Capital, Picpus, was chosen after the guillotine had been relocated to the Place du Trône Renversé—today's Place de la Nation—in the east of Paris, close to the city walls. Picpus, the site of a convent since the seventeenth century, was nationalized and sold to a private citizen early in the Revolution. Its new owner opened a *maison de santé*, or convalescent home, there. During the Terror, the *maisons de santé* served as a kind of refuge for affluent citizens, who paid considerable sums to stay in them with the tacit understanding that they would be relatively safe from persecution. The philosopher Volney, the novelist Choderlos de Laclos, and the Marquis de Sade all whiled away some part of the Terror in Picpus.[24] In June 1794, two large mass graves were dug in the corner of the courtyard. The graves at Picpus would eventually receive the bodies of some 1,300 people who had been guillotined nearby during the Great Terror.[25]

Other parts of the country had their own *cimetières des suppliciés*. The 300 or so victims who were executed on the orders of the Popular Commission of Orange were buried in the fields of Laplane, outside of the city.[26] In Lyon, more than two thousand men were executed by cannon or firing squads following the fall of the rebellious city to the revolutionary armies in November 1793. They were buried in several mass graves where they had been shot, on the grounds of Brotteaux outside the city walls.[27] There were, of course, other mass graves and other burial sites—in the Vendée, in particular, the landscape of burial was quite varied—but these are the main sites that are discussed in this chapter.[28]

The *cimetières des suppliciés* occupied a troubling place in the mental topography of city dwellers during and after the Terror. The nineteenth-century historian Jules Michelet sensed as much. He devoted an entire chapter to the cemeteries of the Terror in his magisterial history of the French Revolution, which was written over several years from 1847 to 1853. In that chapter, Michelet mentioned the complaints sent in by residents of Paris living near these places. They were worried that the putrid air emanating from the open pits would have pernicious effects on their health. It was an unseemly topic to be writing about, and Michelet knew it. "I touch here on a sad subject," he wrote in an apologetic tone, "but history makes it necessary. . . . Pity itself was extinguished or muted; horror spoke, disgust, and the anxiety of the great city, which feared an epidemic. The living became alarmed, believing themselves to be encircled by the dead."[29]

What was it about these cemeteries that so alarmed Parisians in the late eighteenth century? This might seem like a strange question, but burial in mass graves that remained open for some time was actually quite common in early modern Europe. Only the wealthy and the noble were buried in individual, marked graves, and these were usually located in churchyards. The majority of men and women were buried in common graves. This state of affairs began to change in the eighteenth century, largely due to the Enlightenment. The emergence of the miasmatic theory, which contended that diseases spread through putrid air, led to the demand for individual tombs and for reducing overcrowding in cemeteries. These expectations, rooted in concerns over hygiene, "rapidly became a requirement of dignity and piety."[30] In 1738, Voltaire wrote about the war of the dead against the living and demanded that something be done about the state of burial places in Paris.[31] Fifty years later the French naturalist Vicq-d'Azyr warned about the "mephitic odors" emanating from decomposing corpses and proposed that graves be separated from one another by at least four feet.[32] In 1785, the bodies interred in Les Innocents, the largest cemetery in Paris, were dug up and transferred to the catacombs. The cemetery itself was closed down. Therefore, at least one explanation for the concern of Parisians living near the mass graves of the Terror is that tombs came to be seen as dangerous places for one's health in the course of the eighteenth century.

But this was not all. The reaction of Parisians to the *cimetières des suppliciés* must be seen in the context of older attitudes toward criminal corpses. In early modern European culture, the blood and clothes of criminals who had been executed were seen at times as relics and attributed with healing qualities.[33] Criminal corpses were often punished in a variety of ways after death—dismembered, displayed, dissected for anatomical purposes—and they were buried crudely outside of consecrated ground. There was a fascination with the mortal remains of criminals well into the nineteenth century. They were kept as curios and sometimes seen as possessing curative or totemic powers.[34]

According to some reports about the execution of Louis XVI, a number of spectators made their way to the foot of the scaffold after the moment of the beheading to dip their handkerchiefs in royal blood.[35] Burial places of those who were executed as criminals were troubling because they were inherently ambivalent. They were abject and revered, repulsive and fascinating at the same time. In this sense, they bring to mind Emil Durkheim's concept of the impure sacred. Durkheim contended that at the heart of religious ritual stands the relationship between two categories: the sacred and the profane. At first glance, the relationship is one of opposition, even mutual exclusion. But upon closer examination, it appears that many objects occupy a kind of middle ground between the sacred and the profane, which Durkheim referred to as the impure sacred. Perhaps a better way of understanding this is that some powers or things that were originally seen as impure or evil can become tutelary when the circumstances change, and vice versa. This ambivalence was especially true in regard to the corpse, "which at first inspires only terror and distance, but is later treated as a venerated relic."[36]

Hygiene and the ambivalent status of the criminal corpse are part of the explanation for the concern over *les cimetières des suppliciés*, but to this we must add the political resonance of these sites in the revolutionary context. This political resonance is evident in the petitions sent from the residents living near the mass grave at Picpus. The first petition on this matter was sent several weeks before the fall of Robespierre, at the height of the Great Terror. "Justly alarmed by the proximity of these graves, destined for the burial of conspirators who were struck down by the blade of the law," the residents went on to complain about the odor emanating from the graves and to demand that the authorities not allow "those who had been declared enemies of the people and the Republic while they were still alive . . . to assassinate the people after their death."[37] In another petition, sent several months after 9 Thermidor, the "conspirators" and "enemies of the people" in the first petition have been redefined as victims. "The patriots in the vicinity [of Picpus] demand in the strongest terms the disappearance of the chasm that was dug on the orders of Robespierre and his accomplices in order to bury their victims." The sight of this open mass grave, the petitioners wrote, aroused "horror . . . in the minds of good citizens."[38] The demand to cover up the *cimetières des suppliciés* was thus part of a general desire to bridge the gulf of the Terror after the fall of Robespierre.[39] Before 9 Thermidor, the burial places of victims of the Terror were disturbing, at least in part, because of the alleged political crimes of those who were buried in them. After 9 Thermidor, they were disturbing because they were physical reminders of the Terror.

The First Commemorations

The *cimetières des suppliciés* were visible remnants of the Terror. After 9 Thermidor, their presence became intolerable. Anthropologists and media scholars have noted that new regimes of visibility emerge in the context of mass violence and its aftermath.[40] What can and cannot be seen gets redefined. In this sense, dealing with the legacies of the Terror after 9 Thermidor meant, at least in part, creating new ocular realities, disappearing certain things, and making other things appear. The proprietor of Picpus complained to the authorities that his wife had fallen gravely ill "from horror and fear" at the sight of the mass graves in the courtyard of their property.[41] The mass graves at Picpus still received the bodies of those who were guillotined nearby for some time after 9 Thermidor, but the rate of executions had decreased significantly. Burial in the mass graves of the Terror became less common, but the sites themselves remained visible, and accessible to the public. In November 1794, a member of the Municipal Council of Orange, department of the Vaucluse, reported that several of the graves that were used during the Terror remained open. Large crowds were attracted to the site and the authorities worried that these public visits would "reawaken fanaticism."[42] An architect by the name of Poyet, who had worked for the Commission of Public Works during the Terror, wrote that the ongoing presence of the *cimetières des suppliciés* was a "repulsive spectacle to the eyes of humanity."[43] Eventually, the authorities in Paris had the mass graves covered and enclosed within high walls, rendering them inaccessible and hidden from view.[44]

In the years after the Terror, there was a general concern with the state of burial sites and funerary rites. A citizen by the name of Delamalle published a pamphlet about the burial of his mother, who had died of natural causes in 1793. He recounted the disrespectful conduct of the gravediggers, who were drunk. "Horror took hold of me at the sight of humanity itself being dishonored." For Delamalle, this lack of respect for the dead was indicative of a general moral crisis brought about, at least in part, by the policies of the revolutionary government. Referring to his ability to discuss these matters openly after the fall of Robespierre, Delamalle wrote: "Only tyranny could keep these justified grievances stifled in oppressed hearts, but thought broke its chains eventually."[45] He was not alone. François Antoine Daubermesnil, a member of the Council of Five Hundred under the Directory, argued that "the political movement in France has destroyed things instead of reforming [them]. . . . The religious respect for the dead, this moral link has been broken; eyes have grown accustomed not to see, hearts not to feel."[46] Wherever urban residents looked around them in the late 1790s, they saw cemeteries in a state of neglect. This negligence, noted Philippe Ariès, was "generally blamed on the Revolution, that is, the Reign of Terror."[47]

If the neglect of funerary rites was seen as indicative of a general crisis of values, it follows that the path to the moral renewal of French society after the Terror would pass through the mass graves and the bodies in them. The chemist Antoine François Fourcroy, for example, took advantage of the new political climate generated by the Reaction in order to deliver a proper eulogy to his friend and collaborator Lavoisier, who had been guillotined in 1794 and interred in the mass grave at Monceaux. Fourcroy preceded the tribute with a speech on the dire state of funerary rites in France. "Bestowing on man funerary honors when he departs from life, taking special care of the burial places of the dead, enveloping them with the respect of the living—these are duties that cannot be ignored by any policed nation."[48] The disposal of corpses during the Terror without name, without last rites, thrown pell-mell into a common grave—these things amounted to a barbarization of mores. It was necessary to restore respect for the dead in order to return to the path of virtue and civilization. "The tomb is the cradle of immortality for a virtuous man," said Claude-Emmanuel Pastoret, a member of the Council of Five Hundred.[49] Cemeteries needed to be places where people could remember their loved ones and, in so doing, reflect on the common fate of all human beings. As one administrator put it in a report on the condition of tombs in the area of Paris: "The French must feel at present the need for sweet and sentimental ideas, for social ties of every kind, so as not to fall again into the absolute destitution which had nearly led them into barbarism."[50]

The first commemorations of victims of the Terror took place in the context of this quest for moral renewal. In some places, commemoration began as an impromptu gathering. In other places, citizens purchased the land that contained the graves, or took some other steps that marked and separated the place from the surrounding environment. These actions transformed the mass graves into "fields of care," to use a phrase coined by cultural geographer Kenneth Foote.[51] Foote meant by this places that are clearly bounded, maintained carefully over time, and attract continuous ritual commemoration, often in some form of pilgrimage. This general description does not fit the aftermath of the Terror exactly. The maintenance of burial sites of victims of the Terror advanced in fits and starts from 1794 to the 1840s, waxing and waning alongside the frequent regime changes of the time. Nevertheless, the overall trajectory of commemoration around the mass graves of the Terror does fit the model of sanctification; that is, the transformation of these places that were associated with the profane—troublesome, disorderly, contagious—into sacred sites.[52]

In the town of Orange, spontaneous gatherings at the site of the mass graves began several months after the fall of Robespierre. The Popular Commission, which had sentenced hundreds of residents of the town to death during the Terror, was suspended on August 4, 1794. In October, the *représentant en mission* Jean-François Goupilleau, who had been sent to the area after 9 Thermidor, received reports of nightly gatherings in the fields of Laplane, just outside the town, where the mass graves were located. The report referred to these events as "meetings of fanatics" and urged the authorities to take the necessary measures to preserve "public tranquility."[53] Further inquiries found that the crowds gathering in Laplane consisted of both men and women, about six hundred in total. A dispatch of one hundred gendarmes was sent to the place, led by Goupilleau himself. It seems that the crowd dispersed without the need for force. A pamphlet sent to the surrounding areas explained these gatherings as attempts to reawaken discord after the revolutionary government had restored peace on 9 Thermidor. If these gatherings were allowed to continue, argued the authors of the pamphlet, "torrents of blood would have reddened our lands again." By taking prompt measures to bring these spontaneous gatherings to an end, the local authorities were "saving the region."[54] Very early on then, the commemoration of victims of revolutionary violence was seen as a threat to public order.

But things were changing rapidly, and with them the attitude of the authorities toward grassroots remembrance. Several months after the suppression of the nightly gatherings in Orange, a commemorative pedestal was placed where the guillotine used to stand in the city. It was unveiled in a public ceremony.[55] In Lyon, a cenotaph on the grounds of Brotteaux was inaugurated in the presence of a large crowd on May 29, 1795, the anniversary of the insurrection of the city against the National Convention.[56] The librarian of Lyon, Antoine-François Delandine, who had survived the prisons of the Terror himself, wrote a detailed account of the event. According to him, more than six thousand people attended the ceremony. They included the families of the victims, residents of the city, local dignitaries, soldiers of the National Guard, delegations from neighboring communes, and, somewhat surprisingly, representatives of the National Convention. For Delandine, the ceremony marked a transition from a time of conflict to a time of reconciliation and rebuilding: "An unfortunate generation . . . agitated in every way, having passed rapidly from hope to terror, from success to the scaffold, from one extreme to another, the latter as violent as the former . . . having outraged all fatal divinities—fear, vengeance, war, ambition, fury—now raises its hand to embrace peace."[57] The representatives from Paris extended the ultimate gesture of reconciliation—*le baiser fraternel*, the kiss of fraternity—to the members of the delegation from the neighboring village of Saint-Etienne.[58]

These reconciliatory tones stood in contrast to events that were unfolding in the Midi at the same time. Three weeks before the inauguration of the ceno-taph, a group of armed men in Lyon massacred several prisoners that they identified as Jacobins and "terrorists." This launched the cycle of retributive violence that came to be known as the White Terror.[59] Echoes of this popular violence were heard in the inauguration ceremony itself; some participants used the occasion to denounce certain people for their role in the Terror. One of the names mentioned was that of Claude Javogues, who had been a *représent-ant en mission* in the area, and who would be executed a year later in connec-tion with the *affaire Babeuf*.[60] Other participants swore "a war to the death against the infamous terrorists."[61] Vengeance and forgiveness thus operated side by side in these early commemorations. But none of this mattered to Delandine. For him, the inauguration of the cenotaph marked a great deliv-erance. He described how a circle of light appeared around the sun precisely as the ceremony was taking place. It was "like a celestial crown, which pre-saged the glory awaiting our cause, and was a sure sign of the immortality achieved by the friends whose ashes we were honoring."[62] It is of, course, impossible to know whether the natural phenomenon Delandine was de-scribing actually took place, but this is neither here nor there. It is clear that, for him, the commemoration of the victims in Lyon was vindication on a cosmic scale.

All of the men involved in the design of the cenotaph had been imprisoned as suspects at one point or another during the Terror. They included the ar-chitect Claude Cochet, whose brother was executed in 1794; the sculptor Jo-seph Chinard; and Delandine himself, who wrote the verses that were engraved on the façade. The design boasted a big marble coffin, which was empty. Four gargoyle-like figures adorned the corners of the edifice and a funerary urn was placed on top of a pillar. At the base of the pillar were "two statues of women shedding tears into lachrymatory vases; they seem to be in the throes of de-spair."[63] The design, which borrowed elements from Greek and Egyptian fu-nerary cultures, was somewhat outdated, certainly when compared to the modern and more daring cenotaphs designed at the same time by Cochet's teacher, the architect Étienne-Louis Boullée.[64] Be that as it may, unknown hands demolished the cenotaph in Lyon several months after its inauguration, a sign of its contested political significance.

Figure 4. The cenotaph at Brotteaux, Lyon, c. 1795. Credit: Bibliothèque nationale de France.

The Problematic Space of Memory in the Napoleonic Period

The Napoleonic period is generally underrepresented in the literature on the memory of revolutionary violence. Existing studies tend to focus on the immediate aftermath of the Terror—that is, on the Thermidorian Reaction and the Directory—or on the Restoration.[65] One gets the impression that grief and mourning for victims of the Terror came pouring out after 9 Thermidor, subsided under Napoleon, and resurfaced with force after the return of the Bourbons. There are good reasons for this. The Napoleonic state tended to suppress explicit recollections of the more incendiary aspects of the Revolution. Authorities worried that memories of this kind would disturb the peace. Civic life was stifled under Napoleon. The number of newspapers was reduced dramatically in the early 1800s, and those papers that continued to operate had to take their political articles from the *Moniteur*, where Napoleon himself controlled the content. Literary and theatrical works that appeared to criticize the emperor or advance ideas that could disrupt public order were censored. In short, the public sphere, which had expanded dramatically in the decades leading up to the French Revolution, contracted significantly under Napoleon.[66] Veterans of the revolutionary and Napoleonic wars wrote detailed accounts of massacres, pillaging, and other instances of violence, but they did so privately for the most part. They did not intend for their memoirs to be published.[67] It may also be the case that by the time the historiography reaches the Napoleonic period, it simply moves on from questions that dominated the study of the Revolution to other subjects, such as the Napoleonic wars or Napoleon himself. However one explains the paucity of scholarship on memories of the Revolution, and especially memories of the Terror under the Napoleonic regime, the result is a history that does not make sense. The individual life span of those who experienced the Terror did not mirror the political periodization of the time. Most relatives of victims also lived through the Napoleonic era and the Restoration. It makes little sense to assume that they stopped caring about the commemoration of loved ones in 1799 or in 1804, and then started caring about it again in 1814. The space for remembering revolutionary violence in the Napoleonic era was problematic, but it was not empty.

One arena for scrutinizing the ongoing presence of the revolutionary past was literature. Several novels bearing the names of the mass graves of the Terror as their titles were published in the early 1800s. The most famous of them was *Le cimetière de la Madeleine*, written by Jean Joseph Regnault-Warin. A prolific early nineteenth-century author, he is little known today outside of scholarly circles. The plot device is a series of conversations between the protagonist, a sensitive young man, and an old man, whom he encounters during an impromptu visit to La Madeleine, and who turns out to be the Abbé Edgeworth, Louis XVI's confessor at the time of the regicide. The Abbé Edgeworth recounts scenes from the death of Louis XVI to the protagonist, who responds emotionally. In spite of the title and the plot device, the novel was not written from a royalist point of view. Its politics remain ambivalent, hard to define. What mattered more to Regnault-Warin was the emotional effect of his writing on the readers. In the third section of the novel, there is a climactic scene in which the Abbé Edgeworth narrates the execution of the king in detail. After that scene, the plot shifts to the grave itself, where "women, enveloped in sorrow and calamities, arrive at this desolate place." The writer addresses the readers directly, inviting them to share the emotions awakened in him by the cemetery of La Madeleine. "Come, sweet, naïve girls and virtuous young men, listen to me. . . . May I make your breasts heave delicious sighs! May these pages, confidantes of my feelings, be moistened by your tears!"[68] Literary historian Julia Douthwaite describes the exchanges between the two narrators and between the text and the readers as an "echo chamber of sorrowful telling and tearful listening."[69] According to some accounts, the novel caused nervous breakdowns among women and opened old wounds that the government would have preferred to remain closed. Perhaps for this reason, the novel became the target of a veritable seize-and-destroy campaign that lasted for two years. The Napoleonic police seized copies of the book in cities all over France, and Regnault-Warin was arrested briefly. He was also criticized in literary circles for having chosen to write a work of fiction about the cemetery of La Madeleine, a subject that, the critics argued, was better left to historians and to "political writers."[70]

Regnault-Warin's novel was so notorious that it spawned imitators. The Grub Street author Jean-François Villemain d'Abancourt published in 1801 two novels in quick succession: *Le cimetière de la Madeleine* and *Le cimetière de Mousseaux*. The plots in both were taken from Regnault-Warin's book. A woman and her daughter stroll by the cemetery and notice a commotion. The cause of the commotion is a young boy, about fifteen years of age, who has fainted at the gate. The lady and her daughter revive the boy, and, in return, he tells them his story of woe and misfortune. He comes from a family of the nobility. His father was arrested as a suspect during the Terror and the family's property was confiscated. A loyal servant hid the boy and kept him safe. His father was then sentenced to death. The boy witnessed the execution, after which he followed the tumbrels carrying his father's headless corpse to the cemetery of Mousseaux, "known for receiving in its bosom both the executioners and the victims of the Revolution, whose cadavers were thrown there pell-mell."[71] The novels exhibit the same sentimentalist mise en abyme as in Regnault-Warin's book. There is much lifting of arms toward the heavens, tears, and sighing. Villemain d'Abancourt seems to have employed these emotional manipulations self-consciously; there are hints that he was aware of the commercial potential of the genre. The preface to his novel on La Madeleine notes: "The cemetery of La Madeleine! What a title! It makes one shudder. Couldn't we have chosen a less revolting title? But this one is new and piquant. . . . This is no small advantage."[72]

In all of these novels, the mass graves of the Terror are the setting for catharsis. It is on these burial grounds that the characters in the novels share stories of hardship with each other, shed tears together. And of course, the readers are invited to share in the outpouring of emotion as well. At times, the recollection of scenes from the Terror is morbid. In one part of Villemain d'Abancourt's *Le cimetière de la Madeleine*, the boy recounts how he returned to the cemetery several days after having followed the tumbrels carrying his father's body for burial. He wanted to find the cadaver, to see his father one last time. He approached the open mass grave. There was a burial under way and the victims of that day's executions were being brought to the place. The boy describes the "ferocious cries of the drunken soldiers" who were in charge of burying the bodies. In and around the grave, he sees "livid corpses, bloody and disfigured heads, rolling on the ground with a terrified look." Somehow, he recognized his father's head. "I threw myself violently to kiss him for the last time, but my powers failed me."[73] It is a grotesque scene, which brings to mind images of hell. It also inverts, perhaps unconsciously, an early instance of revolutionary violence. I am referring to the lynching of Foullon de Doué, an official in the Ministry of War, and his son-in-law, Bertier de Sauvigny, the *intendant* of Paris, in the days after the storming of the Bastille. According to contemporary accounts, and there are many, the crowd dragged Bertier, who was still alive at this point, toward Foullon's severed head, which was on a pike, chanting "Kiss papa! Kiss papa!"[74] The scene described in Villemain d'Abancourt's novel relates unspeakable horror—heads rolling on the ground, retaining a terrified visage—but there is also something carnivalesque about it. Much like Mikhail Bakhtin's original elaboration of this term, the boy's encounter with his father's severed head in the mass grave of Monceaux brings together jubilation—the drunk soldiers—and terror, laughter, and violence, all occasioned by overturning the normal order of things.[75] The mass graves of the Terror emerge from these novels as liminal spaces, the loci of a world gone topsy-turvy, where the rules, hierarchies, and institutions that make up the everyday have been suspended.

As for the actual commemoration at the mass graves, this too seems to have been suspended during the Napoleonic period, but not entirely. The cemetery of Picpus is a case in point. In 1796, the princess Amélie de Salm-Kyrburg of the House of Hohenzollern-Sigmaringen purchased the land that contained the mass graves. Her brother had been one of the victims buried there. Several years later, two noble sisters, the Marquise de Montagu and Madame Lafayette, whose mother was one of the victims of the Terror, formed a network of families of victims. They collected donations for the construction of a memorial on the site. The association of Picpus went on to buy the property adjacent to the mass graves, and began using it as a private cemetery. The family members of the victims who were buried in Picpus were the only ones who could purchase a burial plot there. Madame Lafayette, the wife of the celebrated general, was the first to be buried in the new cemetery in 1807.

Picpus was a problem for Napoleonic authorities. In 1804, a general reform of funerary practices stipulated the relocation of all cemeteries outside city walls. The responsibility for matters of burial was transferred from the church to municipal authorities.[76] Picpus, however, was a private cemetery within the city walls of Paris. As such, it attracted the attention of the authorities. In 1808, Napoleon's minister of police, Joseph Fouché, who had himself been a *représentant en mission* during the Terror and in that capacity had overseen the extensive reprisals in Lyon, ordered a stop to the activities in Picpus. The letter he wrote on this matter notes that "all future requests for inhumation in this cemetery shall be refused, a measure that he considers necessary so as not to perpetuate the memory of revolutionary misfortunes, *and also not to make out of the relatives of the victims a class apart*, thus to prevent the resurfacing of old hatreds."[77] In 1810, the minister of police "expressed his strong discontent" over the continued annual commemoration of the victims in Lyon, fearing that "this commemoration would reawaken dormant hatreds."[78] The mass graves of the Terror were seen as dangerous places because they had the potential to reignite civil war. In spite of Fouché's wishes, activities in Picpus continued, albeit in a subdued manner. The main cause of this tolerance was probably Napoleon himself. When Napoleon married Josephine in 1796, she was a widow with two sons. Her former husband, the vicomte de Beauharnais, was one of the victims buried in Picpus. It is probably thanks to Napoleon's personal connection to Picpus, and to his desire to make it possible for his adopted children to visit their father's burial site, that the place was allowed to exist at all.[79]

Thus, the space for commemorating the victims of the Terror during the Napoleonic era was restricted, but not void. In some parts of the country, citizens continued to commemorate their loved ones. These private instances of remembrance often took the form of little more than an improvised cross on an unmarked grave.[80] A *cimetière des suppliciés* like Picpus, which was an anomaly in the funerary landscape of the Napoleonic state, continued to function, but quietly. Works of fiction that used the mass graves of the Terror as the backdrop for a cathartic retelling of the violence of Year II sold numerous editions. But eventually, even these novels were censored by the Napoleonic police, on account that "the generations being educated currently require other historical notions, and these souvenirs of the past must cede the way to the brilliance of the present."[81]

The Construction of Expiatory Chapels during the Restoration

The return of the Bourbons to the throne in 1814 opened up space for the public remembrance of victims of the Terror. The Catholic newspaper *L'ami de la religion et du Roi* reported that within months of Louis XVIII's ascendancy to the throne, "everywhere people make haste to repay the debt that we have accrued to those who had been sacrificed to the fury of factions." Writing about a wave of commemorations and religious services—especially those devoted to the ecclesiastic victims of the September Massacres—the paper added that "everyone joins this concert of regrets, homage, expiations and prayer with zeal."[82] An eschatological narrative of French history was bound up with this commemorative revival. In this narrative, the Enlightenment was cast as the original sin, the revolutionary and the Napoleonic period as the chastisement of the French people through blood, and the Restoration as deliverance.[83]

The cult of the dead assumed a new political significance in this period. As noted at the start of this chapter, in 1815 the bodies of Louis XVI and Marie-Antoinette were exhumed from the common grave in La Madeleine and transferred in a royal procession for reburial in Saint-Denis. The construction of an expiatory chapel in their honor began that same year. Funerals of royal figures such as the Duc de Berry, who was assassinated in 1820, were carefully staged events. They were meant to endow the new regime with an aura of sacredness.[84] The sanctification of certain deaths and certain bodies went hand in hand with the erasure of others. Maréchal Ney, who was executed in 1815 for his part in Napoleon's return from exile, was buried in an unmarked grave. The four sergeants of La Rochelle, who were executed in 1822 for plotting to overthrow the monarchy, were exhumed and used for medical purposes, as were the "patriots of 1816," who were executed for similar reasons.[85] Louis

XVIII's politics of *oubli* aimed at suppressing the memory of the twenty-five years when the Bourbons were not on the throne.[86] There was a concerted effort to remove images and symbols that reminded the population of the revolutionary era. Religious burials and royal processions fostered a message of pacification and reconciliation, a return to an idyllic—and, one must add, fictive—period of peace before 1789. The *restaurateur*, or restorer, noted the psychoanalyst Paul-Laurent Assoun, imagined himself to have surpassed political conflict.[87] Yet as Emmanuel Fureix has shown, funerals, exhumations, and reburials were important during the Restoration precisely because they were supreme sites of political contestation. The exhumation and reburial of Louis XVI; the funerals of former *conventionnels* such as Jean-Jacques Cambacérès (d. 1824) and Jean-Denis Lanjuinais (d. 1827); the funeral of the revolutionary and Napoleonic soldier General Foy (d. 1825), which is said to have been attended by more than a hundred thousand spectators in Paris; the burial of François-Joseph Talma, the celebrated actor of the Comédie-Française, who had been affiliated with the Girondins and became an intimate friend of Napoleon—all were occasions for the exploration of conflicts, tensions, and reconciliation in a society that "had become opaque to itself."[88]

The commemoration of victims of the Terror, be they celebrated or ordinary, posed particular problems in this context. On the one hand, bringing those who were killed by the guillotine or by the firing squads in Lyon to proper burial served the agenda of the regime well. In 1826, for example, a religious monument to the victims of revolutionary violence was inaugurated in the commune of Feurs, not far from Lyon. The report on the inauguration noted that it was impossible to bring the "victims of the anarchy of 1793" to rest before the return of "legitimate order." The exhumation and reburial of their mortal remains—referred to as "relics"—provoked a strong emotional reaction, but it also allowed those present to, finally, "cross the abyss of the Revolution." The exhumation and reburial of the victims in Feurs was thus presented as legitimizing the restored monarchy. This was, according to the report, "an act of justice and piety in the service of public order."[89] On the other hand, all of this digging up of the past threatened to bring difficult memories back to the surface and reignite civil strife. The construction of the expiatory monument for Louis XVI and Marie Antoinette necessitated extensive excavations at the site of La Madeleine. In 1818, a concerned citizen complained to the police about what he perceived to be the disrespectful treatment of the cadavers of republican soldiers. "An upsetting spectacle is before my eyes at this very moment. The ground in the cemetery of La Madeleine is being elevated. . . . The corpses of the unfortunate victims [*condamnés*] buried there are mixed with debris and disposed of [in a similar manner]. . . . One of our friends has seen a whole head and even a skeleton still dressed in blue uniform. This is horrifying profanation."[90] The blue uniform mentioned in the letter probably belonged to a member of the National Guard or to a soldier in the revolutionary armies. The architect of the expiatory chapel wrote in response to the citizen's complaint, demanding that "religious respect" be shown to any human remains discovered during the excavations.[91] A letter sent from the chamber of peers to the police prefect, instructing him to keep this entire matter confidential "because of the great inconvenience that would be caused by a public scandal," illustrates the political sensitivity of the subject.[92]

The tension between pacification and agitation, which was caused by the commemoration of victims of the Terror, derived, at least in part, from the concept of expiation itself. The *Encyclopédie* defined expiation as "the action of suffering the punishment meted out against a crime. . . . Thus, it is said that a crime has been expiated by the effusion of blood of the one who has committed it."[93] It further identified expiation with religious rituals aimed at purifying sinners, cleansing desecrated places, and appeasing the gods. Expiation then is a concept that traverses the juridical and theological fields. It aims at the restoration of a moral order, but this restoration is carried out, in some measure at least, through the effusion of blood, that is, through violence. The commemoration of the victims of the Terror was problematic because it both contributed to the legitimacy of the new order and threatened to reawaken the civil strife the regime had been anxious to leave behind. If the monuments to the victims of revolutionary violence were to find a place in the political landscape of the Restoration, they needed to "recall without representing (the regicide), expiate without accusing (the nation), and recount without reawakening (civil conflict)."[94]

In 1814, an anonymous pamphlet announced the construction of a funerary chapel in Picpus. The pamphlet began with a geographic description of the site. According to this description, thirteen hundred victims lay buried "near the old village of Picpus, today enclosed by the Faubourg Saint-Antoine, under the walls of a garden, which belonged to the Chanoinesses nuns of Saint-Augustin."[95] This geographic precision inscribed an entire history of conflict in the built environment. The convent of the Chanoinesses nuns became famous in the seventeenth century as a retreat for noble ladies. After the revolutionaries closed down the convent and confiscated the property, it stood surrounded by the Faubourg Saint-Antoine, the quintessential district of workers and artisans, and a stronghold of the sansculottes during the Revolution.[96] The author of the pamphlet went on to express hope that "this monument becomes the sad reparation of the past and an imposing lesson for the future."[97] A desire for reparation and the persistence of conflict, which is inscribed in the geography of the city, thus operated side by side in the foundation of the monument.

Burials in Picpus were renewed a year later but under an awkward arrangement, which required the affiliated families to obtain a special authorization for each funeral. The requests for burial offer a glimpse at what the place meant for these families. In 1823, the Duc de Damas applied for a burial permit for his wife. Before her death, he wrote, she "had formed the religious project . . . of reuniting in one place all the remains of her deceased family members . . . [among them] her brother, who died [during the Revolution] while defending the cause of the throne and altar."[98] The Duc de Damas was a diehard royalist. He was one of the organizers of the flight to Varennes in 1791, and had fought against the revolutionaries as a general in the armies of the émigrés. His reference to the "throne and altar" is thus to be expected. Another nobleman émigré, Amable de Baudus, who had been the founder and editor of the monthly *Le spectateur du Nord* that was published in Hamburg from 1797 to 1803, and whose father had been one of the victims buried in Picpus, left a record of his annual pilgrimage to the site during the Restoration: "Wednesday, May 13, 1819, at Picpus with my brother; Monday, July 5, 1819, the anniversary of my father's death. Travel to Picpus. I attended mass and then prayed on the grave of the victims; Wednesday, July 5, 1820, I heard mass said in honor of my father at Picpus." In a letter to his son, de Baudus wrote that, "July 14, 1821, three days ago, my dear friend, I made the pilgrimage to Picpus, as I do every year in this month."[99] For returning noble émigrés like the Duc de Damas and Amable de Baudus, Picpus became the locus of a lost identity. Most members of the nobility made their way back to France between the late 1790s and the early 1820s, and many regained possession of land and property that they had held before the Revolution, but their status under the Old Regime could not be resurrected. The social structure had changed too much. Their position in early nineteenth-century France is best described as "socially marginal, yet symbolically central."[100] It was probably the Old Regime that they were mourning in Picpus as much as their own family members. But the references to reunification, and the temporal regularity that governs the mentions of the pilgrimage—Wednesday, July 13, 1819; Monday, July 5, 1819; Wednesday, July 5, 1820—suggest an effort to establish continuity in death where there had been rupture in life.

The monument in Picpus was unusual in its exclusiveness. The families involved in its maintenance from its origins and throughout the Restoration were almost all of the old nobility.[101] Expiatory monuments in other parts of the country had a broader social base. In Lyon, the reconstruction of the monument at Brotteaux was funded through donations. Some five hundred people gave money for this project in 1814–1815. They included Louis XVI's daughter, the duchesse d'Angoulême, and Louis XVIII's brother, the comte d'Artois, who each donated several thousand francs. But they also included subscribers who were identified simply as "priest, arborist, grocer," and even "orphan." Their contributions were much smaller, ranging from three to ten francs.[102] In Orange, the project for the construction of an expiatory monument began in 1824; it too was funded by subscriptions. Forty percent of the subscribers donated five francs or less.[103] By comparison, Gabriel de Vidaud, a local nobleman, donated six hundred francs.[104] The construction of expiatory monuments in the provinces was led by local elites, and much of the funding came from public sources such as the municipality or the regional council, but members of the lower classes were included as well, and they took an active part in supporting these projects, albeit with the meager means at their disposal.

Those involved in the creation and maintenance of expiatory monuments during the Restoration described their efforts as necessary for the reconstruction of social ties and the pacification of past conflicts. The comte d'Artois attended the cornerstone ceremony for the monument in Lyon. He promised those present that "we will not see such days of mourning and despair anymore. . . . All Frenchmen should be friends . . . and be as one family."[105] The participants in the ceremony included the civil, judicial, and military authorities of the city, public functionaries, members of the local *sociétés savants*, and members of the clergy. They marched from the city to the site of the mass graves, accompanied by the sound of artillery charges fired by the National Guard. Upon arrival, the comte d'Artois blessed a white ribbon—symbol of the restored monarchy—and attached it to the cornerstone, which was then sprinkled with holy water. The victims buried in Brotteaux, who were described in 1795 as having fought for the Republic, were now described as having died defending "the altar and the throne."[106] The repositioning of bodies was thus a form of rewriting history.

The conciliatory message of the monuments was expressed in their design. In 1816, the commission in charge of the project in Lyon called on architects and artists to submit their ideas for the monument to a competition. In the call for participants, the members of the commission specified the purpose of the edifice. Future generations, they wrote, "would say to themselves: our fathers have seen here the man that repents and the man that pardons at the foot of the same altar. . . . They [our children] will engrave here together these words, under the renewed charm of social ties: repent, pardon."[107] Reports about the inauguration of the monument emphasized its potential to lay a troublesome past to rest. "The consolation of having finally acquitted ourselves of this scared debt . . . softens profound afflictions, and leaves no more room

FIGURE 5. The expiatory monument in Brotteaux, Lyon, c. 1821. Credit: Bibliothèque nationale de France.

for resentment."[108] The architect Cochet, who had also been behind the cenotaph of 1795, was eventually chosen to design the new expiatory monument. His design consisted of a simple, pyramid-like structure, with a cross on the façade and a vaulted crypt that was to contain the remains. Engravings from the 1820s show a teacher guiding a student through the site, asking him, "Have you seen this somber view, these funerary ornaments, a tribute of our regret to the celebrated souls of the dead?"[109] Other engravings of the monument show women and children in poses that suggest prayer and mourning.

The conciliatory tone of the expiatory monuments clashed with the agitation occasioned by their construction. Building these monuments involved excavating, digging up bodies, moving soil and dirt out of the way, moving cadavers from one location to another. This was physical labor, but it was also mnemonic work. It exposed, physically and symbolically, that which had been hidden under the surface.[110] In seeking closure for the families of the victims, it threatened to bring the past back into the present. In this sense, it was destabilizing, even dangerous, work.

In 1821, for example, the body of the comte de Précy, one of the leaders of the Lyonnais rebellion in 1793, was transferred to Brotteaux for reburial in a mausoleum built especially for that purpose. A police spy present at the ceremony noted that there was much bitterness shown toward the "extraordinary pomp" of this event. Some members of the public mumbled that the

Lyonnais had fought under the *cocarde tricolore*—that is, for the Revolution—and not for the king. In any case, "it was found that such publicity awakened angry memories." These comments, the police spy noted, were made not only by "ultraliberals," but also by "wise, well-intentioned men, devoted to public order and tranquility."[111] When the actual bodies of the victims in Lyon were exhumed and transferred to the crypt of the expiatory monument, the crowd witnessing the work made note of disturbing details, such as the mismatch between the number of skulls and the number of skeletons. This was attributed to the "nature of the execution suffered by these unfortunate victims." The entire process was found to have aroused "sad and painful memories."[112] The mass graves of victims of the Terror were thus at one and the same time pacifying and agitating. The police spy who was present in the reburial of the comte de Précy noted in the same report that there were meetings of the Carbonari under way in Lyon at the same time. The Carbonari was a network of secret societies with origins in the Revolution.[113] Their meetings had nothing to do with the commemoration of victims of the Terror. But the fact that the police spy mentioned the two issues in the same report indicates that, perhaps without intending to, he was establishing a relationship between the political conflicts around the exhumation and burial of victims of the Terror and the subversive elements that operated under the restored monarchy.

In the town of Orange, the persistence of conflict around the monument to victims of the Terror took a particularly concrete form. The construction of this monument began in 1826 and it remained incomplete when the July Revolution broke out in 1830. In November of that year, the Ministry of the Interior wrote to local authorities in the area to express concern over political conflicts that had erupted around the incomplete edifice. It seems there were reports that certain groups in the town were threatening to destroy the monument, possibly with explosives. "The location of this edifice," said the letter from the ministry, "which perpetuates painful memories, seems to have been the pretext for *culpable attempts*," a euphemism for criminal conspiracies. The letter urged local authorities to relocate the monument, preferably somewhere outside the city center, "in the interests of public order and national glory."[114] The authorities in Orange failed to comply with this request. In 1831, an explosion damaged the façade of the edifice, and in 1836 there was another attempt to sabotage the structure. Eventually, after the Revolution of 1848, the city council of Orange ordered the demolition of the monument, which was now described as "counterrevolutionary."[115] The expiatory monument in Orange was never completed. The political conflicts that erupted around it show the tension between conciliation and provocation, which was caused by the public commemoration of victims of the Terror in the early nineteenth century.

Conclusion

The mass graves of the Terror had a long afterlife. The politicization of the memory of the dead during the Revolution invested them with meanings that became intolerable after 9 Thermidor. The quest for moral renewal after the fall of Robespierre expressed itself in a vigorous debate on the dire state of cemeteries and funerary rites. The first commemorations of victims of the Terror took place in this context. These were spontaneous, grassroots affairs for the most part. In some cases, there was an effort to incorporate these commemorations into revolutionary political culture, but, more often than not, these initial rituals were met with disapproval. The Napoleonic state proved especially inhospitable to anything that called public attention to the revolutionary violence of the past. While the space for remembering the victims of Year II was limited under Napoleon, it was not completely vacant. Actual commemoration may have lessened or gone underground, but works of fiction that chose the mass graves of the Terror as their subject matter cemented the presence of these troubling sites in the public imagination. The Restoration of the Bourbons opened a new era for the memory of the victims of revolutionary violence. Multiple expiatory monuments were constructed on the sites of mass graves. Their ostensible aims were conciliatory and pacifying, but they often reignited civil discord. This tension between laying a difficult past to rest and opening old wounds is inherent to the concept of expiation itself, which seeks to restore a moral equilibrium through the effusion of blood.

The question that crystallized around the mass graves of the Terror during the Restoration was how to remember the past without reawakening it. This question was not resolved. Perhaps it could not be. But its urgency says something about the changes brought about by the Revolution. Those who were involved in the creation and maintenance of expiatory monuments—at least most of them—subscribed to traditional values. The sacredness of the monarchy, Catholic practices of burial and commemoration, even the status of the old nobility—all were inscribed somehow in the sanctification of the mass graves. Yet these efforts unfolded in a political, social, and physical landscape that had been transformed by the Revolution. What may have been a private need to bring loved ones to proper burial took on a public, even political, significance that the families of the victims could not control. The desire for closure thus clashed with a social and political reality that made it difficult to leave the past behind.

The story of the mass graves of the Terror did not end with the Restoration. The bodies of the victims in Lyon, which were exhumed and reburied in

1823, were exhumed and reburied yet again in 1906, when the monument in Brotteaux was relocated to make way for urban redevelopment. The cemetery of Picpus became bound up with the Holocaust, albeit in a strange, circuitous way. During the Nazi occupation of France, some Jews—mostly mentally ill patients and pregnant women—found temporary refuge from deportation in an adjacent hospital. Furthermore, the annual commemoration of victims of the Terror and the burial of affiliated family members in the private cemetery there continue to this day. But this chapter is not really a history of these specific sites.[116] Rather, its purpose was to examine how those who had lived through the Revolution struggled to come to terms with its violence by, among other means, exhuming, reburying, and commemorating the victims of Year II. The rich afterlife of the mass graves discussed in this chapter shows that the victims of the Terror were certainly dead, but they refused, literally and figuratively, to remain buried.

CHAPTER 5

Haunting

The Ghostly Presence of the Terror

Dead that refused to remain buried appeared in one of the strangest documents I've come across in the course of my research. It is a pamphlet that tells the story of a correspondence, an exchange of letters between the living and the dead. The pamphlet was published anonymously in 1795, and it went through several editions. At its center was an exchange of letters, which took place after the Terror, between two friends who had been imprisoned together during the Terror. While in prison, they promised each other that, were they to survive, they would make sure that the whole world heard about what they had been through, and that the people who had been responsible for their misfortune would receive their just rewards. One of the friends survived, but the other was guillotined. After 9 Thermidor, the friend who had been executed appeared in the dream of the one who had survived. He reproached him for having forgotten the promise they had made each other, and subsequently, the two friends embarked on a correspondence between the world of the living and the world of the dead, where they discussed politics, gossip, and what they had been through. The pamphlet is a straightforward illustration of the notion that the memories of the Terror haunted those who had survived the experience.

This chapter explores the ghostly presence of the Terror in postrevolutionary France. So far, this book has focused on attempts to leave the Terror behind. Trials of *représentants en mission* like Joseph Le Bon placed the blame for the repression of Year II on the shoulders of the few while absolving the many. In so doing, they aimed at putting an end to the debate on the responsibility for the violence. The restoration of property to widows of victims, partial and problematic as it may have been, was meant to undo the damage caused by the policies of the revolutionary government in 1793–1794, thus closing the books on this matter. The exhumation and reburial of victims, and the construction of expiatory monuments in different locations across the country, provided some sort of closure to affiliated families. At least that was the hope. One can situate these various measures on the spectrum between vengeance and forgiveness. As Martha Minow pointed out, the various measures between vengeance and forgiveness are never perfect. They never achieve the closure they purport to bring about. But they all have this in common: "They depart from doing nothing."[1] The various ways of facing the legacies of mass violence discussed in this book so far illustrate Baczko's argument that one of the most urgent political tasks facing revolutionary France after the fall of Robespierre was liquidating the heritage of the Terror.[2] This meant freeing people who had been incarcerated wrongly, reestablishing faith in the organs of government and in the rights of man, restoring trust between citizens, in short, turning the page forever on this revolutionary episode.

Yet the figure of the ghost in the *Correspondance entre les vivans et les morts* suggested that the Terror would come back, not necessarily as an actual revival of the repression, but rather in spectral forms. This chapter discusses the appearance of these spectral forms in various arenas of social and cultural life in the late 1790s and early 1800s. From rumors concerning possessed wolves to physicians debating whether the victims of the guillotine died immediately or not; from a new type of multimedia performance that featured images of spirits rising from the grave to debates about the abolition of the death penalty in the 1830s—the thread connecting these distinct sites of social and cultural life in postrevolutionary France was the vague but all too real awareness that the Terror was over but not gone; that the violence of Year II would return to haunt French society in a variety of ways for some time to come.

The notion of ghostly presence is amorphous, but it is essential for understanding the persistence of difficult pasts in modern societies. As social theorist Avery Gordon pointed out, just because something is invisible does not mean it is not there. The traces of the past remain behind and beneath the surface of the quotidian. "Haunting," Gordon writes, "is a constituent element of modern social life . . . a generalizable phenomenon of great import."[3] In modern societies, the concept of trauma makes it possible to discuss the persistence of the past in the present, and it does so in a medical and scientific language. This concept was not available to contemporaries of the revolutionary era, but as this chapter will try to show, the notion that the Terror retained a troubling presence in the postrevolutionary landscape was already there; vague, to be sure, and not articulated fully, but there. To illuminate this notion, this chapter draws on the ideas of cultural critic Raymond Williams, and especially on his concept of the "structure of feeling," by which he meant new formations of thought that have not been articulated fully, but that compete with each other to emerge in certain historical moments in the gap between official and popular discourse.[4]

An Excursus on Terror and Trauma

Let us return to the exchange of letters between the living and the dead that opened this chapter and take a closer look at the details. The pamphlet begins with the narrator, who is not identified by name, recounting how he had been on his way one evening to the Café des Chartres in the Palais-Royal in Paris. The narrator and several of his friends used to meet at the café regularly to discuss politics and other matters of the hour. On that particular evening, he stopped by the home of his friend, C.P., whom the narrator describes as an *"enragé."* Normally, we are told, nothing could hold C.P. back from attending these meetings, but this time the narrator found him in his study in what appears to have been a state of reverie. This trance-like condition was not broken even by the sound of the song "Le Réveil du Peuple," which came from the street below.

The narrator describes C.P. as being surrounded by an "incredible quantity" of paper. Letters, pamphlets, and manuscripts were scattered all around him. He was shuffling through them like a man possessed. These papers were so white that their glare had a blinding effect on the narrator. At the same time, the script on them was written in a color so dark that it formed the "most striking contrast." The lines of writing were very neat and precise; they could even be read clearly from six or seven steps away. When the narrator stepped closer, he noticed the strangest thing: the lines of writing appeared to be quivering and changing shape, "like clouds" scattered by the wind across "the silvery face of the nocturnal deities." When the narrator tried to grab the sheets of paper in his hand to take a closer look at this strange phenomenon, the writing on them disappeared completely, only to reappear "when I placed myself at a respectful distance."[5]

At this point in the story, C.P. begins to talk, and he tells a story, a story within a story. He recounts how he had come to be in possession of these mysterious letters. He had been arrested as a suspect during the Terror and held at the Luxembourg Prison, where he became friendly with one of his cell-mates, a certain A.C. The two promised each other that, were they to survive, they would tell the world about what they had been through and would pursue "the executioners of France," even from beyond the grave. A.C. was executed, but C. P. survived and was released from prison after 9 Thermidor. One night, the ghost of his cellmate appeared in a dream. It congratulated him on his "public success" since his release from prison, but reproached him for having forgotten the promise they had made each other. For his part, A.C. was determined to keep the promise he had made, "and to instruct the living with the experience and counsel of the dead."[6] When C.P. woke up from his dream, he found this jumble of papers with their animated script in his study. It turns out these were letters sent by A.C. from the netherworld, and the two friends embarked on a correspondence, an exchange of letters between the living and the dead. The pamphlet reproduced these letters in full, and the publishers assured the readers that they were authentic and that the originals were kept in their office.

The content of the letters is not very interesting. They contain the usual combination of rudimentary political commentary with gossip about some of the celebrated figures in Paris at the time of the Thermidorian Reaction. It is the framing device that is of interest here, the story of the narrator finding C.P. amidst the jumble of papers and in a state of delirium. Several details stand out. First, there are the political clues: *enragé*, Café des Chartres, "Le Réveil du Peuple." The *enragés* were a loose coalition of radical democrats from the popular classes of Paris.[7] They had neither a clear agenda nor a clear leadership, but, being more radical than the Jacobins, they were persecuted during the Terror. The Café des Chartres was a popular meeting place for them after 9 Thermidor. Other disaffected groups such as the *jeunesse dorée*—the gilded youth of Thermidor—also met there. These groups had little in common apart from their resentment toward the Jacobins. Meeting in these cafés, they often engaged in a battle of songs with supporters of the latter. The pro-Jacobin groups would sing "La Marseillaise," whereas the *enragés* and the *jeunesse dorée* would drown them out by singing "Le Revéil du Peuple," which called on the people to repudiate the revolutionary government of Year II.[8] Based on these details, we can deduce that C.P.—and perhaps also the anonymous author of the pamphlet—was a republican who had difficulties accommodating his political views to the changing realities of the moment. He was certainly against the government of Year II, but he was not necessarily a reactionary. Like many men and women who had been involved in one way or another in the revolutionary maelstrom, he was struggling to redefine his politics after the bloodshed of 1793–1794.[9]

The second detail that stands out is the jumble of papers. The narrator describes C.P. as being surrounded by texts, submerged in words. The French Revolution was, among other things, an explosion of language.[10] Speeches, songs, debates, newspapers, pamphlets, and memoirs; those living through the Revolution wrote, talked, and read about it incessantly. The image of C.P. drowning in the written word raises the possibility of being overwhelmed by language, driven to a certain form of madness by a lexical cacophony. But the most puzzling detail is the one of distance. The narrator can only read the mobile script on the letters from the world of the dead if he stands far enough away from them. If he gets too close, the writing disappears. This is a puzzling detail because it seems paradoxical. Normally, proximity begets legibility. We see and read better up close. But here, proximity makes things illegible, hence incomprehensible, and distance becomes the condition of legibility and, by implication, knowledge. What shall we make of this rather startling proposition?

The letters reproduced in the pamphlet, it seems to me, are bearers of trauma. They tell a story that cannot really be told to an audience who cannot really understand it. Trauma is, of course, a concept rich in connotations. At its most fundamental level, it refers to experiences that are so horrifying—most notably those involving a close encounter with terror, violent death, and the threat of bodily harm—that the mind cannot process them through the normal mechanisms of memory and cognition.[11] They become split off, giving rise to a host of symptoms that take on a life of their own, disconnected from the original event. This is a somewhat simple description of a complicated, controversial concept, to say nothing of the elaborate body of scholarship that has grown around it.[12] But there are really two points that are relevant to my interests here. First, trauma is a certain attitude toward time. It is a term that describes a disruption of linear temporality, a past that has not passed. For the traumatized person, writes psychiatrist Judith Herman, "it is as if time stops at the moment of trauma."[13] Second, trauma designates the inability to tell the story of that which has taken place. People who have lived through traumatizing experiences often recount what they had been through in a fragmentary, incoherent manner.[14] Indeed, a crucial part of the healing process is regaining the power to narrate the traumatic experience.[15] As Cathy Caruth pointed out, this presents us with a paradox: "that the most direct seeing of a violent event may occur as an absolute inability to know it; that immediacy, paradoxically, may take the form of belatedness."[16] On both counts, as an attitude toward time and as a form of impossible knowledge, the concept of trauma seems apposite to the story of C.P. and the letters from the dead.

Still, trauma is a loaded term. The concept first entered the purview of historians in relation to the Holocaust. The Nazi catastrophe was of such magnitude, it was argued, that it challenged the very ability of historians to tell a coherent story about the past. The Holocaust, in other words, created a crisis of representation. For many scholars, "the Holocaust in particular is the watershed event of the modern age because, uniquely terrible and unspeakable, it radically exceeds our capacity to grasp and understand it. . . . The Holocaust is held to have precipitated, perhaps caused, an epistemological-ontological crisis of witnessing, a crisis at the level of language itself."[17] This crisis of representation, this inability to narrate the past, is what makes trauma a theoretically significant concept for historians.[18] One result of this is that using the concept of trauma to interpret the past almost always creates an association with the Holocaust. It is problematic to employ this term in order to analyze the aftermath of the Terror, because doing so implies some kind of analogy between the Revolution and modern genocide, an analogy that makes most historians deeply uncomfortable.[19]

Another problem with applying the concept of trauma directly to the experiences of men and women in the late eighteenth century is that it was not a part of their intellectual landscape. This is problematic because it implies that trauma is a timeless, universal category, applicable to all periods and places. Doing so ignores the fact that trauma is a historically specific concept. It emerged in a particular context in order to account for particular phenomena.[20] Recently, historians have used the term to analyze the decision-making process of revolutionary leaders or to explain the turn from the moderate politics of 1789 to the radicalism of 1793.[21] These accounts highlight the experiential dimension of the Revolution. They remind us that revolutionary actors were not political abstractions, but rather human beings. They were influenced by emotions, not just ideas, and susceptible to pain, not just ideological fervor.[22] But the extent to which the concept of trauma is necessary to illuminate these dimensions of the revolutionary experience remains unclear. Thus, we find ourselves in something of a conceptual bind. On the one hand, the concept of trauma is invaluable for thinking about the aftermath of events of mass violence like the Reign of Terror. On the other hand, applying the term in any straightforward manner to the revolutionary era is problematic methodologically and normatively.

Perhaps another term would serve better. The Marxist cultural critic Raymond Williams coined the phrase "structure of feeling." It is a term that tries to grasp the fluidity of lived experience and of culture. Marxist approaches to culture tend to reduce it to fixed social forms: institutions, class, and so forth. In contrast, Williams tried to characterize social experience that is not yet recognized or articulated clearly as such. A structure of feeling is a sense of a shared present "in embryonic phase before it can become fully articulate." It is a "particular quality of social experience . . . which gives the sense of a generation or a period."[23] It refers to the tension between consciousness, which is always social in Williams's view, and lived experience. This tension often gives rise to a sense of unease or discomfort. A structure of feeling is an interpretation of the world that has not yet crystallized as such, and thus exists as a general, vague, but altogether real, awareness.

The term structure of feeling refers to different ways of thinking that are competing to emerge at any particular moment in history. Williams writes of feeling rather than thought because he is talking about something that has not yet been articulated in a fully worked-out form, and so has to be inferred between the lines.[24] Williams believed that new structures of feeling emerge in the gaps between official discourse and popular culture. He saw the arts, and especially literature, as privileged sites for the formation of these new ways of thinking *avant la lettre*. He gives the example of novels in the early Victorian era. The dominant ideology in the early Victorian era, Williams argued, attributed the miseries of poverty and illegitimacy to the moral failings of individuals. By contrast, later Victorian novels written by Charles Dickens and Emily Brontë described these predicaments as part of the general social condition. In these novels, the misfortunes of the protagonists did not derive from their moral failures or deviance, but rather from the existing social order. An explicit ideology that would articulate this thought in a fully formed manner would only emerge later, in the form of mature Marxist theory. In this sense, the novels of Dickens and Brontë, respectively, gave expression to a vague structure of feeling that would emerge as a fully formed body of thought only later.[25]

In the remainder of this chapter I would like to explore a similar notion to Williams's structure of feeling. The notion that the dead of Year II were not really dead—that the Terror had not ended when it ended—emerged in various arenas of social life in the decades after the fall of Robespierre. In one area of social life, peasants believed that a wolf seen in their region was possessed by the soul of a former *représentant en mission*. In quite another area of social life, physicians argued about the effects of public executions on the mental health of the population. Seemingly, these different things have nothing to do with each other. But seen from the perspective of Williams's ideas, they amount to a vague but real awareness of the reverberations of the Terror in the post-revolutionary landscape. In other words, they constitute ways of thinking about trauma before the concept of trauma and its entire medical-philosophical language were fully formed.[26]

Visual Culture and Specters

Writing about a new style of literature that emerged in the 1790s, the Marquis de Sade noted that "it was the inevitable result of the revolutionary shocks, which all of Europe has suffered." He was referring to novels such as *The Monk* by Matthew Lewis (1796) or Ann Radcliffe's story about supernatural terrors in an old castle, *The Mysteries of Udolpho* (1794.) These are, of course, classics of Gothic fiction. Sade thought that their main merit was in their elements of "sorcery and phantasmagoria." Why did writers become preoccupied with evil, the occult, ghosts, haunted castles, and fear at the end of the eighteenth century? For Sade the answer was clear: revolutionary violence. He argued that the sentimental novel of the eighteenth-century became irrelevant against the background of the guillotine, the September Massacres, the popular lynchings of 1789, and the revolutionary wars. "There was not a man alive who had not experienced in the short span of four or five years more misfortunes than the most celebrated novelist could portray in a century." To retain their relevance as a genre of literature after the Reign of Terror, novels had to "call upon the aid of hell itself."[27]

It has since become commonplace to attribute the popularity of Gothic fiction in the late 1790s and early 1800s to the anxieties caused by the French Revolution.[28] Not all literary critics agree with this correlation, however.[29] After all, the description "a Gothic story," and many of the elements that would come to characterize this rather unstable genre, emerged in Britain in the decades before the Revolution. Nevertheless, the connection between the violence of the Revolution and the popularity of Gothic fiction seems rather clear. As Joseph Crawford argued recently, the French Revolution, and especially the Reign of Terror, made it necessary to invent new ways of talking about the impact of difficult events, and it was this need that endowed the Gothic with its valence in this period.[30] Haunting, specters, and various forms of "apparently dead people" became widespread themes in the culture of the late 1790s.[31]

Consider here the following anecdote, taken from a dictionary that was published in 1801. The villagers in the area of Nantes were alarmed at the appearance of a wolf that took to roaming nearby forests, making occasional forays into their communities in search of food. When the mutilated bodies of two little girls were discovered nearby, the peasants in the area began spreading a rumor that this wolf was actually possessed by the spirit of Jean-Baptiste Carrier. Carrier had been executed for his role in the Terror in 1794, but now, the villagers believed, he had come back in the body of this wolf, "and it is he, who is still causing distress in the region."[32] This story about Carrier and the wolf includes certain elements that are no longer part of most modern belief systems. One is metempsychosis, the belief in the transmigration of souls. The other is lycanthropy, the belief in the transformation of humans into wolves. It is difficult to know how widespread these beliefs were in the rural population of late eighteenth-century France. Certainly, wolves were a cause for concern in the countryside late into the nineteenth century.[33] But it is debatable whether one could take this anecdote as representing rural culture in this period. Be that as it may, it is a striking manifestation of the notion that the threat posed by the repression of Year II did not end on 9 Thermidor, that it would haunt French society for some time to come.

For the most part however, the attitude toward supernatural phenomena in the late eighteenth century was very different, certainly among the urban elite. Under the influence of the Enlightenment and of secularization, the belief in occult forces came to be seen as a form of vulgar credulity. Rather than defining supernatural experiences—ghosts and possessions—as part of an external reality, they were redefined as signs of an internal pathology. Apparitions came to be seen by medical science as evidence of hallucinations, not the return of the dead.[34] In the aftermath of the Terror, there were those who played on this tension between popular beliefs in ghosts and the scientific refutation of ghost sightings in order to create new ways of visualizing the effects of mass violence on society.

One of them was Etienne-Gaspard Robert, creator of the phantasmagoria. The phantasmagoria was a new type of lantern show that debuted in Paris several years after the fall of Robespierre. Robert, or, as he was more commonly known, Robertson, was a physicist, balloonist, and showbiz entrepreneur. The word "phantasmagoria" is composed of the Greek words *phantasma*, meaning "ghost," and *agora*, referring to the public spaces in Greek city states.[35] Robertson's shows consisted in the projection of images of spirits rising from the dead, a spectral gathering of sorts. The ghosts in these shows were mostly of celebrated men like Voltaire and Rousseau, but also, significantly, Robespierre and Jean-Paul Marat, the Jacobin martyr whose assassination in July 1793 became a major catalyst for the Terror. The shows usually opened with a demonstration of scientific experiments. They were a great success, attracting such figures of Parisian high society as the future empress Josephine and Madame Tallien, who ran a famous literary salon and whose husband was among the prominent leaders of the Thermidorian Reaction. The shows took place in an appropriately Gothic setting, the abandoned convent of the Capuchin Order in Paris, whose former inhabitants had been driven out by the revolutionaries and whose chapel housed the mortal remains of, among others, the marquise de Pompadour, mistress of Louis XV.[36]

What shall we make of the appearance of this curious apparatus for the projection of images of the dead coming back to life several years after one of the most emblematic events of mass death in modern history? The story practically lends itself to discussions of trauma and of coming to terms with the past. Moreover, it brings to mind recent efforts to theorize the intimate links between terror and visuality. As Bruce Hoffman observed, terror is inherently theatrical: its effectiveness depends on its ability to produce dramatic spectacles.[37] Allen Feldman's ethnographic study of terror in Northern Ireland found that violence creates new perceptual possibilities; that is, it redefines what can and cannot be seen at a given moment. More recently, W. J. T. Mitchell analyzed the images produced in the context of America's so-called War on Terror and found that they take on a life of their own, reproducing and spreading terror "often in the very act of trying to destroy it."[38] The ubiquity of images in the digital age, and the unprecedented proliferation of technologies for their reproduction, dissemination, and alteration create a strangely contradictory effect with regard to terror: it is more tangible and more amorphous at once, everywhere and thus nowhere.

Current theories of visual culture are relevant for thinking about the aftermath of the Terror in France in that they draw our attention to the fact that the Reign of Terror was a profoundly visual and visible event. Unlike modern totalitarian regimes, which tend to carry out the business of political repression in secret, the violence of the French revolutionaries took place in broad daylight, in the full gaze of the public. In the aftermath of the Terror, the authorities in revolutionary France engaged in what could be described as a process of erasure. The guillotine was removed from its central location in Paris to the outskirts of the city. The names of public spaces that were identified with some of the most famous scenes of revolutionary repression were changed to reflect a new atmosphere of stability or reconciliation. Mass graves of victims of the Terror, which remained open for much of the time in 1793–1794, were covered up and surrounded by high walls, thus removed from public view. Current theories of visual culture suggest that dealing with the legacies of the Terror in late eighteenth-century France meant, among other things, creating new ocular realities.

The phantasmagoria is particularly interesting here, because of the combination it created between the supernatural and modern visual technology. The novelty of the phantasmagoria, in terms of visual culture, was that the images moved, and the projecting apparatus was hidden from view, thus creating the impression that the images appeared out of nowhere. Early newspaper reports about the phantasmagoria, such as the following one from London in 1801, drew attention repeatedly to this technological aspect of the experience:

Figure 6. The phantasmagoria at the Capuchin Convent, Etienne-Gaspard Robertson's *Mémoires récréatifs, scientifiques, et anecdotiques du physicien-aéronaute*, c. 1798. Credit: University of Minnesota Libraries.

"These images appear without any surrounding circle of illumination and the spectators, having no previous knowledge or view of the screen . . . are each left to imagine the distance according to their own respective fancy. . . . This part of the exhibition . . . appeared to be much the most impressive."[39]

Of course, one should be cautious when applying current theories of visual culture to late eighteenth-century France. Images and image making were extremely important during the French Revolution, yet most French men and women probably never saw them.[40] Moreover, explicit representations of the Terror were discouraged and sometimes censored in its immediate aftermath. Nevertheless, the phantasmagoria was a new visual medium that constituted a sight for dealing with the legacies of the Terror. It emerged from, on the one hand, the intellectual traditions of the Enlightenment, with their emphasis on reason, science, and technology, and, on the other hand, from much older cultural beliefs in the occult and the supernatural. The phantasmagoria embodied and played on these tensions between contrasting forces. As cultural critic Terry Castle wrote about the shows: "One knew ghosts did not exist, yet one saw them anyway, without precisely knowing how."[41] The phantasmagoria was a new way for imagining and, indeed, imaging the effects of the Terror on self and society. The images that it produced occupied an ambiguous space between speech and silence, giving visual expression to the notion that postrevolutionary society was spectral in some sense, illegible to itself, haunted by the past that the Revolution had destroyed.

These claims should be elaborated by looking closely at the three fields that the phantasmagoria brought into contact with each other, namely, science, the Gothic, and visual culture. But first, a few words about Robertson, the creator of this spectacle. Etienne-Gaspard Robert was born in Liège in 1763. He had been destined for a career in the priesthood, but was distracted by other, more fashionable pursuits, namely, art and the sciences. Robertson combined these two passions by focusing on optics, a field of physics concerned with the properties of light. He published his first scientific essay in 1789, on electrical experiments.

According to his memoirs, published in 1831, Robertson developed an interest in specters, apparitions, and natural magic early in life: "I must confess that I believed in the devil, in invocations, in infernal pacts. . . . I believed that an old woman, my neighbor, had regular exchanges with Lucifer."[42] It was modern science that disabused the young Robertson of such notions. As we shall see, one of the goals of the phantasmagoria was to use science in order to prove that all beliefs in supernatural forces were rooted in ignorance and irrationality. The point here is that in his autobiographical tale of a conversion from superstition to enlightenment, Robertson embodied in a sense the discrediting of early modern popular beliefs in occult forces by modern scientific and rational thought.[43]

There is another reason for reproducing Robertson's biography: he had experienced the Terror personally. Robertson arrived in Paris in 1791 to pursue his studies and to make his name and fortune. He found employment as a tutor for the children of Madame Chevalier, wife of the former governor of India. This association with a family of the French nobility put Robertson in a dangerous position once the Jacobins took power. In his memoirs he recounts how his employer's conduct during the execution of Marie-Antoinette, in October 1793, put them both at risk. Apparently, Madame Chevalier fainted upon seeing the tumbrel that carried the queen to her death passing in the streets, and in general carried on in a manner that attracted unwanted attention from the Parisian militants, who were suspicious of any behavior that suggested royalist sympathies. Years later Robertson wrote that it seemed to him as if this incident, "present in my imagination ever since, was but yesterday."[44] He had to flee Paris subsequently and returned only after the fall of Robespierre. Robertson described the scene that he found in Paris after the Terror as one of a cautious revival: "Order, sincerity, liberty reemerged gradually; family members and friends that have been dispersed were being reunited; society, so to speak, was reconstituting itself."[45] Robertson then created the phantasmagoria at a time when the memories of the Terror were particularly immediate and visceral, for him as well as for many others in France.

But it was probably science rather than terror that was on Robertson's mind when he inaugurated the phantasmagoria in January 1798. In his memoirs, Robertson insisted that the goal of the phantasmagoria was to combat superstition and spread enlightenment.[46] It would provide spectators with a scientific explanation for apparitions and ghosts by showing how these could be produced through simple optical means. Newspaper reports indicate that people were aware of the scientific aspects of Robertson's shows. One account heralded this "spectacle of a new kind that should destroy once and for all the strange effect of an imagination influenced by absurd tales that one hears in childhood; we are talking of the terror inspired by the shadows, the spells, and the occult tales of magic."[47] The shows were thus described as being an experiment in the education of the senses.

Reality, however, was somewhat more complex. A newspaper report about one of the earliest shows described the opening monologue, in which Robertson presented himself as a man of science and promised those present that "I am not among those charlatans, those adventurers who promise what they cannot deliver." He went on to declare: "I have promised to resurrect the dead, and I shall resurrect them."[48] Advertisements for the show placed specters and science side by side: "apparitions of specters, phantoms and *revenants* (ghosts), as they should have and did appear in all times and places. Experiments with the new fluid known by the name of galvanism, whose application can introduce brief movements in dead bodies."[49] Robertson thus played deliberately on the ambiguity between credulity and reason, superstition and science.

The reference to galvanism is particularly interesting here. The term referred to the theories developed by the Italian physician and man of science Luigi Galvani (1737–1798). Galvani maintained that the principle of life was an invisible "electric fluid" that existed in living things. He was particularly famous for an experiment in which he connected the nerves and the legs of a dead frog through an electric conductor and showed that he could produce movement in that way.[50] Galvanism was one theory among many that sought to shed light on the invisible forces of nature in the late eighteenth century. Anton Mesmer's notion of animal magnetism is another example from the same period.[51] One implication of such early theories of electricity was that invisible yet very real forces connected things and events, even those distant from each other in space and time. Emotions and sensations could spread in a manner akin to contagion, even to those far from the originating event.[52] Robertson was steeped in this scientific culture; he was a member of the Galvanic Society and repeated many of Galvani's experiments in his shows.[53] This connection between the phantasmagoria and galvanism suggests the following point: Robertson's shows took place in the context of a scientific culture that sought to make the invisible, intangible forces that connected all things visible and tangible.[54] Furthermore, the phantasmagoria emerged at a particular juncture when the notion of the afterlife, just for a moment, was a real scientific possibility.

The phantasmagoria must also be seen in the context of the Gothic. The shows took place in an abandoned convent and they obviously involved ghosts. On this level alone, the affinities are clear, but they were even deeper and more explicit. One of the scenes created by the phantasmagoria depicted the poet Edward Young burying his daughter. Young was a founding figure of the Gothic genre. This particular scene was a reference to his well-known poem *Night Thoughts on Life, Death and Immortality* (1742). Even more tellingly, Robertson explained his choice of the abandoned convent as an appropriate site for his shows by referring to the "religious terror" that the place inspired in visitors.[55]

The ghosts that Robertson chose to conjure tell us something about the connections between the phantasmagoria and the aftermath of the Terror. They included such celebrated figures as Mirabeau, Rousseau, Voltaire, and the great scientist Lavoisier, who was guillotined in 1794. But they also included figures more directly identified with revolutionary violence. The description of one such show, involving the "resurrection" of Marat, is particularly interesting. Robertson often invited members of the audience to request the appearance of spirits of specific people that were dear to them. On one such occasion, a man in the audience, described as being "in a state of disorder, with disheveled hair and sad eyes," got up and declared: "Since I cannot reestablish the cult of Marat in an official journal, I would at least like to see his apparition."[56] In a scene reminiscent of sorcery, Robertson then threw blood, sulfuric acid, and some documents into a flame, and a figure appeared in the air. The man who made the request identified the apparition as Marat, but as he tried to get near and hug it, the figure's face contorted hideously and it disappeared.

As this scene suggests, Robertson's shows often flirted with politically sensitive issues. In one of the shows, a man described as an "amnestied rebel (chouan)" apparently asked whether Robertson could resurrect Louis XVI. Robertson replied tactfully to this indiscreet request: "I had the recipe for this before 18 Fructidor, but I am afraid I lost it. I'll probably never find it again, and so from now on, it will be impossible to resurrect the kings of France."[57] The mention of 18 Fructidor in this quote is a reference to an internal seizure of power within the republican government of France in 1797, in response to a perceived threat of a royalist revival. By referring to this event, Robertson was trying to distance himself from any association with royalism, but his wit did not help him in this case. Several days after this incident, the police halted his shows temporarily and confiscated his equipment.

We learn several things from Robertson's ghosts. First, the phantasmagoria sometimes referred explicitly to figures that were identified with revolutionary violence, whether as its victims or perpetrators. Second, ghosts signify the persistence of the past in the present. They are a twist in time, the return of that which should have been gone forever. This is captured well in the French term for ghosts, revenants, or "those that have come back."[58] As literary critic Leslie Fiedler argued, their popularity in the 1790s was related to the guilt of revolutionaries haunted by the past, which they had destroyed, but which, they sensed, would return to haunt them.[59] The phantasmagoria suggested in visual form that the past had not passed, that it would return to haunt the future. Finally, and most importantly, Robertson's ghosts embodied the ambivalence regarding the legacies of the Terror in late eighteenth-century France. They were a way of talking and not talking about a difficult past that many in France would have preferred to, but could not, leave behind. Specters offered a way for talking around official silences, saying in visual form what was forbidden and dangerous to say in words. As John Borneman put it, in the aftermath of political brutality "we need interlocutors—imagined and real spirits, ghosts, djins, therapists, even anthropologists—who might provide access to memory's speech, a speech about our duty to address loss."[60]

The third area of social life that Robertson's shows engaged was visual culture. Here, the phantasmagoria was an innovation. Magic lanterns had been used for the projection of images on a screen since the seventeenth century.[61] But the phantasmagoria was an improvement on magic lantern shows in several ways. First, the images moved. Robertson created movement by placing the Fantascope—the name he gave to his projection apparatus—on rails. When the device moved backwards, away from the screen, the image grew in size, and when the device moved nearer, the image decreased in size, creating the illusion that it was coming nearer or farther away from the spectators.

Second, the phantasmagoria shows were truly multimedia events. Visitors entered the venue through the darkened corridors of the convent. On their way, they passed through rooms that displayed scientific curiosities and wonders. Once inside the actual room used for the phantasmagoria, they sat in rows, in the dark. The doors were locked behind them. The images were projected to the accompaniment of the eerie sounds of a glass harmonica, a musical instrument invented by Benjamin Franklin, which was believed to have curious effects on the nerves of listeners.[62] Everything was done to increase the effect of horror. In earlier lantern shows the device itself had been at the center of interest, but here the projecting apparatus was hidden from spectators, creating the impression that the images appeared by themselves, out of thin air.[63] In the words of historian of cinema Laurent Mannoni, the impression created by the phantasmagoria was of an "assault of images."[64]

It is difficult to know what this assault of images meant to those who experienced it. Examples of audience reception in the eighteenth century are hard to come by, especially for the shows created by Robertson. Nevertheless, anecdotal evidence suggests that, at times, the links between the phantasmagoria and the Reign of Terror were quite explicit. Consider the following description of one of the scenes created by Robertson. This time, he threw into the flames a series of objects that connoted various moments of revolutionary violence: the proceedings of the National Convention's session of May 31, 1793, when the Jacobins purged the moderate faction of the Girondins from the leadership of the Revolution; scenes of prison massacres from the White Terror; collections of denunciations or judgments passed by revolutionary tribunals; a list of suspects; several issues of "a demagogic and aristocratic journal"; and an exemplar of "Le Réveil du Peuple." Robertson then pronounced the following words, in a manner akin to the incantation of witches: *"conspirators, humanity, terrorist, justice, Jacobin, public safety, alarmists, exagéré, girondin, moderate, orleaniste* . . . whereupon a group of shadowy figures appeared, covered in bloody shrouds."[65]

Obviously, Robertson was not a stickler for political coherence. The reference to revolutionary violence in his shows drew on all sides of the political spectrum. But this is not surprising. The phantasmagoria was first and foremost a form of entertainment.[66] Nevertheless, and perhaps precisely because of that, it had the capacity to sanitize, or maybe even exorcise, memories of revolutionary violence by transforming them into aesthetic objects. Contemporaries were well aware of the connections between the phantasmagoria and revolutionary violence. According to reports in the papers, the scene described above involved two members of the Committee of Public Safety, who were present in the audience that day: Bertrand Barère and Pierre-Joseph Cambon, both identified with Jacobin repression. Apparently, Robertson directed the images at them, so that the two appeared to be encircled by the blood-drenched apparitions of victims of revolutionary violence. The two then left the venue angrily, accompanied by the sounds of insults hurled at them by other spectators. I have my doubts about the truth of this story. Nevertheless, it suggests that in the aftermath of the Terror the shows of the phantasmagoria could amount at times to an indictment of sorts.

We know very little about the responses of the audience to the shows. Some commentators expressed concern over the harmful effects that the shows might exert on those with heightened sensibilities, especially pregnant women.[67] Robertson responded to these concerns by arguing that "the terror [caused by the apparitions] is much diminished by the presence of many people and by the certitude of having before one's eyes nothing but shadows, and does not produce dangerous effects."[68] This quote suggests that, at least in Robertson's mind, the nature of his shows was a collective experience, and the agreement of spectators to suspend their disbelief in order to participate in a scary, yet ultimately entertaining spectacle meant that the phantasmagoria could play a role in exorcising the ghostly presence of the Terror.

The Debate on Decapitation

The figure of the ghost, featured in the Gothic fiction of the late eighteenth century or in an innovative visual device like the phantasmagoria, was one way of expressing the awareness that the Terror retained a haunting presence long after the fact. Another arena of social life where this notion was expressed, albeit in a less direct manner, was medicine. In the late 1790s, a debate erupted among physicians on the question of whether death by the guillotine was instantaneous, or whether consciousness persisted for some time in the bodies of the beheaded. The participants in the debate were concerned mostly with scientific questions such as the nature of pain, the definition of consciousness, and the precise determination of the moment of death. For these scientists, the Terror constituted a laboratory of sorts.[69] Furthermore, the debate took place in the context of much broader concerns about the certainty or uncertainty of signs of life. The French surgeon Antoine Louis published a book on the signs of death in 1752, in response to widespread concerns at the time about people being buried alive.[70] Louis would later play a key role in the invention of the guillotine.[71] But the timing of this scientific debate, taking place immediately after the fall of Robespierre, meant that it could not be dissociated from this particular historical moment. The physician Paul Loye, who wrote a thesis on the debate in 1888, noted: "Following the massacres of the Terror, one was preoccupied exclusively with the question of the survival of consciousness. Above all, one wanted to know whether the victims of revolutionary tribunals suffered after their executions. All other questions were superfluous."[72]

The debate on decapitation was sparked by the renowned German anatomist Samuel Thomas von Sömmering. In a text published in 1795, which circulated widely among French readers, Sömmering argued that "in the head severed from the body by this mode of punishment [decapitation by the guillotine], the sentiment, the personality, the self (*moi*) remain alive for some time, thus enduring the after-pain (*arrière-douleur*) by which the neck is affected."[73] Sömmering's argument was based on the premise that the brain was the seat of consciousness and that the head could retain its "vital force" for some time after the circulation of blood had ceased, that is, after decapitation. Indeed, Sömmering even thought that it was possible to make the severed heads talk by using a pump to circulate air through the vocal cords. The French physician Jean-Joseph Sue, father of the novelist Eugène Sue, took Sömmering's arguments a step further. Sue believed that the heads of those executed by the guillotine retained the ability of "after-thought" (*arrière-pensée*) for some time.[74] These ideas led to the startling possibility that the victims of the Terror were able to perceive their own deaths.

The debate on decapitation was public enough to merit notice by that essential chronicler of Parisian daily life, Louis-Sébastien Mercier, who contended that it threatened to undo the humanitarian sentiments that motivated the invention of the guillotine.[75] The debate had been animated by popular anecdotes about severed heads that continued to exhibit signs of life after decapitation. The most famous of these anecdotes concerned Charlotte Corday, whose cheeks, so the story goes, blushed after the executioner slapped her severed head.[76] Long after the Revolution, military physicians who took part in the conquest of Algeria performed various experiments on the severed heads of Muslim convicts.[77]

But it is the way in which this scientific debate played a part in the process of dealing with the legacies of the Terror that is of primary interest here. It did this in two ways. First, the entire discussion could be read as a political allegory. Sömmering's position, which identified the brain as the seat of consciousness, fit a monarchical perception of the body politic, with the king at its head. There is some evidence that Sömmering was highly critical of the French Republic. In the closing lines of his text on decapitation, he wrote that "such abominable spectacles have not been seen even among the savages, and it was republicans who created and attended them!"[78] Similarly, those who disagreed with Sömmering's propositions did so from a scientific standpoint that accorded well with a republican image of the body. The renowned French physician and idéologue Pierre Jean George Cabanis argued that death by the guillotine was immediate because human consciousness cannot be located physiologically in a specific organ.[79] Rather, human consciousness, according to Cabanis, lies in the coordination of the totality of body parts. The linchpin of the system was the spinal cord. Since the guillotine severs the spinal cord at the neck, it follows that loss of sensation and death are instantaneous. This holistic view of the human body corresponded to a republican perception of the political community, which saw power as diffused among all its members. Several years after the debate on decapitation, Cabanis, now a member of the legislative assembly, compared society to an animated machine, "whose every part must be vivified."[80] Cabanis also berated Sömmering for adding to the sorrows of those who had lost loved ones on the scaffold by implying that the victims of the guillotine had suffered a great deal but were unable to express their pain because their vocal chords had been severed.

The possibility that life persisted for some time in victims of decapitation became an indictment of the Terror and its iconic instrument, the guillotine. Konrad Engelbert Ölsner, the publicist who first brought Sömmering's ideas to the attention of the French public, expressed his wishes that in the future the guillotine should remain nothing but a "horrible symbol of political fanaticism and its auto-da-fé."[81] The writer Philibert Nicolas Hemey d'Auberive, whose collection of anecdotes on the survival of sentiment in severed heads through the ages did much to popularize the debate, argued that even the mere possibility that death by decapitation was not instantaneous should suffice to "proscribe forever the detestable instrument of the furies of our modern tyrants."[82] Even Jean Sédillot the Younger, a physician who was critical of

Sömmering's arguments, ended his pamphlet with an emotional recounting of the experiences of the Terror. Writing of women, children, and the elderly being led to the blood-drenched site of the guillotine, and of the scandalous treatment of their remains, Sédillot asked his readers: "Until when will juridical assassination, which debases and demoralizes man, be regarded as a means of government? Who will burn publicly the instrument of so many cruelties, which have dishonored the French Revolution?"[83] So the first point about this debate is that, in addition to its scientific dimensions, it had clear political echoes that had to do with the question of facing the legacies of the Terror.

The second point is that the debate on decapitation condensed the amorphous structure of feeling of the time into one iconic image: the severed head. The public display of severed heads had a long history, of course.[84] But as Regina Janes has shown, this display took on a particularly modern meaning during the revolution. In fact, there were two competing displays of severed heads at this time. One was the head on a pike, marched through the streets of Paris by the angry populace. This kind of display signified archaic, popular violence, and the uncontrollability of the crowd. The second was the guillotine, which connoted principles of Enlightenment rationality—science, mechanical precision, and the law—and which symbolized the institutional form of revolutionary violence.[85] The heads discussed by physicians in this debate on decapitation retained then a troubling ambiguity. On one hand, here was a rational, scientific debate in the best traditions of the Enlightenment. Terrible as its subject matter might have been, it served to further the cause of knowledge. On the other hand, more than a tinge of horror colored the entire discussion. Talking heads, heads coming back to life—such images echoed the aesthetic sensibilities of the Gothic. As Julia Douthwaite pointed out, they depicted the postrevolutionary mood as a "nightmarish landscape."[86]

A series of experiments conducted by the Italian physician Giovanni Aldini during the Napoleonic era illustrate this point well. Aldini was interested in proving the theories of Luigi Galvani, his father-in-law. To that end, he conducted public experiments on bodies of convicts who had been guillotined in Bologna in 1802. Like Galvani's experiments with frogs, Aldini connected the severed heads of the convicts to their bodies by way of a metallic conductor. In the book that he published on the subject, which was dedicated to Emperor Bonaparte, Aldini described the "terrible grimaces" that he managed to produce in the faces of these beheaded convicts by using electricity.[87] He described movements of the tongue and eye pupils in the severed heads. For Aldini, these experiments proved that vital forces persisted for a while in the bodies of people who had died suddenly and violently.[88]

Aldini's experiments captured the complex meanings of the legacies of the Terror in a particularly tangible, visual manner. For one thing, the arena of these experiments became a theater of horror of sorts, where the line between the rational, scientific aspects of these practices and their disquieting, horrifying visual effects was blurred. Aldini described how he positioned the heads of two decapitated convicts in front of each other and, through the application of electricity, obtained powerful movements of their facial muscles. "It was marvelous, and at the same time terrifying, to see these two heads making horrible grimaces at each other; so much so that several of the spectators present . . . were truly terrified."[89] The experiments also raised moral concerns. One of Aldini's colleagues sent him a letter in which he expressed his concern that the experiments were "unjust and immoral," because if indeed they proved the persistence of vital forces after decapitation, then they necessarily prolonged the suffering of their unfortunate subjects.[90]

Aldini's book also contained engravings. We see the metallic conductor that connects the head to nerves that have been exposed in various parts of the body. We see two severed heads connected to each other by way of this early version of a battery (*pile*). In one of them the brain is exposed. Hovering over these objects are presumably men of science, dressed respectfully, and going

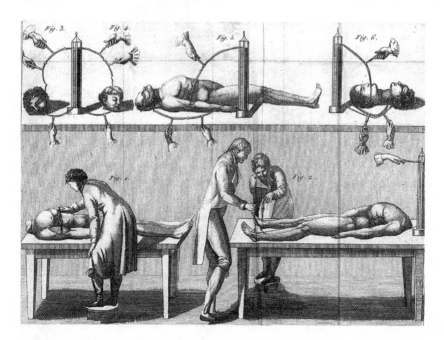

FIGURE 7. Experiments on severed heads, Giovanni Aldini's *Essai théorique et expérimental sur le galvanisme*, 1804. Credit: BIU Santé, Paris.

about their business in a somber manner that suggests detachment and seriousness.

The image brings to mind the laboratory in Mary Shelley's *Frankenstein*, which was published in 1818. In both, the rationality of science, of enlightenment, meets the irrationality of horror and the atavistic in a particularly potent mixture. The debate on decapitation captured the haunting presence of the Terror by foregrounding the iconic image of the severed head, which, as it turned out, might be alive after all.

Physicians and the Effects of the Terror

It is no coincidence that physicians occupied a central place in discussions about the effects of the Terror on self and society. Medical language and metaphors had a significant influence on the political culture of the Revolution. This was especially true after 9 Thermidor; physicians participated in debates on how to stabilize society after the Terror. They advocated hygiene, the moral "rehabilitation" of women, and strategic choices around reproduction designed to create "a new generation of rejuvenated citizens."[91] New representations of the political community and of popular sovereignty after the fall of Robespierre drew frequently on medical terms, and medical texts of the period tended to generalize from individual to public health.[92]

This, for instance, was the case of the Lyonnais surgeon Marc-Antoine Petit. In 1796, Petit delivered the inaugural lecture for the school of surgery in the city. The subject of his lecture was the influence of the Revolution on public health. He argued that the experience of revolutionary violence might feel painful while actually being beneficial, for the individual as well as for the social body. "Revolutions," Petit said, "act on the political body as medicine acts on the human body. In one as in the other, the first effect is disorder, the first sensation is pain."[93] Petit recounted numerous anecdotes about patients whose symptoms disappeared due to the effects of the Terror. This was the case of a young woman who had been suffering from palpitations of the heart, which the doctors could not resolve. The turning point came in May 1793, when she found herself caught in the bombardment of Lyon by revolutionary armies. In the sudden commotion of battle, she lost consciousness and was carried off to the hospital. After several days in which she threw up repeatedly and had high fever, she was completely cured of her previous condition. Another case involved a respectable resident of Lyon, whom Petit described as "one of the last victims of the Terror."[94] The man had been suffering from swelling in various organs for some time when he was arrested as a suspect of counterrevolutionary offenses. While in prison, his symptoms completely disappeared, but they reappeared after his miraculous liberation, which was brought about by the events of 9 Thermidor. According to Petit, then, a brief period of incarceration in one of the prisons of the Terror might actually have beneficial effects on one's health.

Petit's arguments sound strange in our day and age. Generally speaking, we tend to see the effects of terror and mass violence as negative; from the perspective of modern medicine and psychiatry, terror increases the incidence of pathology.[95] It is tempting to attribute Petit's arguments to ideology. Surely, people who were committed to the revolutionary cause would have been at pains to find some redeeming feature in its considerable violence. Yet there is little reason to assume that Petit was particularly well disposed toward the Revolution. He witnessed the siege and bombardment of Lyon, which was one of the more brutal episodes of the Reign of Terror, and he even fled the city briefly for fear of falling victim to the extensive reprisals carried out against the Lyonnais by revolutionary forces. Most of the anecdotes he drew on as evidence during his lecture were taken from his personal experiences as a surgeon in Lyon during those troubled times, a position which brought him into direct, visceral contact with the realities of revolutionary repression. Petit's views on the positive effects of the Terror cannot then be explained by his political views because his experiences gave him many reasons to resent rather than defend the revolutionary cause, certainly in its more radical form.[96]

A better explanation for his views has to do with one of the dominant medical philosophies of the eighteenth century, namely, vitalism. Vitalism involved a holistic approach to medicine, emphasizing the harmonious coordination of mind and body that together constituted what physicians referred to as "the animal economy."[97] The key to health was in the balance of the various parts of this system. Vitalist physicians attributed great importance to a person's sensibility, a rather mysterious concept that could perhaps be understood as a generalized capacity for sensation, having the necessary equipment as it were for receiving impressions from external sources and processing them through the body.[98] A person could have too much or too little sensibility. In the latter case, vitalist physicians often used terror and pain as a way to stimulate one's sensibility back into action.

In the eighteenth century, vitalist physicians developed an early form of shock therapy. In 1777, for example, the English medical student Thomas Pemberton recounted the case of a young, depressed girl who refused to get out of bed or cooperate with her doctors. Her physician then left the room, undressed, and proceeded to jump naked into the girl's bed. She, in turn, jumped out in a panic and, we are told, was subsequently cured of her melancholy.[99]

One of the major theoreticians of vitalism, the physician Théophile de Bordeu from Montpellier—where Petit had studied medicine—developed a "therapeutics of perturbation," whereby terror and pain would be used in order to induce a state of "crisis" that could cure patients by jolting their sensibilities.[100] The point of this rather lengthy detour into the history of medicine is that in the late eighteenth century there was a major medical approach in place that saw terror as having potentially positive effects on people's health.

Petit probably drew on vitalism when he argued that the effects of the Terror on public health were contradictory—simultaneously pernicious and salutary—depending on a patient's preexisting condition. The experience of terror tended to worsen the symptoms of patients suffering from various afflictions associated with stress. Thus, Petit noted that during the Terror there was a marked increase in cases of voice loss, asthma, depression, toothaches, migraines, convulsions, and hysteria. Aneurysms of the heart increased "under the tyranny of Robespierre," as did suicides.[101] Like most physicians in the eighteenth century, Petit thought that women in particular were susceptible to these maladies of stress. On the other hand, terror had therapeutic effects on patients suffering from poor circulation of blood, swollen lymph nodes, various forms of paralysis, and the debility of nerve fibers.

Petit's examples of the positive effects of revolutionary violence were not limited to Europe. According to him, physicians in North America recorded a sudden increase in the birth rate after the American Revolution. In an early version of the baby-boom theory, Petit hypothesized that perhaps "in times of great calamity, in the midst of storms that threaten to knock off all heads, people's souls long for sweet embraces."[102] For Petit then, revolutionary violence could have a rejuvenating effect on society.

Vitalism was largely on the wane by the early nineteenth century, yet some influential physicians were still making arguments about the positive effects of the Terror. In 1811, a physician by the name of J.-F. Guitard won an essay competition on the question of the effects of the Terror on the animal economy.[103] Terror, according to Guitard, operated mainly on the nervous system, producing effects that were both destructive and constructive. "The sentiment of Terror, having in a way destroyed all faculties, appears subsequently to terminate this state of stupor and to breathe new life into organs that seem to have been paralyzed previously."[104]

In the early decades of the nineteenth century, under the Napoleonic regime and then during the Restoration, it became less and less acceptable to attribute any beneficial impact to the Terror. The legacy of the Revolution was a matter of considerable debate, but revolutionary violence became anathema on virtually all sides of the political spectrum. Even for the socialists, who in general saw Robespierre as a hero, the Reign of Terror posed a moral and political conundrum.[105] And when the Second Republic was founded in 1848, on the ruins of the restored monarchy, one of its first acts was to abolish the death penalty for political crimes, in order to signal to the public that this republic will not go down the path of the first one.

At the same time, the rise of psychiatry changed the way physicians and state authorities understood the effects of the Terror on the mental health of the French. Psychiatry, or as the French referred to it at the time, moral medicine, began to emerge as a distinct field of knowledge in the late eighteenth and early nineteenth centuries. As a new branch of science that challenged long-held views in the medical community, moral physicians struggled to gain legitimacy. The revolutionary era created the conditions that allowed their claims to take hold in public. As Jan Goldstein has shown, it was precisely the anxieties occasioned by the Terror and the collapse of moderate republicanism that led to a demand for a new kind of self, less susceptible to the turmoil of the imagination.[106] After what many in France had come to see as the emotional excess of the Terror, there was a need to cultivate new values: restraint, respectability, and secularism, in a word, the ethos of the bourgeoisie.[107] Psychiatry contributed to the reproduction of these values and so became a main source of support for the liberal state, which in turn afforded it ever greater power and acceptability.[108]

In this context, the argument that experiences like the Terror, while painful, could have beneficial effects became politically untenable. Instead, there was a growing recognition of the possibility that the turmoil of Revolution could literally drive people insane. Thus, in 1819 the young physician J. F. Bonfils observed that more cases of insanity were diagnosed in France than in other European countries. The explanation for this was to be found, he argued, in "patriotic exaltations on one hand and, on the other hand, the profound regrets over the fate of the old regime, whose downfall dragged so many fortunes with it, the crisis, the anguish of the time of the Terror, of wars."[109] In 1839, the influential psychiatrist Brièrre de Boismont noted that fifty-eight patients admitted into Bicêtre between 1803 and 1819 were suffering from "intense *revolutions* of the mind," while twenty-four had been driven insane by "political events." "The Political crises," Boismont declared, "which shake the social order to its foundations from time to time . . . do not belong to history alone. They are also the domain of medicine."[110] In other words, the tumultuous history of the revolutionary era was responsible for a predilection among the French to, quite simply, go mad.

In the early decades of the nineteenth century, we begin to see descriptions of the effects of the Terror on mental health that resemble modern notions of trauma and PTSD. Philippe Pinel, one of the founders of modern psychiatry, included in his *Treatise of Insanity* a story about a watchmaker who had suffered some sort of mental breakdown "during the storms of the Revolution." His mania took on a most unusual form. He became convinced that he had been decapitated during the Terror. In his elaborate fantasy, the magistrates of the revolutionary tribunal soon realized that he had been condemned wrongly and ordered that his head be reattached to his body. But because his original head had been thrown pell-mell with other corpses into a mass grave, a mistake occurred, and he received someone else's head, one that was much less fine than his. In conversations with Pinel, the watchmaker implored: "Look at my teeth. Mine were so nice, but these are all rotten. My mouth was clean, but this one is totally infected. Look at my hair. What a difference between this and the hair I had before I received this new head."[111] The fact that the patient in this anecdote was a watchmaker is interesting in and of itself for, on some level, trauma is a particular attitude toward time. Anecdotes like those found in Pinel's account illustrate how the emerging interest in mental health led contemporaries of the revolutionary era to a new awareness of the ways in which the Terror continued to reverberate in France long after the fact. Physicians even noted that revolutionary violence appeared frequently in people's dreams.[112]

The Debate on the Death Penalty in the 1820s

One instance in which the Terror reverberated loudly was in the debate on the death penalty that erupted in the early 1820s and continued into the 1830s. Debates on the abolition of the death penalty had been taking place in Europe in fits and starts at least since the publication of Cesare Beccaria's *On Crimes and Punishments* in 1764. The revolutionaries argued about the death penalty during the reform of the penal code in 1791. The Convention discussed abolition again in October 1795, in its last session as the legislative assembly. The revival of the debate on the death penalty in the 1830s had to do less with revolutionary politics and more with liberalism and the growing popularity of philanthropic causes in this period, but the echoes of Year II were never far from the mind of those who took part in the discussion.[113]

The original impetus for the 1820s–1830s debate was a wave of political repression that followed the assassination of the heir to the throne, the Duc de Berry, in 1820. This wave of repression, which, like the wave of reprisals against Jacobins in 1795, came to be known as the White Terror, pitted liberals and conservatives against each other in a conflict over the legacies of the French

Revolution and the limits of political power.[114] Arguing for the abolition of the death penalty was one way in which liberals could claim the heritage of the Revolution, while at the same time dissociating themselves from the Terror.[115] Consequently, François Guizot, the future liberal prime minister of France, whose own father had been executed during the Reign of Terror, penned one of the first texts in the debate on the death penalty, in which he held that the memories of the Revolution's frequent recourse to capital punishment made the case for abolition all the more cogent.[116]

One of the recurring arguments for the abolition of the death penalty, which drew directly on the echoes of the Terror, was that public executions led to the barbarization of society. The early nineteenth-century woman of letters Elizabeth-Félicie Bayle-Mouillard wrote that "a terrible spiral is observed in all the places where the executioners spill blood, a fatal circle that explains why the view of the executions hardens and depraves the soul, for around the scaffold a base and cruel instinct develops with the vapors of blood."[117] The physician Claude Charles Pierquin de Gembloux declared that "the public murders, which have soiled the French Revolution through the furies of parties are the principal cause of the murderous monomanias and the crimes that we see every day."[118] Describing the effects of the Terror in a manner similar to traumatic repetition, Gembloux's point was that capital punishment, far from deterring crime, actually led to an increase in its incidence.

Such arguments were derived from a mixture of old theories that had been largely discredited by this time with new ideas that were very much in vogue. For example, Gembloux observed that the number of miscarriages had increased during the Terror, and he attributed this to the presence of pregnant women among the spectators of public executions. One woman who had attended one of these bloody spectacles, he claimed, gave birth six months later to a baby with a perfect imprint of the guillotine on his cheek.[119] Such ideas might have derived from the theory of maternal impression, which had been popular in the early modern period but still had some resonance in the early 1800s.[120] According to this theory, pregnant women were particularly susceptible to impressions from external sources. Gembloux also referred to galvanism in order to make the argument that the sentiment of life persisted for some time in victims of the guillotine, thus causing them unspeakable pain, which they could not express because their vocal cords had been severed.

At the same time, Gembloux derived his arguments about the damaging impact of the Terror on French society by drawing on theories of contagion that were very much part of his time.[121] Many physicians in nineteenth-century France thought that emotions were contagious, particularly extreme emotions like fear. The physician Jean-Baptiste-Félix Descuret, for example, who had published an influential book on emotions in 1844, thought that "of all our affections, fear is the most contagious. . . . We see that it persists long after the danger had passed."[122] Accordingly, Gembloux made the case that the emotional energies unleashed by the Revolution were contagious and pathological: "Is not enthusiasm one of the more contagious diseases of the soul, as are fear and terror? How many examples of this have been provided by the multiplicity of our political events?"[123]

The violence of the Revolution, Gembloux seemed to be saying, left an indelible imprint on the psyche of an entire generation. "If we observe the increasing number of individuals charged with murder today," he stated, "we will see that it is precisely those whose childhood had been spent around the scaffolds of the Terror."[124] Positions like the ones held by Gembloux were probably the exception rather than the norm, but they do show how the coincidence of the revolutionary era with the emergence of the psychiatric profession gave rise to new ways of thinking about the effects of events of mass violence like the Terror on self and society.

Conclusion

In the years after the fall of Robespierre, the notion that the dead of Year II were not really dead, and that the Terror retained a haunting presence in the postrevolutionary landscape, appeared in various areas of social and cultural life. Playing on the ambiguity between credulity and reason, the Enlightenment and the occult, Robertson's phantasmagoria endowed the ghostly presence of the Terror with a concrete, visible quality. The debate on decapitation encapsulated the legacies of the Terror in the iconic image of the severed head, which, physicians suggested, might be alive after all. More directly, physicians and other men of science discussed the effects of the Terror on individual psyches as well as on public health. In the immediate aftermath of the Terror, physicians influenced by vitalist theories argued that the effects of revolutionary violence on public health were contradictory, simultaneously beneficial and pernicious. As the political landscape changed in the early decades of the nineteenth century, and as the French medical and psychiatric profession changed along with it, such claims became less tenable politically and scientifically. They gave way to arguments that the difficult experiences of Year II had left an indelible imprint on the psyche of an entire generation. These arguments began to resemble what we today refer to as trauma and PTSD.

Exploring the ghostly presence of the Terror is thus a way of thinking about how men and women in the revolutionary period perceived the effects of mass violence on self and society in their own terms, before the advent of modern trauma-talk. The various manifestations of this ghostly presence amount to only a vague "structure of feeling." The striking thing, however, about the distinct arenas of social and cultural life discussed in this chapter is their position between the early modern and the modern, the superstitious and the rational. Processes identified with modernity—the emergence of medicine and psychiatry, or the rise of cinematic visual culture—were not fully realized at the time of the Revolution, but they were already transforming the way contemporaries of the revolutionary era imagined the effects of massive violence on themselves as well as on others. Ultimately, this chapter has tried to illustrate that the broad structural transformations unleashed by the French Revolution were intertwined with the emergence of new ways of reckoning with a difficult past.

Conclusion

The National Convention held its last session on October 26, 1795. Fifteen months after the fall of Robespierre, it was time for this body to dissolve itself and to do what it had wanted to do for a long time, namely, bring the Revolution to an end. The legislators spent much of the session discussing proposals put forward two days earlier by one of its members, Pierre Baudin, on the subject of amnesty. Baudin proposed that in its last acts as the legislative assembly, the Convention should abolish the death penalty, burn the guillotine publicly, change the name of the Place de la Révolution—the main site of executions during the Terror—to Place de la Concorde, and terminate all investigations into matters related directly to the Revolution. "There are evils that are inseparable from a great revolution," Baudin told his colleagues, "and among these evils are some which, by their very nature, can no longer be remedied."[1] Two of Baudin's proposals were adopted. The Place de la Révolution was renamed Place de la Concorde. The Convention voted in favor of a sweeping amnesty decree, effectively ensuring that most of its members—several, like Joseph Le Bon, had already been put on trial—would not be brought to justice for their role in the repression of Year II. It rejected, however, the abolition of the death penalty, or rather it deferred the discussion on the matter to a later, unspecified date. In its ambiguous, cautious way, the Convention thus devoted its last session to closing the books on the Reign of Terror.

Yet French society was struggling with the legacies of revolutionary violence years and even decades later. The period of the Restoration saw multiple exhumations and reburials of victims of the Terror. Conflicts around *les biens des condamnés* continued well into the nineteenth century.[2] Physicians argued about the effects of the Terror on the physical and mental well-being of the population. Children of *conventionnels* changed their names, so as to hide their relation to the men who had been in power during the repression. The son of Antoine Claire Thibaudeau, a former Montagnard, was the subject of police surveillance, even though his actions had nothing to do with the radicalism of his father.[3] Emile Le Bon, a magistrate in Chalon-sur-Saône, was still struggling to clear his father's name in the 1850s.[4] In 1863, Gustave Flaubert, then forty-two years old, told his dinner hosts, the famous writers Edmond and Jules de Goncourt, how his father, as a seven-year-old boy, had saved his grandfather from being sent to the prisons of the Terror by reciting a moving poem, which, as the story goes, swayed the members of the Revolutionary Society of Nogent-sur-Marne.[5] A project to construct an expiatory monument for Louis XVI in the center of Paris was abandoned because the construction site reminded his daughter too much of the scaffold that had stood there in the days of the guillotine.[6] That daughter, Marie-Thérèse, was the only surviving child of Louis XVI and Marie-Antoinette; she died in exile in 1851. Her tombstone bore the inscription: "All you who pass this way, behold and see if there be any sorrow like unto my sorrow."[7] Gothic literature and new visual technologies like the phantasmagoria represented in concrete ways the notion that French society would be haunted for years to come by the Terror.

Why was this so? Why was it so difficult to leave the Terror behind? On some level, the answer to this question is obvious. Events of mass violence leave in their wake traces that affect survivors, perpetrators, and observers long after the fact. They defy the human capacity to transform past experiences into a coherent narrative. Having conducted interviews with Japanese war criminals years after World War II, literary scholar James Dawes wrote: "Trauma represents an impossibility in language because it is primarily an assault on meaning rather than a kind of meaning. There is no final understanding. There is no transcendence. There are only momentary stays against confusion."[8] Questions about retribution, redress, remembrance, revenge, reconciliation, and narration are bound to trouble societies emerging from periods of massive repression for a long time. "There is no closure," wrote the South African psychologist Pumla Gobodo-Madikizela, about the aftermath of such events.[9]

Yet as I have tried to show in this book, the reasons for the difficulties with facing the legacies of mass violence in postrevolutionary France were more historically specific. The democratization of responsibility in the French

Revolution led to a new kind of dilemma after 9 Thermidor, namely, how to hold individuals accountable for mass crime. The revolutionary politics of property and expropriation led to specific problems with redress after the Terror. It proved difficult, therefore, to undo the past in the context of a movement focused on the future. The politicization of memory and the revolutionary cult of the dead invested the burial places of victims of the Terror with meanings that went far beyond the realm of private, familial grief. The pacifying, conciliatory tone of the expiatory monuments constructed on these sites clashed with their potential to reawaken civil discord. The political and social transformations that were launched in 1789 made it difficult to come up with a coherent narrative about the Terror in its aftermath because they rendered the everyday illegible, unfamiliar, in search of a name.

Many of these changes did not begin or end in the revolutionary decade. Secularization and the rise of the public sphere had changed the way Europeans processed cataclysmic events. The emergence of accountability as a central moral and political feature of European states was the result of a process that had been unfolding at least since the fourteenth century. The expansion of capitalism in the centuries leading up to the French Revolution had transformed notions of property, ownership, politics, and the relation between them, developments that in turn influenced the revolutionary view of the link between possession and participation.[10] Changes in attitudes toward the dead and the dying in European culture, which had been under way since the Middle Ages, invested burial sites and rituals of mourning with new meanings and made them into protean symbols in moments of radical, political change. The rational ethos of the Enlightenment and the emergence of science and medicine as distinct areas of expertise and authority influenced the way men and women in late eighteenth-century France thought about, imagined, and dealt with the effects of massive violence on self and society.[11] The story of how those who had experienced the Terror firsthand struggled to come to terms with it must be situated then in a context that is much broader than the revolutionary era itself.

But the French Revolution accelerated, inflected, and made these transformations visible in dramatic ways. "The French Revolution brought about the invention of modern politics," according to Marisa Linton.[12] More and more people could express their will and demand their rights in an ever-expanding arena of political participation. The Revolution opened up and diversified political life, making space for the emergence of plural and competing voices that influenced the decision-making process of elites. This was not a perfect beginning. Many parts of the population, such as women and people of color, were excluded from political and civil life for decades and even centuries after the overthrow of the Old Regime. Nevertheless, the Revolution established the plurality of voices and the management of competing interests as a central feature of modern politics. Antagonism, to quote Chantal Mouffe, was transformed into agonism, that is, the view that conflict, rather than consensus, forms the basis of modern democratic life.[13]

In this context, it became increasingly difficult for the state or for any central authority to control memory or to impose amnesia. One of the significant findings of this book is that the period after the fall of Robespierre saw a variety of complicated, painful, and at times surprisingly honest debates about the best way of dealing with the legacies of the Terror. Revolutionary leaders, ordinary citizens, relatives of victims, and men and women of letters took part in difficult, public discussions about accountability, restitution, and commemoration. The inability of the National Convention to "impose silence on posterity," a failure that was lamented by Edgar Quinet, was a result of the democratizing dynamic unleashed in 1789.[14] To put it simply, the overthrow of the Old Regime and the establishment of the new one changed the way French society chose to reckon with its own past. This process of reckoning unfolded in fits and starts, but it continued nonetheless under the surface of the frequent and abrupt regime changes that France experienced between 1794 and the 1830s.

The process examined in this book brings to mind more recent cases of transitional justice. The study of transitional justice is focused overwhelmingly on the present or the recent past. Ruti Teitel has traced the origins of the concept to the Nuremberg trials.[15] There is little question that the concern with difficult pasts, the rule of law, and respect for human rights in the aftermath of genocide and state terrorism is bound up with the memory of World War II, and especially the Holocaust.[16] Yet the process examined in this book suggests that while the concept of transitional justice may be recent, the dilemmas that it articulates are not. Many of the events and debates examined in this book would strike a familiar chord among scholars of transitional justice. Alex Boraine, who is one of the leading voices in the field, and who together with Archbishop Desmond Tutu was one of the architects of South Africa's Truth and Reconciliation Commission, has written recently that transitional justice marks the search for a more equitable order in societies that are emerging from periods of oppression and violence. According to Boraine, this concept offers "a deeper, richer, and broader vision of justice which seeks to confront perpetrators, address the needs of victims, and assist in the start of a process of reconciliation and transformation."[17] This process, according to most practitioners in the field, must combine some measure of retributive justice with some measure of restorative justice. Boraine has proposed four key pillars: accountability, truth recovery, institutional reform, and reparations. Similarly, Martha Minow has emphasized institutional measures that combine punishment with redress, but she has also discussed the importance of commemoration and other less formal and more community-based responses to mass violence.[18]

The similarities between the measures advocated by these scholars and the process discussed in this book are striking. In the aftermath of the Terror, there was a debate on accountability, and there was an effort, albeit a partial and flawed one, to punish some perpetrators for their excessive use of force. The revolutionary government also engaged in some form of restorative justice, particularly around the restitution of property to the surviving relatives of victims. There were ongoing efforts to commemorate those who had died as a result of revolutionary violence. Some of these efforts were grassroots initiatives and some were more public and formal. All of this suggests that transitional justice has a history that goes back farther in time than the Nuremberg trials, but it is a history that remains to be written.

Similarity, however, is not identity, and there are important differences between the agenda of transitional justice at present and the political challenges that French society faced after the Terror. One difference is discourse. The agenda of transitional justice is embedded in a liberal—perhaps even neoliberal—discourse that takes certain things for granted. It is a premise in the field, for example, that the transition in question is, or should be, in one direction, namely, to liberal democracy. It is no coincidence that transitional justice emerged as a concept in the 1990s, after the collapse of the Soviet Union and around the same time that scholars and global leaders were predicting the "end of history," that is, the triumph of Western economic and political liberalism.[19] Democracy, international standards of human rights, and a market economy: these things were not, and could not have been, taken for granted in the late eighteenth and early nineteenth centuries. That there was a process of reckoning with the legacies of the Terror at all in postrevolutionary France should encourage us to question the presumed symbiosis between liberal-democratic regimes and transitional justice, or at least to rethink what we mean by liberal and democratic.[20]

A second, and closely related, difference is the centrality of questions of redistributive justice in the revolutionary era compared to the relatively marginal place these questions occupy in the political and cultural life of our time. As some scholars have argued, the agenda of transitional justice seems to exclude social justice or the redistribution of material resources.[21] In contrast, questions of redistribution and of economic inequality were central to the political culture of the Revolution.[22] This difference between the revolutionary era and our own matters, because redistributive justice is almost always about the future, about the shape of the social and political order to come. As this book has tried to show, the process of reckoning with the legacies of the Terror was of consequence to those who have lived through, or had witnessed in some way, the events of the French Revolution, but there is little doubt that the major political battles of their time were more about shaping the future, and less about the rectification of past wrongs.

It is worth thinking about why historical justice and the rectification of past wrongs are such central subjects in the political culture of our time but were less so in the political culture of the Revolution. As Wendy Brown and others have pointed out, many of the political battles of the present seem to be about the redress of an injury.[23] The victim and the traumatized person are the prime political subjects of our time.[24] Why has there been "a major shift in much progressive thinking from a focus on the future as the proving ground of social change to a preoccupation with the past as the arena in which to seek improvements in the human condition"?[25] It is beyond the purview of this study to answer this question. The reasons, I believe, have something to do with the 1970s; with the emergence of the Holocaust as the "foundational past" of our time and the decline of the great ideologies that had provided competing blueprints for the future for much of the nineteenth and twentieth centuries.[26] The evidence brought forward in this book shows that the experience of mass violence did continue to reverberate in the lives of revolutionary leaders, victims, and ordinary citizens long after the fact, but it does not seem to have become a constitutive element of their identity.

Ever since the French revolutionaries named the political and social system that existed before their arrival the Old Regime, it has become commonplace to identify the French Revolution with rupture, with the audacity to start time itself anew. The revolutionaries repudiated "the accumulated weight of the past in order to inaugurate a new epoch."[27] Two months or so after the fall of Robespierre, Robert Lindet, then a member of the revamped Committee of Public Safety, called on his compatriots to leave the past behind, and let bygones be bygones. "Reason, the welfare of the fatherland does not allow you to look back on the ruins that you have left behind."[28] The revolutionary gaze, Lindet was saying, must be focused on the future, on the realization of the new social and political order. The Republic that was born in Revolution could not afford to face the past. The research that culminated in the writing of this book, however, shows that actually the political need to struggle with the legacies left in the wake of mass violence was among the consequences of the Revolution. Lindet did not have a full understanding of the political and social transformations that he had helped to inaugurate. The same democratizing, radicalizing dynamic that led to civil conflict, repression, and the Terror also gave rise to an unprecedented interrogation of how society is affected by events of massive brutality. The French Revolution, which painted the horizon of modern European politics in utopian colors, also led to a new kind of reckoning with difficult pasts, pasts that did not, and perhaps could not, pass.

Notes

Works frequently cited have been identified by the following abbreviations:

ADHG	Archives Départementales de la Haute-Garonne
ADPC	Archives Départementales du Pas-de-Calais
ADR	Archives Départementales du Rhône
ADS	Archives Départementales de la Somme
ADV	Archives Départementales de Vaucluse
AHR	*American Historical Review*
AHRF	*Annales historiques de la Révolution française*
AML	Archives Municipales de Lyon
AMO	Archives Municipales d'Orange
AN	Archives Nationales
AP	*Archives parlementaires de 1787 à 1860; recueil complet des débats législatifs & politiques des chambres françaises.* 127 vols. Edited by M. J. Mavidal et al. (Paris: P. Dupont, 1862–)
APA	Archives de Paris
APP	Archives de la Préfectures de Police
ARTFL Encyclopédie	ARTFL Encyclopédie Project (Autumn 2017 ed.), ed. Robert Morrissey and Glenn Roe (https://encyclopedie.uchicago.edu/)
BHVP	Bibliothèque Historique de la Ville de Paris
BML	Bibliothèque Municipales de Lyon
Collection Badouin	Décrets et Lois 1789–1795: Collection Baudouin (http://collection-baudouin.univ-paris1.fr)
DAF	*Dictionnaire de l'Académie française*
FHS	*French Historical Studies*
JMH	*Journal of Modern History*
Moniteur	*Réimpression de l'ancien Moniteur, seule histoire authentique et inaltérée de la révolution française depuis la réunion des États-généraux jusqu'au Consulat (mai 1789–novembre 1799),* 32 vols. (Paris: Plon, 1858–1970)

Introduction. Approaching the Aftermath of the Terror

1. There is no consensus in the scholarship about the number of victims of the Terror. Part of this is due to lack of reliable data, but most of it is due to disagreements about what precisely constituted the Terror. The standard quantitative study that is cited most often is Donald Greer, *The Incidence of the Terror during the French Revolution: A Statistical Interpretation* (Cambridge, Mass.: Harvard University Press, 1935). According to Peter McPhee, about 40,000 people were executed during the Terror. See Peter McPhee, *Liberty or Death: The French Revolution* (New Haven, Conn.: Yale University Press, 2016), 271. For a discussion of the problems in establishing the statistical record of the Terror, see Jean-Clément Martin, *Violence et Révolution. Essai sur la naissance d'un mythe nationale* (Paris: Seuil, 2006), 243–247.

2. See Yuval Neria et al., eds., *9/11: Mental Health in the Wake of Terrorist Attacks* (Cambridge: Cambridge University Press, 2006).

3. On this notion of "working through," see Dominick LaCapra, *Writing History, Writing Trauma* (Baltimore: Johns Hopkins University Press, 2000), esp. 141–153. See also Jean Laplanche and Jean-Bertrand Pontalis, *The Language of Psychoanalysis* (New York: Norton, 1973), 488–489.

4. See Martha Minow, *Between Vengeance and Forgiveness: Facing History after Genocide and Mass Violence* (Boston: Beacon Press, 1998).

5. See Tina Rosenberg, "Tipping the Scales of Justice," *World Policy Journal* 12, no. 3 (1995): 55–64; Elazar Barkan, *The Guilt of Nations: Restitution and Negotiating Historical Injustices* (New York: Norton, 2000); and Jennifer Lind, *Sorry States: Apologies in International Politics* (Ithaca, N.Y.: Cornell University Press, 2008).

6. See Nancy Scheper-Hughes, "Undoing: Social Suffering and the Politics of Remorse in the New South Africa," *Social Justice* 25, no. 4 (1998): 114–142; and Frank Trommler, "Stalingrad, Hiroshima, Auschwitz: The Fading of the Therapeutic Approach," in *Catastrophe and Meaning: The Holocaust and the Twentieth Century*, ed. Moishe Postone and Eric Santner (Chicago: University of Chicago Press, 2003), 136–153.

7. See Ian Buruma, "The Joys and Perils of Victimhood," *New York Review of Books* 46, no. 6 (April 1999): 1–9; Wendy Brown, *States of Injury: Power and Freedom in Late Modernity* (Princeton, N.J.: Princeton University Press, 1995).

8. See Didier Fassin and Richard Rechtman, *The Empire of Trauma: An Inquiry into the Condition of Victimhood* (Princeton, N.J.: Princeton University Press, 2009); Jeffrey Alexander et al., *Cultural Trauma and Collective Identity* (Berkeley: University of California Press, 2004); Shoshana Felman, *The Juridical Unconscious: Trials and Traumas in the Twentieth Century* (Cambridge, Mass.: Harvard University Press, 2002); Ann Kaplan, *Trauma Culture: The Politics of Terror and Loss in Media and Literature* (New Brunswick, N.J.: Rutgers University Press, 2005).

9. John Torpey, *Making Whole What Has Been Smashed: On Reparation Politics* (Cambridge, Mass.: Harvard University Press, 2006), 5.

10. Edgar Quinet, *La Révolution*, 2 vols. (Paris: Belin, 1987), 2:829.

11. Ibid., 2:834, 832.

12. See Michel-Rolph Trouillot, *Silencing the Past: Power and the Production of History* (Boston: Beacon Press, 1997). In 2014 I attended a conference in South Africa on the subject of silence after violence. The goal of the conference was to examine

whether silence and forgetting are pathologies or whether, indeed, they may be the appropriate response in the aftermath of certain cases of violence and loss. For a selection of papers from the conference, see Anja Henebury and Yehonatan Alsheh, eds., "Silence after Violence and the Imperative to 'Speak Out,'" Special Issue, *Acta Academica* 47, no. 1 (2015).

13. See Keith Baker, "Sovereignty," in *A Critical Dictionary of the French Revolution*, ed. François Furet and Mona Ozouf (Cambridge, Mass.: Harvard University Press, 1989), 844–859.

14. On electoral behavior during the French Revolution, see Patrice Gueniffey, *Le nombre et la raison. La Révolution française et les élections* (Paris: EHESS, 1993); and Malcolm Crook, *Elections in the French Revolution: An Apprenticeship in Democracy, 1789–1799* (Cambridge: Cambridge University Press, 1996).

15. See William Rogers Brubaker, "The French Revolution and the Invention of Citizenship," *French Politics and Society* 7, no. 3 (1989): 30–49. See also Sudhir Hazareesingh, *From Subjects to Citizens: The Second Empire and the Emergence of Modern French Democracy* (Princeton, N.J.: Princeton University Press, 1998).

16. Lynn Hunt, *Politics, Culture, and Class in the French Revolution* (Berkeley: University of California Press, 1984), 56.

17. Quinet, *La Révolution*, 2:833.

18. See Alan Spitzer, *The French Generation of 1820* (Princeton, N.J.: Princeton University Press, 1987). See also Paul Viallaneix, *Michelet, les travaux et les jours, 1798–1874* (Paris: Gallimard, 1998) and Stanley Mellon, *The Political Uses of History: A Study of Historians in the French Restoration* (Stanford, Calif.: Stanford University Press, 1958).

19. See François Furet, *La gauche et la Révolution au milieu du XIXe siècle. Edgar Quinet et la question du jacobinisme, 1865–1870* (Paris: Hachette, 1986).

20. Quinet, *La Revolution*, 2:829–830.

21. See Dan Edelstein, "What Was the Terror?," in *The Oxford Handbook of the French Revolution*, ed. David Andress (Oxford: Oxford University Press, 2015), 453–470.

22. See Martin, *Violence et Revolution*, esp. chap. 5.

23. See Mircea Eliade, *Myth and Reality* (New York: Harper Torchbooks, 1963).

24. See Albert Mathiez, *The French Revolution* (New York: Russell and Russell, 1962); Albert Soboul, *The Sans-Culottes: The Popular Movement and Revolutionary Government, 1793–1794* (Princeton, N.J.: Princeton University Press, 1972); D. M. G. Sutherland, *France 1789–1815: Revolution and Counterrevolution* (Oxford: Oxford University Press, 1986); Arno Meyer, *The Furies: Violence and Terror in the French and Russian Revolutions* (Princeton: Princeton University Press, 2001).

25. See François Furet, *Interpreting the French Revolution* (Cambridge: Cambridge University Press, 1981); Keith M. Baker, *Inventing the French Revolution: Essays on French Political Culture in the Eighteenth Century* (Cambridge: Cambridge University Press, 1990); Carol Blum, *Rousseau and the Republic of Virtue: The Language of Politics in the French Revolution* (Ithaca, N.Y.: Cornell University Press, 1986); Dan Edelstein, *The Terror of Natural Right: Republicanism, the Cult of Nature, and the French Revolution* (Chicago: University of Chicago Press, 2009); Mary Ashburn Miller, *A Natural History of the French Revolution: Violence and Nature in the French Revolutionary Imagination, 1789–1794* (Ithaca, N.Y.: Cornell University Press, 2011).

26. See Simon Schama, *Citizens: A Chronicle of the French Revolution* (New York: Knopf, 1989), xv, 767, 789, 836.

27. See Mayer, *Furies*, chap. 3.

28. Adrien de Lezay-Marnésia, *Des causes de la Révolution et de ses résultats* (Paris: L'imprimerie du journal d'Économie publique, 1797), 24.

29. John Wilson Croker, "The Guillotine," review of *Notice Historique et Physiologique sur le Supplice de la Guillotine* by Guyot de Fère and of *Recherches Historiques et Phsyiologiques sur la Guillotine; et détails sur Sanson, ouvrage rédigé sur pieces officiels* by Louis de Bois, *Quarterly Review* 73, no. 145 (December 1843), 235.

30. Timothy Tackett, *The Coming of the Terror in the French Revolution* (Cambridge, Mass.: Harvard University Press, 2015), 12.

31. David Andress, *The Terror: Civil War in the French Revolution* (London: Little, Brown, 2005), 104.

32. See Colin Lucas, "Revolutionary Violence, the People, and the Terror," in *The French Revolution and the Creation of Modern Political Culture*, 4 vols., ed. Keith M. Baker et al. (New York: Pergamon Press, 1987–1994), 4:57–80.

33. Louis Sebastien Mercier, *Paris pendant la Revolution*, 2 vols. (Paris: Poulet-Malassis, 1862), 2:8.

34. For an example of the first kind of interpretation, see Biard, ed., *Les politiques de la Terreur, 1793–1794* (Rennes: Presses Universitaires de Rennes, 2008). For an example of the second kind of interpretation, see Patrice Gueniffey, *La politique de la Terreur. Essai sur la violence révolutionnaire, 1789–1794* (Paris: Fayard, 2000). I take the term "continuum of destruction" from Ervin Staub, *The Roots of Evil: The Origins of Genocide and Other Group Violence* (Cambridge: Cambridge University Press, 1992), 17–18.

35. Peter Fritzsche, *Stranded in the Present: Modern Time and the Melancholy of History* (Cambridge, Mass.: Harvard University Press, 2004), 16.

36. Lynn Hunt, "The World We Have Gained: The Future of the French Revolution," *AHR* 108, no. 1 (2003), 4.

37. Quoted in Reinhart Koselleck, *Futures Past: On the Semantics of Historical Time* (New York: Columbia University Press, 2004), 244.

38. See Sergio Luzzatto, *Mémoire de la Terreur. Vieux montagnards et jeune républicains au XIXe siècle* (Lyon: Presses Universitaires de Lyon, 1991).

39. See Mellon, *The Political Uses of History*; and Linda Orr, *Headless History: Nineteenth-Century French Historiography of the Revolution* (Ithaca, N.Y.: Cornell University Press, 1990).

40. Bronislaw Baczko, *Ending the Terror: The French Revolution after Robespierre* (Cambridge: Cambridge University Press, 1994), 34.

41. *Moniteur*, 26 Fructidor, an 2 (September 12, 1794), no. 356.

42. Baczko, *Ending the Terror*, 34.

43. See Suzanne Desan, "Reconstituting the Social after the Terror: Family, Property, and the Law in Popular Politics," *Past and Present* 164 (August 1999): 81–121; James Livesey, *Making Democracy in the French Revolution* (Cambridge, Mass.: Harvard University Press, 2001); Isser Woloch, *The New Regime: Transformations of French Civic Order, 1789–1820s* (New York: Norton, 1994); Sergio Luzzatto, *L'automne de la Révolution. Luttes et cultures politiques dans la France thermidorienne* (Paris: Champion, 2001); Andrew Jainchill, *Reimagining Politics after the Terror: The Republican Origins of French Liberalism* (Ithaca, N.Y.: Cornell University Press, 2008); Laura Mason, ed., "Thermidor and the French Revolution," Special Forum, *FHS* 38, no. 1 (2015) and 39, no. 3 (2016).

44. Howard Brown, *Ending the French Revolution: Violence, Justice, and Repression from the Terror to Napoleon* (Charlottesville: University of Virginia Press, 2006), 235. See also Howard Brown and Judith Miller, eds., *Taking Liberties: Problems of a New Order from the French Revolution to Napoleon* (Manchester: Manchester University Press, 2003). Brown's work has been influenced by the work of Richard Cobb, his doctoral adviser. In the 1960s and 1970s, it was mostly Cobb's research that highlighted the unique configuration of political and social conditions that took shape after the Terror, emphasizing in particular the harmful impact of revolutionary politics on the everyday life of *le menu peuple*. Before the recent wave of interest in the period, which has been inspired by Baczko's work, it was mostly Cobb's students who carried out research in this area, at least in the English-speaking world. See Richard Cobb, *Reactions to the French Revolution* (Oxford: Oxford University Press, 1972); and Gwynne Lewis and Colin Lucas, eds., *Beyond the Terror: Essays in French Regional and Social History, 1794–1815* (Cambridge: Cambridge University Press, 1983).

45. Denis Woronoff, *The Thermidorean Regime and the Directory, 1794–1799* (Cambridge: Cambridge University Press, 1984), xix. The classic interpretation of the Reaction is Albert Mathiez, *After Robespierre: The Thermidorian Reaction* (New York: Grosset and Dunlap, 1965).

46. Baczko, *Ending the Terror*, 224.

47. See Ronen Steinberg, "Reckoning with Terror: Retribution, Redress, and Remembrance in Post-Revolutionary France," in *The Oxford Handbook of the French Revolution*, ed. David Andress (Oxford: Oxford University Press, 2015), 487–502.

48. I take the notion of "difficult pasts" from Eva Hoffman, "Complex Histories, Contested Memories: Some Reflections on Remembering Difficult Pasts," Townsend Center for the Humanities at the University of California Berkeley, accessed April 17, 2017, http://townsendcenter.berkeley.edu/publications/complex-histories-contested-memories-some-reflections-remembering-difficult-pasts. For the future-orientation not only of the Revolution, but of revolutionary historiography as well, see Dorinda Outram, "Revolution and Repression," *Comparative Studies in Society and History* 34, no. 1 (1992): 58–67.

49. Alon Confino, *Foundational Pasts: The Holocaust as Historical Understanding* (Cambridge: Cambridge University Press, 2011), 5–6.

50. The argument is Confino's, but the quote is from Dan Diner, *Cataclysms: A History of the Twentieth Century from Europe's Edge* (Madison: University of Wisconsin Press, 2008), 48.

51. Jan Goldstein, "The Future of French History in the United States: Unapocalyptic Thoughts for the New Millennium," *FHS* 24, no. 1 (2001), 5.

52. Martin, *Violence et Révolution*, 8.

53. Lynn Hunt, "The Experience of Revolution," *FHS* 32, no. 4 (2009): 671–678. See also Ronen Steinberg, "Somber Historiographies: The French Revolution, the Holocaust, and Alon Confino's Concept of Foundational Pasts," *Storia della storiografia* 66, no. 2 (2014): 87–100.

54. "Instructions to Authors," *International Journal of Transitional Justice*, accessed April 19, 2017, https://academic.oup.com/ijtj/pages/General_Instructions.

55. See Minow, *Between Vengeance and Forgiveness*. See also Neil Kritz, ed., *Transitional Justice: How Emerging Democracies Reckon with Former Regimes*, 3 vols. (Washington D.C.: United States Institute of Peace, 1995); Ruti Teitel, *Transitional Justice* (Oxford:

Oxford University Press, 2000); Jon Elster, *Closing the Books: Transitional Justice in Historical Perspective* (Cambridge: Cambridge University Press, 2004); Naomi Roht-Arriaza and Javier Mariezcurrena, eds., *Transitional Justice in the Twenty-First Century: Beyond Truth versus Justice* (Cambridge: Cambridge University Press, 2006).

56. Of the many books that have made the concept of trauma accessible to the general public and that have had an impact on its use across a variety of disciplines in the medical and social sciences as well as in the humanities, the following one is probably the most influential: Judith Herman, *Trauma and Recovery: The Aftermath of Violence—from Domestic Abuse to Political Terror* (New York: Basic Books, 1992).

57. See Michael Trimble, *Post-Traumatic Neurosis: From Railway Spine to the Whiplash* (New York: Wiley, 1981); and Ruth Leys, *Trauma: A Genealogy* (Chicago: University of Chicago Press, 2000).

58. See "Post-Traumatic Stress Disorder," in *The Diagnostic and Statistical Manual of Mental Disorders*, 3rd ed. (Washington D.C.: American Psychiatric Association, 1980), 236–238; and N. C. Andreasen, "Posttraumatic Stress Disorder," in *Comprehensive Textbook of Psychiatry*, 4th ed., ed. H. I. Kaplan and B. J. Sadock (Baltimore: Williams and Wilkins, 1985), 918–924.

59. See Bessel A. van der Kolk and Onno van der Hart, "Pierre Janet and the Breakdown of Adaptation in Psychological Trauma," *American Journal of Psychiatry* 146, no. 12 (1989): 1530–1540.

60. Fassin and Rechtman, *Empire of Trauma*, 15. See also Allan Young, *The Harmony of Illusions: Inventing Post Traumatic Stress Disorder* (Princeton, N.J.: Princeton University Press, 1995); Michael Rothberg, "Decolonizing Trauma Studies: A Response," *Studies in the Novel* 40, nos. 1–2 (2008): 224–234; Mark S. Micale and Paul Lerner, eds., *Traumatic Pasts: History, Psychiatry, and Trauma in the Modern Age, 1870–1930* (Cambridge: Cambridge University Press, 2001).

61. These terms often figure together in the literature on difficult pasts. See Judy Barsalou, "Trauma and Transitional Justice in Divided Societies," United States Institute of Peace, accessed July 10, 2018, https://www.usip.org/publications/2005/04/trauma-and-transitional-justice-divided-societies.

62. See Julia Douthwaite, *The Frankenstein of 1790 and Other Lost Chapters from Revolutionary France* (Chicago: University of Chicago Press, 2012). See also Debora Jenson, *Trauma and Its Representations: The Social Life of Mimesis in Post-Revolutionary France* (Baltimore: Johns Hopkins University Press, 2001); and Katherine Astbury, *Narrative Responses to the Trauma of the French Revolution* (London: Magenta, 2012).

63. Avery Gordon, *Ghostly Matters: Ghosts and the Sociological Imagination* (Minneapolis: University of Minnesota Press, 1997), 7.

64. See Geoffrey Hartman, *The Longest Shadow: In the Aftermath of the Holocaust* (New York: Palgrave Macmillan, 1996); Bernhard Schlink, *Guilt about the Past* (Toronto: Anansi, 2009).

65. I take the term "democide" from R. J. Rummel, *Death by Government: Genocide and Mass Murder since 1900* (New York: Routledge, 1997).

66. Just like with the Reign of the Terror, there is no agreement on the number of people who were killed during the White Terror of 1795. Jean-Clément Martin estimates that at least 2,000 people were killed, whereas according to Jean Tulard the number is closer to several hundred. See Jean-Clément Martin, *La Terreur. Part Maudite de la Révolution* (Paris: Découvertes/Gallimard, 2010), 84; and Jean Tulard, "La terreur

blanche est-elle le symétrique de la terreur jacobine?," in *La Vendée. Après la Terreur, la reconstruction. Actes du colloque ténu à la Roche-sur-Yon les 25, 25, et 27 Avril 1996* (Paris: Perrin, 1997), 187–190.

67. Bronislaw Baczko, *Politiques de la Révolution française* (Paris: Gallimard, 2008), 169.

68. Chemin-Dupontès, *Que-ce que la théophilanthropie?* (Paris: Bureaux du journal La Libre Conscience, 1868 [1797]), 13. See also Albert Mathiez, *La Thépophilanthropie et la culte décadaire, 1796–1801. Essai sur l'histoire religieuse de la Révolution* (Paris: Félix Alcan, 1903).

69. Joseph Crawford, *Gothic Fiction and the Invention of Terrorism: The Politics and Aesthetics of Fear in the Age of the Reign of Terror* (London: Bloomsbury, 2013), x.

70. See Luzzatto, *Mémoire de la Terreur*, chap. 6.

71. Keith M. Baker, "Enlightenment and the Institution of Society: Notes for a Conceptual History," in *Main Trends in Cultural History: Ten Essays*, ed. Willem Melching and Wyger Velema (Amsterdam: Rodopi, 1994), 96.

72. See Brian C. J. Singer, *Society, Theory, and the French Revolution* (New York: St. Martin's Press, 1986).

73. Hunt, *Politics, Culture, and Class*, 56.

1. Nomenclature

1. Quoted in François Gendron, *The Gilded Youth of Thermidor* (Montreal: McGill-Queen's University Press, 1993), 7.

2. Georges Duval, *Souvenirs thermidoriens*, 2 vols. (Paris: Victor Magen, 1844), 2:69.

3. Here and throughout the book, when I use the word "Terror" with a capital T, I am referring to the revolutionary Reign of Terror. When I use the word "terror" with a lowercase t, I am referring to the concept of terror in general.

4. Jean-Claude-Hippolyte Méhée de la Touche, *La queue de Robespierre, ou les Dangers de la liberté de la presse* (Paris: Imprimerie de Rougyff, 1794).

5. See Michel Biard, "Après la tête, la queue! La rhétorique antijacobine en fructidor an II—vendémiaire an III," in *Le tournant de l'an III. Réaction et Terreur blanche dans la France révolutionnaire*, ed. Michel Vovelle (Paris: CTHS, 1997), 201–214.

6. *AP*, 96:55. The original quote from Tallien refers to "three *décadi*" rather than a month. A *décadi* was the ten-day week instituted by the revolutionaries in 1793, when the revolutionary government adopted the Republican Calendar. I opted for English usage in my translation for reasons of consistency and because three *décadi* are, basically, a month.

7. Ibid., 96:55–58.

8. I am not certain that Tallien's speech was the first time the word *terrorisme* was used, but it was the first time it was used in an official setting, and it is common to attribute the appearance of this term to this moment. See Annie Geffroy, "Terreur et terrorisme. Les mots en héritage, du néologisme au concept," in *La Vendée: après la Terreur, la reconstruction. Actes du colloque tenu à la Roche-sur-Yon les 25, 26, et 27 Avril 1996* (Paris: Perrin, 1997), 143–161.

9. See Bruce Hoffman, *Inside Terrorism* (New York: Columbia University Press, 2006), 15–16; Gérard Chaliand and Arnaud Blin, *The History of Terrorism, from Antiquity to Al Qaeda* (Berkeley: University of California Press, 2007), chap. 5. See also

Walter Laqueur, *A History of Terrorism* (New Brunswick, N.J.: Transaction, 2001), 6; and Randall D. Law, *Terrorism: A History* (Cambridge: Polity, 2009), chap. 4.

10. The literature one could cite here is virtually endless. For some recent historiographic interventions in this debate, see Gueniffey, *Politique de la Terreur;* Mayer, *Furies;* Sophie Wahnich, *In Defence of the Terror: Liberty or Death in the French Revolution* (London: Verso, 2012); D. M. G. Sutherland, ed., "Violence and the French Revolution," Special Issue, *Historical Reflections/Réflexions historiques* 29, no. 3 (2003). For some paradigmatic theoretical statements, see Maurice Merlau-Ponty, *Humanism and Terror: An Essay on the Communist Problem* (Boston: Beacon Press, 1969); Jean-Paul Sartre, "Preface to Fanon's *Wretched of the Earth*," in *Violence in War and Peace: An Anthology,* ed. Nanchy Scheper-Hughes and Philippe Bourgeois (Oxford: Blackwell, 2004), 229–235; Walter Benjamin, "Critique of Violence," in *Reflections: Essays, Aphorisms, Autobiographical Writings,* ed. Peter Demetz (New York: Schocken Books, 1986), 277–300; Hannah Arendt, *On Violence* (New York: Harcourt, Brace and World, 1969).

11. Annie Jourdan, "Les discours de la terreur à l'époque révolutionnaire (1776–1798): Etude comparative sur une notion ambiguë," *FHS* 36, no. 1 (2013), 80. On the many meanings of the term terror during the revolutionary era, see Gerd van der Heuevel, "Terreur, Terroriste, Terrorisme," in *Handbuch politisch-sozialer Grundbegriffe in Frankreich, 1680–1820,* ed. Rolf Reichardt and Eberhard Schmitt, 21 vols. (Munich: Oldenbourg, 1985–), 3:89–132.

12. *AP,* 96:56.

13. According to modern psychiatry, traumatic events impact communities as well as individuals. This observation is similar to Tallien's claims about the individual and collective effects of terror. "Traumatic events," writes Judith Herman, "call into question basic human relationships. They breach the attachments of family, friendship, love, and community." Herman, *Trauma and Recovery,* 52.

14. See Julius Ruff, *Violence in Early Modern Europe, 1500–1800* (Cambridge: Cambridge University Press, 2001); Robert Muchembeld, *A History of Violence: From the End of the Middle Ages to the Present* (Cambridge: Polity, 2012); Yves Michaud, *La violence apprivoisée* (Paris: Hachette, 1996).

15. I realize this is a controversial statement. It is, however, supported by demographic evidence. See Massimo Livi Bacci, *The Population of Europe* (Oxford: Blackwell, 2000). It is also part of a view—one might even say, something of a master narrative—that equates the transition to modernity with a decline in violence. Many scholars point out that although it has become something of a commonplace to say that our time is the most violent of all, the fact is that, when taking the long view, our time is decidedly less violent than previous periods. In other words, there is a telling gap, even contrast, between reality and representation here. Much of the argument about the decline in violence is based on Norbert Elias, *The Civilizing Process: Sociogenetic and Psychogenetic Investigations* (Oxford: Blackwell, 1994). For a more recent rendition of similar arguments, see Steven Pinker, *The Better Angels of Our Nature: Why Violence Has Declined* (New York: Viking, 2011). For a book that provides a decidedly less rosy picture of the relationship between modern times and violence, see Joanna Bourke, *An Intimate History of Killing: Face-to-Face Killing in Twentieth Century Warfare* (London: Granta, 1999).

16. See John Theibault, "The Rhetoric of Death and Destruction in the Thirty Years War," *Journal of Social History* 27, no. 2 (1993): 271–290.

17. Matthew White, *The Great Big Book of Horrible Things: The Definitive Chronicle of History's 100 Worst Atrocities* (New York: Norton, 2012), 256.

18. See Alexandra Witze and Jeff Kanipe, *Island on Fire: The Extraordinary Story of Laki, the Volcano That Turned Eighteenth Century Europe Dark* (London: Profile, 2017); Mark Molesky, *This Gulf of Fire: The Destruction of Lisbon, or Apocalypse in the Age of Science and Reason* (New York: Knopf, 2015).

19. Susan E. Neiman, *Evil in Modern Thought: An Alternative History of Philosophy* (Princeton, N.J.: Princeton University Press, 2015), 1.

20. See Max Weber, "The Meaning and Value of Science: Disenchantment, 'Progress,' and Civilized Man's Meaninglessness," in *Max Weber: Readings and Commentary on Modernity*, ed. Stephen Kalberg (Oxford: Blackwell, 2005), 321–327. See also Peter L. Berger, *The Heretical Imperative: Contemporary Possibilities of Religious Affirmation* (New York: Doubleday, 1979); and Owen Chadwick, *The Secularization of the European Mind in the Nineteenth Century* (Cambridge: Cambridge University Press, 1975).

21. See Jonathan Sheehan, "Enlightenment, Religion, and the Enigma of Secularization: A Review Essay," *AHR* 208, no. 4 (2003): 1061–1080; Peter L. Berger, ed. *The Desecularization of the World: Resurgent Religion and World Politics* (Washington D.C.: Ethics and Public Policy Center, 1999); Rodney Stark, "Secularization, R.I.P.," *Sociology of Religion* 60, no. 3 (1999): 249–273.

22. See Jeffrey Burson and Ulrich Lehner, eds., *Enlightenment and Catholicism: A Transnational History* (South Bend, Ind.: University of Notre Dame Press, 2014).

23. See John McManners, *Church and Society in Eighteenth Century France*, 2 vols. (Oxford: Oxford University Press, 1998); Nigel Aston, *Religion and Revolution in France, 1780–1804* (Washington D.C.: Catholic University of America Press, 2000); Suzanne Desan, *Reclaiming the Sacred: Lay Religion and Popular Politics in Revolutionary France* (Ithaca, N.Y.: Cornell University Press, 1990); Caroline Ford, *Divided Houses: Religion and Gender in Modern France* (Ithaca, N.Y.: Cornell University Press, 2005); Carol Harrison, *Romantic Catholics: France's Postrevolutionary Generation in Search of a Modern Faith* (Ithaca, N.Y.: Cornell University Press, 2014); Dale van Klay, "Christianity as Causality and Chrysalis of Modernity: The Problem of Dechristianization in the French Revolution," *AHR* 108, no. 4 (2003): 1081–1104; Thomas Kselman, "Challenging Dechristianization: The Historiography of Religion in Modern France," *Church History* 75, no. 1 (2006): 130–139.

24. Pippa Norris and Ronald Ingelhart, *Sacred and Secular: Religion and Politics Worldwide* (Cambridge: Cambridge University Press, 2011), 2.

25. See Arlette Jouanna, *The Saint-Bartholomew Day Massacre: The Mysteries of a Crime of State* (Manchester: Manchester University Press, 2015), esp. chap. 7. See also Denis Crouzet, *Les guerriers de Dieu. La violence au temps des troubles de religion, vers 1525–vers 1610*, 2 vols. (Paris: Champ Vallon, 1990); Natalie Zemon Davis, "The Rites of Violence: Religious Riot in Sixteenth Century France," *Past and Present* 59 (1973): 51–91.

26. Molesky, *This Gulf of Fire*, 336.

27. On religious explanations for the violence of the French Revolution, see Richard Burton, *Blood in the City: Violence and Revelation in Paris: 1789–1945* (Ithaca, N.Y.: Cornell University Press, 2001); Jesse Goldhammer, *Headless Republic: Sacrificial Violence in Modern French Thought* (Ithaca, N.Y.: Cornell University Press, 2005).

28. I borrow the phrase "secularization of catastrophe" from the Israeli philosopher Adi Ophir. See Adi Ophir, *Divine Violence: Two Essays on God and Disaster* [Hebrew]

(Tel-Aviv: Hakibbutz Hameuchad, 2013), 193. On the failure of theological explanations for evil in the eighteenth century, see Berber Bevernage, "The Past is Evil/Evil Is Past: On Retrospective Politics, Philosophy of History, and Temporal Manichaeism," *History and Theory* 54, no. 3 (2015): 333–352. See also the introduction to Elinor Accampo and Jeffrey H. Jackson, eds., "Disaster in French History," Special Issue, *FHS* 36, no. 2 (2013): 165–174.

29. Jürgen Habermas, *The Structural Transformation of the Public Sphere: An Inquiry into a Category of Bourgeois Society* (Cambridge, Mass.: MIT Press, 1989), 69.

30. See Dena Goodman, *The Republic of Letters: A Cultural History of the French Enlightenment* (Ithaca, N.Y.: Cornell University Press, 1996); Sarah Maza, *Private Lives and Public Affairs: The Causes Célèbres of Prerevolutionary France* (Berkeley: University of California Press, 1995); Colin Jones, "The Great Chain of Buying: Medical Advertisement, the Bourgeois Public Sphere, and the Origins of the French Revolution," *AHR* 101, no. 1 (1996): 13–40; Rebecca Spang, *The Invention of the Restaurant: Paris and Modern Gastronomic Culture* (Cambridge Mass.: Harvard University Press, 2000). See also Roger Chartier, *The Cultural Origins of the French Revolution* (Durham, N.C.: Duke University Press, 1991), chap. 2.

31. See Joan Landes, *Women and the Public Sphere in the Age of the French Revolution* (Ithaca, N.Y.: Cornell University Press, 1988); Baker, *Inventing the French Revolution*; Dena Goodman, "Public Sphere and Private Life: Toward a Synthesis of Current Historiographical Approaches to the Old Regime," *History and Theory* 31, no. 1 (1992): 1–20; Harold Mah, "Phantasies of the Public Sphere: Rethinking the Habermas of Historians," *JMH* 72, no. 1 (2000): 153–182.

32. See Sara Maza, *The Myth of the Bourgeoisie: An Essay on the Social Imaginary, 1750–1850* (Cambridge, Mass.: Harvard University Press, 2005). I borrow the notion of metaphor from Victor Turner, *Dramas, Fields, and Metaphors: Symbolic Action in Human Society* (Ithaca, N.Y.: Cornell University Press, 1974), 25–26. See also Anthony J. La Vopa, "Conceiving a Public: Ideas and Society in Eighteenth Century Europe," *JMH* 64, no. 1 (1992): 79–116.

33. See Robert Mandrou, *De la culture populaire aux 17e et 18e siècles. La bibliotheque bleue de Troyes* (Paris: Imago, 1985). On one such figure that gained widespread celebrity or, if one prefers, notoriety, in the eighteenth century thanks to the *bibliothèque bleue*, see Michael Kwass, *Contraband: Louis Mandrin and the Making of a Global Underground* (Cambridge, Mass.: Harvard University Press, 2014).

34. See Koop W. Koopmans, "The 1755 Lisbon Earthquake and Tsunami in Dutch News Sources: The Functioning of Early Modern News Dissemination," in *News in Early Modern Europe: Currents and Connections*, ed. Puck Fletcher and Simon Davies (Leiden: Brill, 2014), 19–40.

35. James Van Horn Melton, *The Rise of the Public in Enlightenment Europe* (Cambridge: Cambridge University Press, 2001), 82.

36. See Robert Darnton, "The History of Reading," in *New Perspectives on Historical Writing*, ed. Peter Burke (Cambridge: Polity Press, 1991), 157–186.

37. See Ruff, *Violence in Early Modern Europe*, 40.

38. See Marian Hobson, *The Object of Art: The Theory of Illusion in Eighteenth Century France* (Cambridge: Cambridge University Press, 1982); Sophia Rosenfeld, *A Revolution in Language: The Problem of Signs in Late Eighteenth Century France* (Stanford, Calif.: Stanford University Press, 2001); Paul Friedland, *Political Actors: Representative Bodies and*

Theatricality in the Age of the French Revolution (Ithaca, N.Y.: Cornell University Press, 2002).

39. See Anon., *Sur les moyens de communiquer sur-le-champ au peuple, occupant le dehors du lieu où se tient l'Assemblée, les délibérations qui y sont prises* (Paris: Imprimerie de Vve. Hérissant, 1789). See also Jacques Guillhaumou, "Zeitgenössische politische Lebensgeschichten aus der Französischen Revolution (1793–1794): Autobiographischer Akt und diskursives Ereignis," in *Die französische Revolution als Bruch des gesellschaftlichen Bewusstseins*, ed. Reinhart Koselleck and Rolf Reichardt (Munich: R. Oldenburg Verlag, 1988), 358–378.

40. See Hunt, "Experience of Revolution."

41. Jeremy Popkin, *Revolutionary News: The Press in France, 1789–1799* (Durham, N.C.: Duke University Press, 1990), 39.

42. See William H. Sewell, "Historical Events as Transformations of Structures: Inventing Revolution at the Bastille," *Theory and Society* 25, no. 6 (1996): 841–881.

43. See Nina Rattner Gelbart, "Death in the Bathtub: Charlotte Corday and Jean-Paul Marat," in *The Human Tradition in Modern Times*, ed. Steven K. Vincent and Alison Klairmont Lingo (Lanham, Md.: Rowman and Littlefield, 2000), 17–32; Guillaume Mazeau, *Le bain de l'histoire: Charlotte Corday et l'attentat contre Marat (1793–2009)* (Seyssel: Champ Vallon, 2009).

44. Schama, *Citizens*, xv.

45. See Micah Alpaugh, *Non-Violence and the French Revolution: Political Demonstrations in Paris, 1787–1795* (Cambridge: Cambridge University Press, 2015), 4–5.

46. "Révolution," *DAF*, ARTFL Project, accessed July 12, 2017, http://artflsrv02 .uchicago.edu/philologic4/publicdicos/query?report=bibliography&head =revolution.

47. D. M. G. Sutherland, "Introduction," *Historical Reflections/Réflexions historiques* 29, no. 3 (2003), 388.

48. Quoted in McPhee, *Liberty or Death*, 74.

49. Edmund Burke, *Reflections on the Revolution in France* (New Haven, Conn.: Yale University Press, 2003), 60.

50. Alain Corbin, *The Village of Cannibals: Rage and Murder in France, 1870* (Cambridge, Mass.: Harvard University Press, 1992), 92. See also Regina Janes, *Losing Our Heads: Beheadings in Literature and Culture* (New York: New York University Press, 2005), chap. 5.

51. See William Doyle, *The Oxford History of the French Revolution* (Oxford: Oxford University Press, 2002), 113.

52. Jean-Lambert Tallien, *La vérité sur les événemens du 2 septembre* (Paris: n.p., 1792), 5.

53. On this paradox of popular violence during the Revolution, see Colin Lucas, "Revolutionary Violence, the People and the Terror," and Colin Lucas, "Talking about Urban Popular Violence in 1789," in *Reshaping France: Town, Country, and Region during the French Revolution*, ed. Alan Forrest and Peter Jones (Manchester: Manchester University Press, 1991), 122–136.

54. *Le patriot François*, July 25, 1791, no. 715.

55. See Dominique Godineau, *The Women of Paris and Their French Revolution* (Berkeley: University of California Press, 1998). See also Dominique Godineau, "Femmes et violence dans l'éspace politique révolutionnaire," *Historical Reflections/Réflexions historiques* 29, no. 3 (2003): 559–576.

56. See Lynn Hunt, *The Family Romance of the French Revolution* (Berkeley: University of California Press, 1992), 152.

57. *Moniteur*, June 1, 1791, no. 152. On Brillat-Savarin's role in the rise of modern gastronomy, see Susan Pinkard, *A Revolution in Taste: The Rise of French Cuisine* (Cambridge: Cambridge University Press, 2009).

58. *AP*, 26:721.

59. On criminal reform in the eighteenth century, see Gordon Wright, *Between the Guillotine and Liberty: Two Centuries of the Crime Problem in France* (Oxford: Oxford University Press, 1985); and Marcello T. Maestro, *Voltaire and Beccaria as Reformers of Criminal Law* (New York: Columbia University Press, 1942).

60. *Moniteur*, June 1, 1791, no. 152.

61. Ibid.

62. Paul Friedland, *Seeing Justice Done: The Age of Spectacular Capital Punishment in France* (Oxford: Oxford University Press, 2012), 230.

63. Corbin, *Village of Cannibals*, 93.

64. Louis Antoine de Saint-Just, *Oeuvres completes*, 2 vols., ed. Charles Vellay (Paris: Charpentier et Fasquelle, 1908), 2:8.

65. Quoted in *Dictionnaire des usages socio-politiques (1770–1815). Fasc. 2: notions-concepts* (Paris: Klincksieck, 1987), 129–130.

66. Maximilien Robespierre, "Sur les principes de morale politique qui doivent guider la Convention nationale dans l'administration intérieure de la République," in *Oeuvres de Maximilien Robespierre*, 10 vols. (Paris: E. Leroux, 1912–), 10:353.

67. On this notion of terror as predicated on an absence; that is, on a social and moral order that is not yet there, see Marie-Hélène Huet, *Mourning Glory: The Will of the French Revolution* (Philadelphia: University of Pennsylvania Press, 1997), esp. chap. 2.

68. The phrase "twelve who ruled" is, of course, in reference to R. R. Palmer's classic study of the Terror. See R. R. Palmer, *Twelve Who Ruled: The Year of the Terror in the French Revolution* (Princeton, N.J.: Princeton University Press, 1941).

69. *AP*, 94:30–31.

70. On law of 22 Prairial, see Dan Edelstein, "The Law of 22 Prairial: Introduction," *Telos* 141 (2007): 82–91; and Carla Hesse, "The Law of the Terror," *Modern Language Notes* 114, no. 4 (1999): 702–718.

71. See Cesare Vetter, "'Systeme de Terreur' et 'system de la Terreur' dans le lexique de la Révolution française," Révolution Française.net: L'Esprit des lumières et de la Révolution, accessed December 19, 2017, https://revolution-francaise.net/2014/10/23/594-systeme-de-terreur-et-systeme-de-la-terreur-dans-le-lexique-de-la-revolution-francaise.

72. See Colin Jones, "French Crossings: III. The Smile of the Tiger," *Transactions of the Royal Historical Society* 22 (2012): 3–35; Françoise Brunel, "Bridging the Gulf of the Terror," in Baker et al., *French Revolution and the Creation of Modern Political Culture*, 4:327–346.

73. *Moniteur*, 12 Floréal, an III (May 1, 1795), no. 222.

74. Baczko, *Ending the Terror*, 36.

75. *AP*, 96:58. For the famous statement from September 5, 1793, see *Moniteur*, September 8, 1793, no. 251. Incidentally, Robespierre presided over that famous session of the Convention, and while the original call to "make Terror the order of the day"

was made by Chaumette, who spoke for the Commune of Paris, it was taken up and endorsed by none other than Barère himself.

76. See Martin, *Violence et Révolution*, 213.

77. See Mette Harder, "A Second Terror: The Purges of French Revolutionary Legislators after Thermidor," *FHS* 38, no. 1 (2015): 33–60. Howard Brown's research has also shown that many of the repressive measures that are identified with the Terror were also employed by the Directory and even by the Napoleonic state, at least in its early years. See Howard Brown, *Ending the French Revolution*, chaps. 6–7.

78. Jourdan, *Le discours de la Terreur*, 67.

79. Marc-Antoine Baudot, *Notes historiques sur la Convention nationale, le Directoire, l'Empire, et l'exil des votants* (Geneva: Slatkine-Megariotis, 1974 [1893]), 298.

80. On Tallien's revolutionary career, see Mette Harder, "Reacting to Revolution— the Political Career(s) of J.-L. Tallien," in *Experiencing the French Revolution*, ed. David Andress (Oxford: Voltaire Foundation, University of Oxford, 2013), 87–112. Tallien's common-law wife Thérésia Cabarrus has proven more interesting to scholars and biographers than Tallien himself. See Marie-Hélène Bourquin-Simonin, *Monsieur et Madame Tallien* (Paris: Perrin, 1987); and Françoise Kermina, *Madame Tallien, 1773–1835* (Paris: Perrin, 2006).

81. *AP*, 96:58.

82. Ibid., 96:56.

83. It is possible that much of Tallien's address was actually written by another revolutionary leader, Pierre-Louis Roederer. A later, revised version of Roederer's text appears in his collected writings, where he claims that his text was the origin of Tallien's address. However, the chronology there is confused, and this makes it difficult to determine whether indeed Roederer's reflections on the Terror were the origin of Tallien's ideas. See Pierre-Louis Roederer, "Appendice—de la Terreur," in *Oeuvres du Comte P. L. Roederer*, 8 vols., ed. A. M. Roederer (Paris: Firmin-Didot Frères, 1853–1859), 3:57–65. This is an intriguing possibility, however, because in his capacity as the *procureur général syndic* of Paris, Roederer had been personally involved in the experiments and funding behind the building of the guillotine. His experiences and his proximity to the machine that came to symbolize this moment in the Revolution might be yet another reason for the very different image of the Terror that emerges from Tallien's *discours* of August 1794. On Roederer's revolutionary career, see Kenneth Margerison, "P.-L. Roederer: Political Thought and Practice during the French Revolution," *Transactions of the American Philosophical Society* 73, no. 1 (1983): 1–166.

84. Paul Ricoeur, "Violence and Language," *Bulletin de la Société Américaine de Philosophie de Langue Française* 10, no. 2 (1998): 32–41.

85. See Elaine Scarry, *The Body in Pain: The Making and Unmaking of the World* (Oxford: Oxford University Press, 1985); and Marguerite Feitlowitz, *A Lexicon of Terror: Argentina and the Legacies of Torture* (Oxford: Oxford University Press, 1998).

86. *AP*, 97:175.

87. Jean-Gabriel Peltier, *Paris pendant l'année*, 15 vols. (London: Baylis, 1795–1801), 13:637.

88. Rosenfeld, *Revolution in Language*, 181.

89. On the crisis of representation in the Revolution, see Friedland, *Political Actors*; and Singer, *Society, Theory, and the French Revolution*, esp. chap. 1.

90. Of course, the displacement of religion with the social neither began nor ended with the Revolution, but the Revolution was a particularly dramatic example of this process, and it created the institutions for the management of this new relation to the social. See Lynn Hunt, *Writing History in the Global Era* (New York: Norton, 2014), 81–85.

91. I am borrowing the concept of symbolic order from the psychoanalytic theories of Jacques Lacan. See Adrian Johnston, "Jacques Lacan," *The Stanford Encyclopedia of Philosophy* (Fall 2018 ed.), ed. Edward N. Zalta, accessed July 5, 2018, https://plato .stanford.edu/cgi-bin/encyclopedia/archinfo.cgi?entry=lacan. I believe one can find some parallels between the idea of a rupture in the symbolic order and the concept of liminality, as articulated by the anthropologist Victor Turner. Turner saw liminal moments as a twilight zone between an order of things that is gone and an order of things that has not yet emerged. These moments are characterized by enormous excitement and anxiety at the same time. They are profoundly destabilizing and disquieting, but they also make it possible to see, however briefly, that which is normally hidden under the surface of the everyday. Turner saw revolutions as prime examples of liminal moments. See Victor Turner, *The Ritual Process: Structure and Anti-Structure* (New Brunswick, N.J.: Transaction, 1969), chap. 3.

92. *Citoyen Pindray aux Citoyens Représentants, membres du Comité d'instruction publique*, 24 Pluviôse, an III (February 12, 1795), AN F17 1240.

93. See Ralph Kingston, *Bureaucrats and Bourgeois Society: Office Politics and Individual Credit in France, 1789–1848* (Basingstoke, UK: Palgrave Macmillan, 2012); and Benjamin Kafka, "The Demon of Writing: Paperwork, Public Safety, and the Reign of Terror," *Representations* 98, no. 1 (2007): 1–24.

94. Mercier, *Paris pendant la Révolution*, 2:8.

95. See Wallace Fowlie, *A Reading of Dante's Inferno* (Chicago: University of Chicago Press, 1981), esp. chap. 12; and Theofilio Ruiz, *The Terror of History: On the Uncertainties of Life in Western Civilization* (Princeton, N. J.: Princeton University Press, 2011).

96. See Michael Taussig, *The Nervous System* (New York: Routledge, 1992), chap. 7.

97. Louis-Marie Prudhomme, *Histoire générale et impartiale des erreurs, des fautes, et des crimes commis pendant la Révolution française, à dater du 24 août 1787, contenant le nombre des individus qui ont péri par la Révolution, de ceux qui ont émigré, et les intrigues des factions qui pendant ce tems ont désolé la France*, 6 vols. (Paris: n.p., 1796–1797), 3:4.

98. Ibid., 3:1.

99. Ibid., 3:4.

100. Ibid., 2:254. All in all, Prudhomme's list of victims of the Terror came to about 16,000 names. This number is not too far off from the numbers in Greer's quantitative study of the Terror. See Greer, *Incidence of the Terror*.

101. See Mona Ozouf, "The Terror after the Terror: An Immediate History," in Baker et al., *French Revolution and the Creation of Modern Political Culture*, 4:3–19.

102. Prudhomme, *Histoire générale*, 1:5–6.

103. Joseph Zizek, "'Plumes de fer': Louis-Marie Prudhomme Writes the French Revolution," *FHS* 26, no. 4 (2003), 628. Alain Corbin has also made a case for studying texts like Prudhomme's because they shed light on the place of cruelty and carnage in the social imaginary of the time, a historical subject that he sees as eminently legitimate. "Fastidious and fearful historians," writes Corbin, "appear to have conspired with

the men of the time to cover up horrific events. . . . Historical cruelty has been watered down and cruelty banished from its pages." Corbin, *Village of Cannibals*, 99.

104. See Annie Duprat, "Louis Marie Prudhomme et *l'Histoire Générale et impartiale des erreurs et des crimes commis pendant la Révolution française* (1797). Les réflexions d'un républicain sur la Terreur," in *La Révolution, 1789–1871. Écriture d'une histoire immédiate*, ed. Philippe Bourdin (Clermont-Ferrand: Presses Universitaires Blaise-Pascal, 2008), 111–128.

105. Prudhomme, *Histoire Générale*, 1:ii.

106. There are several editions of the *General History* and there are differences between them. See Duprat, "Louis Marie Prudhomme et *l'Histoire Générale*."

107. Prudhomme, *Histoire Générale*, 2:frontispiece. Capitalized words in the original.

108. Minow, *Between Vengeance and Forgiveness*; Eric Stover and Harvey M. Weinstein, eds., *My Neighbor, My Enemy: Justice and Community in the Aftermath of Mass Atrocity* (Cambridge: Cambridge University Press, 2004); Schlink, *Guilt about the Past*.

109. Prudhomme, *Histoire Générale*, 1:5.

110. François-Barnabé Tisset, *Compte rendu aux sans-culottes de la République française par très-haute, très-puissante, et très-expeditive Dame Guillotine*, 2 vols. (Paris: De l'Imprimerie du Calculateur Patriote, au corps sans tête, 1794), 2:2.

111. See *Liste, par ordre alphabétique, des noms des citoyens députés à la convention nationale, avec leurs demeurs au second mois de l'an 2 de la République* (Paris: Imprimerie nationale, 1794); *Liste generale des individus condamnés par jugemens, ou mis hors de la Loi par Decrets, et dont les biens ont été déclarés confisqués au profit de la République* (Paris: Imprimerie des domaines nationaux, 1794); *Liste générale et alphabetique des noms, ages, qualités, emplois et demeurs de tous les conspirateurs qui ont été condamnés à mort par le Tribunal Revolutionnaire, établi à Paris par la loi du 17 Aout 1792, et par le second Tribunal, établi à Paris par la loi du 10 Mars, 1793, pour juger tous les ennemis de la Patrie* (London: J. Johnson, St. Paul's Church-Yard, 1795). These and many other lists are preserved in the collections of the Newberry Library in Chicago and have been digitized. See the French Pamphlet Collection, Newberry Library, accessed July 27, 2018, https://archive.org/details/newberryfrenchpamphlets.

112. See Antoine de Baecque, *The Body Politic: Corporeal Metaphor in Revolutionary France, 1770–1800* (Stanford, Calif.: Stanford University Press, 1997), chap. 6.

113. François d'Ivernois, *Tableau historique et politique des pertes que la Révolution et la guerre ont causées au peuple français dans sa population, son agriculture, ses colonies, ses manufactures et son commerce* (London: Imprimerie de Baylis, 1799), 10. On the increasing use of mathematical methods to study the social world during the revolutionary era, see Keith M. Baker, *Condorcet: From Natural Philosophy to Social Mathematics* (Chicago: University of Chicago Press, 1974); and Joshua Cole, *The Power of Large Numbers: Population, Politics, and Gender in Nineteenth-Century France* (Ithaca, N.Y.: Cornell University Press, 2000)

114. Prudhomme, *Histoire Générale*, 6:522.

115. Ibid. The last of these identifiers seems to have been in reference to an alleged group of royalist conspirators. Apparently, suspects in one of the prisons in Paris during the Terror were to be given a sign for the beginning of an uprising. The sign was to be an egg painted red and white, colors associated with the monarchy and the city

of Paris. See Augustin Challamel and Wilhelm Ténint, *Les français sous la Révolution* (Paris: Challamel, c. 1843), 175.

116. Prudhomme, *Histoire Générale*, 6:523.

117. Michel Foucault, *The Order of Things: An Archaeology of the Human Sciences* (New York: Vintage, 1970), xv.

118. Jorge Luis Borges, "The Analytical Language of John Wilkins," in *Other Inquisitions, 1937–1952*, trans. Ruth Simms (Austin: University of Texas Press, 1964), 103.

119. Foucault, *Order of Things*, xv.

120. Eric Hazan, *A People's History of the French Revolution* (London: Verso, 2014), 312.

121. Pierre-Henri Billy, "Des prénoms révolutionnaires en France," *Annales historiques de la Révolution française* 322 (October–December 2000), 44.

122. See Miller, *Natural History of the French Revolution*.

123. See Robert Darnton, "What Was Revolutionary about the French Revolution?" *New York Review of Books*, January 19, 1989.

124. See Irving Goffman, *The Presentation of the Self in Everyday Life* (New York: Anchor, 1959).

125. Denise Davidson, "Making Society 'Legible': People-Watching in Paris after the Revolution," *French Historical Studies* 28, no. 2 (2005), 267.

126. *Citoyen Aïgoin au citoyen, President de la Convention nationale*, 11 Thermidor an II (July 29, 1794), AN D III 240.

127. *Reconstitution des actes de l'état civil*, APA, 5 Mi 1 / 87. The name-change files for the late 1790s and early 1800s in Paris were damaged in a fire. All that remains are a few reconstructed documents on microfilm.

128. Jean-Baptiste Dauchez, *Rapport fait au nom d'une commission spéciale, par Dauchez (d'Arras), représentant du peuple, relativement à la suppression des prénoms révolutionnaires donnés aux enfans dont la naissance a été constatée pendant le régime de la terreur: séance du 6 messidor, an V* (Paris: Imprimerie nationale, 1797).

129. Ibid., 3–4.

130. Ibid., 5.

131. One can get a sense of this by following the etymology of the word "term." In archaic usage, the word "term" was defined as that which marks the limit or boundary of anything, be it time, space, or indeed, the meaning of words. This is not how the word is commonly used today, although traces of these more archaic meanings remain in present-day language, as when we speak of an elected official serving their term, or when physicians refer to a woman as being preterm or post-term, meaning before or after thirty-eight weeks of pregnancy. This relationship between the etymology of the word "term" and its present usage is relevant for understanding the deep meaning of the phrase "coming to terms with the past," because it suggests that coming to terms has something to do with ending, with leaving the past behind and setting a limit to its capacity to determine the present. Moreover, there is an etymological connection between the word "term" and the word "name." Late Latin philosophers used the word *terminus* to denote the definition of a word. Thomas Aquinas saw *terminus* as synonymous with *dictio* and *locutio*, words denoting the ability to speak clearly, but also with *nomen*, that is, "name." In this sense, coming to terms with something denotes acts of circumscription, delimitation, and even definition. I see a deep connection here to the title of this chapter, "Naming the Terror." Naming the terror after

9 Thermidor —with the broad understanding of naming that is elaborated in this chapter —was a fundamental part of the effort to leave this past behind; to mark a clear boundary between the course of revolutionary history before and after 9 Thermidor; to limit the influence that the events of Year II exerted over the foundation of the Republic. And as the name of the Terror remained ambiguous, so too the quest to leave it behind remained elusive. Elaborating the relationship between the etymology of the word "term" and the phrase "coming to terms with the past" allows me to highlight the connection between linguistic and temporal instability after the Terror. For the etymology of the word "term" see "term," Oxford Dictionaries, at https://en.oxforddictionaries.com/definition/term, accessed November 23, 2018; and "term," Online Etymology Dictionary, at https://www.etymonline.com/word /term#etymonline_v_10648, accessed November 23, 2018. For a critical view of the notion of coming to terms with, or working through, the past, see Theodor Adorno, "The Meaning of Working through the Past," in *Critical Models: Interventions and Catchwords*, trans. Henry W. Pickford (New York: Columbia University Press, 2005), 89–104.

132. Maurice Blanchot, *The Writing of the Disaster* (Lincoln: University of Nebraska Press, 1986), 28.

133. See Bill Nichols, *Speaking Truth with Films: Evidence, Ethics, Politics in Documentary* (Berkeley: University of California Press, 2016), 113. See also Ann Larabee, *Decade of Disaster* (Urbana, Ill.: University of Illinois Press, 1999).

134. See Françoise Brunel, *Thermidor. La chute de Robespierre* (Brussels: Editions Complexes, 1989).

135. I am referring, of course, to the Baczko's argument in *Ending the Terror*.

2. Accountability

1. Contemporary accounts from the revolutionary period alternate between two spellings of the name: Le Bon and Lebon. In this book I use the former.

2. See Greer, *Incidence of the Terror*, 135.

3. P.-J.-B. Buchez and P.-C. Roux, *Histoire parlementaire de la Révolution française*, 40 vols. (Paris: J. Hetzel, 1834–8), 37:88.

4. Le Bon has been studied less thoroughly than other officials who were put on trial after the Terror. Nevertheless, there are several detailed monographs, most of them quite dated. See A.-J. Paris, *La Terreur dans le Pas-de-Calais et dans le Nord. Histoire de Joseph Le Bon et des tribunaux révolutionnaires d'Arras et de Cambrai*, 2 vols. (Arras: Rousseau-Leroy, 1864); Louis Jacob, *Joseph Le Bon, 1765–1795. La terreur à la frontier (Nord et Pas-de-Calais)*, 2 vols. (Paris: Mellottée, 1934). To these should be added a rather curious attempt at psychohistory analyzing Le Bon's mission in the north as a case of revolutionary insanity. See Yves Dhotel, *Joseph Le Bon, ou, Arras sous la Terreur. Essai sur la psychose révolutionnaire* (Paris: Éditions Hippocrate, 1934).

5. Mathiez, *After Robespierre*, 67.

6. See Albert Soboul, *The French Revolution 1787–1799: From the Storming of the Bastille to Napoléon* (New York: Random House, 1974), 425–426; and Georges Lefebvre, *The Thermidorians and the Directory: Two Phases of the French Revolution* (New York: Random House, 1964), chap. 3.

7. François Furet and Denis Richet, *La Révolution française* (Paris: Fayard, 1973), 261.

8. See Corinne Gomez-Le Chevanton, "Le procés Carrier. Enjeux politiques, péda-gogie collective et construction mémorielle," *AHRF*, no. 343 (January–March 2006): 73–92; and Baczko, *Ending the Terror*, esp. chap. 3.

9. See Howard Brown, "Robespierre's Tail: The Possibilities of Justice after the Ter-ror," *Canadian Journal of History* 45, no. 3 (2010): 503–535; and Howard Brown, *Ending the French Revolution.*

10. See Mary Albon, "Project on Justice in Times of Transition," in Kritz, *Transi-tional Justice*, 1:42–53.

11. See Vida Azimi, "Aux origines de la responsabilité ministérielle," in *1791, la pre-mière constitution française*, ed. Jean Bart et al. (Paris: Economica, 1993), 220.

12. *AP*, 35:511.

13. On the concept of *moeurs*, see Jainchill, *Reimagining Politics after the Terror*, chap. 2.

14. *AP*, 39:12.

15. See Teitel, *Transitional Justice*, chap. 2.

16. See Jacob Soll, *The Reckoning: Financial Accountability and the Rise and Fall of Na-tions* (New York: Basic Books, 2014).

17. See Francis Fukuyama, *The Origins of Political Order: From Prehuman Times to the French Revolution* (New York: Farrar, Straus and Giroux, 2011), chap. 22.

18. See A. W. Bradley, "Personal Responsibility and Government: A Case for Im-peachment?," in *The Impeachment of Warren Hastings: Papers from a Bicentenary Commem-oration*, ed. Geoffrey Carnall and Colin Nicholson (Edinburgh: Edinburgh University Press, 1989), 164–185.

19. Soll, *Reckoning*, 133.

20. On the judicial reforms of the Revolution, especially as these pertain to crimi-nal justice, see Jean-Claude Farcy, *Histoire de la justice française de la Révolution à nos jours. Trois décennies de recherches* (Paris: Presses Universitaires de France, 2001), 364–387. See also Pierre Lascoumes et al., *Au nom de l'ordre. Une histoire politique du code pénal* (Paris: Hachette, 1989); and Robert Allen, *Les tribunaux criminels sous la Révolution et l'Empire, 1792–1811* (Rennes: Presses Universitaires de Rennes, 2005).

21. See Richard Mowery Andrews, *Law, Magistracy, and Crime in Old Regime Paris, 1735–1789: Volume 1, the System of Criminal Justice* (Cambridge: Cambridge University Press, 1994).

22. See Howard Brown, *Ending the French Revolution*, chaps. 3–4. See also Woloch, *New Regime*, chap. 12.

23. "Responsabilité," *DAF*, accessed February 28, 2013, http://artflsrv02.uchicago .edu/cgi-bin/dicos/pubdico1look.pl?strippedhw=responsabilite.

24. See Margueritte Boulet-Sautel et al., *La responsabilité à travers les âges* (Paris: Eco-nomica, 1989), 78.

25. Scholars of transitional justice regard the trial and execution of Louis XVI as a pivotal moment of transitional justice. See Teitel, *Transitional Justice*, 27.

26. Michael Walzer, *Regicide and Revolution: Speeches at the Trial of Louis XVI* (Cam-bridge: Cambridge University Press, 1974), 5.

27. "Constitution de 1791," Conseil Constitutionel, accessed November 11, 2015,http://www.conseil-constitutionnel.fr/conseil-constitutionnel/francais/la -constitution/les-constitutions-de-la-france/constitution-de-1791.5082.html.

28. For a sense of the dramatic debates about this legal and theoretical problem, Albert Soboul, *Le procès de Louis XVI* (Paris: Gallimard, 1973); and David Jordan, *The*

King's Trial: Louis XVI vs. the French Revolution (Berkeley: University of California Press, 1979).

29. François Furet, "A Commentary," *FHS* 16, no. 4 (1990), 795.

30. See François Furet, *Revolutionary France, 1770–1880* (Oxford: Blackwell, 1995).

31. See Baker, "Sovereignty," 844–859; and Paul Hanson, *Contesting the French Revolution* (Oxford: Wiley-Blackwell, 2009), 7.

32. "Plan de travail, de surveillance et de correspondance, proposé par le Comité de Salut Public aux Représentant du Peuple, députés près des Armées de la République," Collection Baudouin, accessed July 1, 2018, http://artflsrv02.uchicago.edu/cgi -bin/philologic/getobject.pl?c.35:87.baudouin0314.

33. It is, of course, controversial to refer to the Reign of Terror as a mass crime. This kind of descriptions flattens what was, according to most historians, a highly complex reality. It is also a moral judgment that is not shared by all scholars of, and commentators on, the Revolution. Still, it was a fairly widespread view after 9 Thermidor, in and beyond France. It remains a term that even historians who are by and large sympathetic to the revolutionary project must adopt sometimes when reflecting on the historiography of the Terror. See Béatrice Pouligny, Bernard Doray, and Jean-Clément Martin, "Methodological and Ethical Problems: A Trans-Disciplinary Approach," in *After Mass Crime: Rebuilding States and Communities*, ed. Béatrice Pouligny et al. (Tokyo: United Nations University Press, 2007), 19–40.

34. See Jon Elster, "Retribution," in *Retribution and Reparation in the Transition to Democracy*, ed. Jon Elster (Cambridge: Cambridge University Press, 2006), 33–56.

35. See Hannah Arendt, *Eichmann in Jerusalem: A Report on the Banality of Evil* (New York: Penguin, 1963), 288; and Mark J. Osiel, *Mass Atrocity, Ordinary Evil, and Hannah Arendt: Criminal Consciousness in Argentina's Dirty War* (New Haven, Conn.: Yale University Press, 2001).

36. See Sophie Wahnich, "La question de la responsabilité collective en l'an III," in *Le tournant de l'an III. Réaction et terreur blanche dans la France révolutionnaire*, ed. Michel Vovelle (Paris: CTHS, 1997), 85–96.

37. Laurent Lecointre, *Les Crimes de sept membres des anciens Comités de salut public et de sûreté générale, ou, Dénonciation formelle à la Convention nationale contre Billaud-Varennes, Barère, Collot-d'Herbois, Vadier, Vouland, Amar et David, suivie de pièces originales existantes dans les comités, preuves et temoins indiqués à l'appui des faits* (n.p., 1795), 19.

38. *Moniteur*, 14 Fructidor, an II (August 31, 1794), no. 344.

39. Ibid.

40. *Moniteur*, 15 Fructidor, an II (September 1, 1794), no. 345.

41. *AP*, 100:134.

42. See William Doyle, *Oxford History of the French Revolution* (Oxford: Oxford University Press, 1989), 282–283; Sutherland, *France 1789–1815*, 251–252.

43. *Extrait du registres des arrêtés du Comité de salut public de la Convention nationale*, 10 Thermidor II (July 28, 1794), AN F7 4772.

44. See Michel Biard, *Missionaires de la République. Les représentants du peuple en mission* (Paris: CTHS, 2002), 350.

45. Robert Lindet, *Rapport fait à la Convention nationale dans la séance du 4ème des Sans-Culottides de l'an 2ème, au nom des Comités de salut public, de sûretè générale et de législation, réunis, sur la situation interieure de la république, par Robert Lindet, Représentant*

du peuple, et membre du comité de salut public (Montauban: chez Fontanel, imprimeur de la société populaire, 1794), 22.

46. *Histoire du terrorisme dans la commune d'Arles, servant de suite au mémoire publié pour cette commune, le 8 Floréal* (Paris: Imprimerie de Guffroy, 1795), 11.

47. Ibid., 2.

48. *Pétition à la Convention nationale des citoyens de la Commune d'Avignon, victimes de la faction Robespierre, sur les atrocités commises dans cette commune et dans le département de Vaucluse, par les agens et les complices de cette faction* (Avignon: V. Raphel, 1794), 1.

49. *Les citoyens d'Arras réunie en assemblée à la Convention nationale*, August 1795, AN, F7 4772.

50. *AP*, 94:61.

51. Baczko, *Politiques de la Révolution française*, 165.

52. De Baecque, *Body Politic*, 209. See also Colin Lucas, "The Theory and Practice of Denunciation in the French Revolution," *JMH* 68, no. 4 (1996): 768–785; Lucien Jaume, *Le discours Jacobin et la démocratie* (Paris: Fayard, 1989).

53. Baczko, *Ending the Terror*, 34.

54. See Gendron, *Gilded Youth of Thermidor*.

55. See Donald M. G. Sutherland, *Murder in Aubagne: Lynching, Law, and Justice during the French Revolution* (Cambridge: Cambridge University Press, 2009), 250.

56. See Stephen Clay, "Vengeance, Justice, and Reactions in the Revolutionary Midi," *French History* 23, no. 1 (2009): 22–46.

57. *AP*, 72:337.

58. There are numerous studies of Carrier's mission in the west and of his trial. The ones I have relied on here are Baczko, *Ending the Terror*, chap. 3; Gomez-Le Chevanton, "Le procés Carrier"; Palmer, *Twelve Who Ruled*, chap. 9; and Jacques Dupâquier, ed., *Carrier. Le procès d'un missionnaire de la Terreur et du Comité révolutionnaire de Nantes, 16 Octobre–16 décembre 1794* (Paris: Editions des Etannets, 1994).

59. Jules Michelet, *Histoire du dix-neuvième siècle*, 3 vols. (Paris: Flammarion, 1898), 1:98.

60. Luzzatto, *L'autumne de la Révolution*, 31.

61. See Gracchus Babeuf, *La guerre de la Vendée et le système de dépopulation* (Paris: Tallandier, 1987).

62. Linda Joan Christian, "The Social Psychological Construction of the Revolutionary State and Fouquier-Tinville's Trial" (PhD diss., University of Manitoba, 2005).

63. *Jugement rendu par le tribunal criminel séant à Avignon, 7 Messidor III* (June 25, 1795), ADV, 7L art. 57.

64. See Henri Dubled, "Une page de la Terreur en vaucluse: le tribunal révolutionnaire d'Orange (1794)," *Bulletins des amis d'Orange*, no. 127 (1994): 4–10.

65. Jacob, *Joseph Le Bon*, 1:30.

66. On the connections between enlightenment and ballooning, see Richard Gillespie, "Ballooning in France and Britain, 1783–1786: Aerostation and Adventurism," *Isis* 75, no. 2 (1984): 248–268; and Michael R. Lynn, "Enlightenment in the Public Sphere: The Musée de Monsieur and Scientific Culture in Late-Eighteenth-Century Paris," *Eighteenth-Century Studies* 32, no. 4 (1999): 463–476.

67. Timothy Tackett, *Religion, Revolution, and Regional Culture in Eighteenth-Century France: The Ecclesiastical Oath of 1791* (Princeton, N.J.: Princeton University Press, 1986), 69.

68. *AP*, 69:475.

69. *Arrêté concernant les objets d'or ou d'argent, bijoux et assignats trouvé chez les suspects*, 22 Ventôse II (March 12, 1794), ADPC, 4L 4.

70. Colin Lucas, *The Structure of the Terror: The Example of Javogues and the Loire* (Oxford: Oxford University Press, 1972), 259.

71. See Biard, *Missionnaires de la République*, chap. 4.

72. See, for example, Jacob, *Joseph Le Bon*, 1:44.

73. See Bernard Bodinier, "Un département sans Terreur sanguinaire: l'Eure en l'an II," in *Les politiques de la Terreur, 1793–1794*, ed. Michel Biard (Rennes: Presses universitaires de Rennes, 2008), 111–126; Paul Hanson, *The Jacobin Republic under Fire: The Federalist Revolt in the French Revolution* (University Park: Pennsylvania State University Press, 2003).

74. *La sentinelle du Nord*, 16 Brumaire II (November 6, 1793), no. 36. On the pedagogic functions of the theater during the Revolution, see Susan Maslan, *Revolutionary Acts: Theater, Democracy, and the French Revolution* (Baltimore: Johns Hopkins University Press, 2005); and Friedland, *Political Actors*.

75. *Arrêté du représentant du peuple Joseph Le Bon*, 13 Brumaire II (November 3, 1793), ADPC 4L3.

76. *Liste des objets réconnus nécessaires aux détenus*, 22 Pluviôse II (February 10, 1794), AN F7 4773.

77. Jacob, *Joseph Le Bon*, 2:164.

78. Dupâquier, *Carrier*, 22–23.

79. *Moniteur*, 4 Messidor, an 3 (June 22, 1795), no. 274.

80. Ibid.

81. *Procès de Joseph Lebon, membre de la députation du Département du Pas-de-Calais à la Convention nationale, condamné à la peine de mort par le Tribunal Criminel du Département de la Somme, Recueilli audit Tribunal, par la Citoyenne Varlé*, 2 vols. (Amiens, 1795), 1:41–42. I am grateful to Howard Brown for making his own reproduction of this book available to me.

82. I am relying on an abridged version of the original novel, which runs to nine volumes. Samuel Richardson, *The Paths of Virtue Delineated, or the History in Miniature of the Celebrated Clarissa Harlowe, Familiarised and Adapted to the Capacities of Youth* (Philadelphia: W. Woodhouse, 1791).

83. See Paris, *La Terreur dans le Pas-de-Calais*, 1:371.

84. See Biard, *Missionnaires de la République*; Lucas, *Structure of the Terror*.

85. See August Kuscinski, *Dictionnaire des conventionnels* (Paris: Société de l'histoire de la Révolution française, 1917), 316.

86. *Censure républicain ou lettre d'A.-B.-J. Guffroy, représentant du peuple, aux françois habitans d'Arras et des communes environnantes, à la Convention nationale, et à l'opinion publique* (Paris: Imprimerie de Rougyff, n.d.), 33.

87. *Rapport fait au nom du Comité de Salut Public, sur les pétitions faites à raison des opérations de Joseph Lebon, Représentant du peuple dans les départements du Pas-de-Calais at du Nord, dans la séance du 21 Messidor, l'an 2 de la République française, une & indivisible, par Barère* (Paris: Imprimerie nationale, 1794), 4.

88. Ibid., 3.

89. *Extrait du registres des arrêtés du Comité de salut public de la Convention nationale*, 10 Thermidor, an II (July 28, 1794) AN, F7 4772.

90. *Encore un crime de Joseph Le Bon, représentant du peuple, La veuve Lallart, demeurant à Arras, à la Convention nationale* (Paris: Imprimerie de Rougyff, 1795), 1, AN, D III 191.

91. *Adresse du citoyen Delelis à la société populaire et ses concitoyens du district de Béthune, Gonneheim,* 11 Brumaire, an III (November 1, 1794), AN, F7 4772.

92. See Blum, *Rousseau and the Republic of Virtue,* 278; Marisa Linton, *The Politics of Virtue in Enlightenment France* (Basingstoke, UK: Macmillan, 2001), 213; Marisa Linton, *Choosing Terror: Virtue, Friendship, and Authenticity in the French Revolution* (Oxford: Oxford University Press, 2013), 270.

93. Jainchill, *Reimagining Politics after the Terror,* 67.

94. Luzzatto, *L'automne de la Révolution,* chap. 1.

95. See Peter Brooks, *The Melodramatic Imagination: Balzac, Henry James, Melodrama, and the Mode of Excess* (New Haven, Conn.: Yale University Press, 1976); Maza, *Private Lives and Public Affairs,* 66–67.

96. *La confession générale de Joseph Lebon et bande, ou prédiction de Jean Sans-Peur, applicable à tous les autres bouveurs de sang et complices du terrorisme* (Arras: Imprimerie du grand Pain d'épice d'Arras, n.d.), 4.

97. Quoniam Bonus, *L'anniversaire ou le libera de Joseph Lebon, éxécuté à Amiens, le 23 Vendémiaire, an 4, ou le 14 Octobre 1795, dédié à Arras et Cambrai* (n.p., 1796).

98. Montgey et Poirier, *Atrocités commises envers les citoyennes, ci devant détenues dans la Maison d'Arrêt, dite la Providence, à Arras, par Joseph Lebon et ses Adhérens, pour servir de suite aux angoisses de la mort ou idées des horreurs des prisons d'Arras, par les citoyens Montgey et Poirier de Dunkerque* (Paris: chez les Marchands des nouvautés, 1795), 26.

99. *L'orateur du peuple par Fréron,* 8 Vendémiaire, an III (September 29, 1794), no. 10.

100. Biard, *Missionaires de la République,* 376–77.

101. Edme-Bonaventure Courtois, *Rapport fait au nom de la Commission chargée de l'examen des papiers trouvés chez Robespierre et ses complices par E. B. Courtois, député du département de l'Aube, dans la séance du 16 Nivôse, an III* (Paris: chez Maret, 1795), 64.

102. "Joseph Le Bon à son collègue Courtois, membre de la Convention nationale, Paris, 2 .Ventôse, an III," reproduced in Louis Jacob, *La défense du conventionnel Joseph Le Bon, présentée par lui-même* (Paris: Mellottée, 1934), 34.

103. Joseph Le Bon, *Lettre justificative no. I,* AN, F7 4774/6.

104. See Charles Walton, *Policing Public Opinion in the French Revolution: The Culture of Calumny and the Problem of Free Speech* (Oxford: Oxford University Press, 2009).

105. See Robert Darnton, *The Forbidden Best-Sellers of Pre-Revolutionary France* (London: Fontana, 1997), 91–95.

106. *L'orateur du peuple par Fréron,* 8 Vendémiaire, an III (September 29, 1794). no. 10.

107. Joseph Le Bon, *lettre justificative no. X,* AN, F7 4774/6.

108. Joseph Le Bon, *Lettre justificative no. IV,* AN, F7 4774/6.

109. Ibid.

110. *Moniteur,* 21 Messidor, an III (July 9, 1795), no. 291.

111. Judith Shklar, *Men and Citizens: A Study of Rousseau's Social Theory* (Cambridge: Cambridge University Press, 1969), 5.

112. This translation of the passage is taken from Jean-Jacques Rousseau, *Emile, or on Education,* trans. Allan Bloom (New York: Basic Books, 1979), 40.

113. Joseph Le Bon, *Lettre justificative no. VIII,* AN F7 4774/6.

114. *Procès de Joseph Lebon,* 2:164.

115. "Joseph Le Bon à sa femme," October 11, 1795, reproduced in Emile Le Bon, *Joseph Le Bon dans sa vie privée et dans sa carrière politique, par son fils Émile Le Bon, juge au Tribunal de 1ère instance de Chalon-sur-Saône* (Paris: E. Dentu, 1861), 289.

116. *Extrait des registres du greffe du tribunal criminel du Departement de la Somme,* 25 Vendemiaire, an IV (October 17, 1795), ADS, L 975.

117. See Antoine Goze, *Histoire des rues d'Amiens,* 3 vols. (Amiens: A. Caron, 1854–58), 3:129.

3. Redress

1. See Alphonse Aulard, *Le culte de la Raison et le culte de l'être suprême, 1793–1794* (Paris: Félix Alcan, 1904), 317.

2. See Christine le Bozec, *Boissy d'Anglas. Un grand notable libéral* (Annonay: Fédération des oeuvres laiques de l'Ardèche, 1995).

3. François-Antoine de Boissy d'Anglas, *Essai sur la vie, les écrits, et les opinions de M. de Malesherbes, adressé à mes enfans,* 3 vols. (Paris: Chez Treuttel et Wurtz, 1819), 1:2.

4. Pietro Sardaro and Paul Lemmens, "Restitution," in *Encyclopedia of Genocide and Crimes against Humanity,* 3 vols., ed. Dinah Shelton (New York: Thomson Gale, 2006), 2:910–913. See also Barkan, *Guilt of Nations,* esp. chap. 6; Nell Jessup Newton, "Compensation, Reparations and Restitution: Indian Property Claims in the United States," *Georgia Law Review* 28, no. 2 (1994): 453–480; Ellen Comisso, "Legacies of the Past or New Institutions? The Struggle over Restitution in Hungary," *Comparative Political Studies* 28, no. 2 (1995): 200–238; Claus Offe, *Varieties of Transition: The East European and East German Experience* (Cambridge, Mass.: MIT Press, 1997), esp. chaps. 5 and 6.

5. Charles S. Maier, "Overcoming the Past? Narrative and Negotiation, Remembering, and Reparation: Issues at the Interface of History and the Law," in *Politics and the Past: On Repairing Historical Injustices,* ed. John Torpey (New York: Rowman and Littlefield, 2003), 296.

6. *Resigstres du comité de legislation de la Convention nationale,* Nivôse–Prairial, an III (December 1794–June 1795), AN, D III 15*–D III 27*.

7. See Louis Bergeron, "National Properties," in Furet and Ozouf, *Critical Dictionary,* 511–518.

8. William Sewell, *Work and Revolution in France: The Language of Labor from the Old Regime to 1848* (Cambridge: Cambridge University Press, 1980), 134. See also Jean-Marc Schiappa, "Les conceptions de la propriété dans le discours politique en l'an IV," in *Propriété et Révolution,* ed. Geneviève Koubi (Toulouse: Editions de CNRS, 1990), 46–94.

9. Rafe Blaufarb, *The Great Demarcation: The French Revolution and the Invention of Modern Property* (Oxford: Oxford University Press, 2016), 120.

10. Quoted in Bernard Bodinier and Éric Teyssier, *L'événement le plus important de la Révolution. La vente des biens nationaux, 1789–1867* (Paris: Société des Études Robespierristes et Editions du CTHS, 2000), 382.

11. "Décret qui met les Biens des Emigrés sous la main de la Nation," February 9, 1792, Collection Baudouin, accessed June 12, 2017, http://artflsrv02.uchicago.edu/cgi-bin/philologic/getobject.pl?c.25:122.baudouin0314.

12. On the social composition of the émigrés, see Donald Greer, *The Incidence of the Emigration during the French Revolution* (Cambridge, Mass.: Harvard University Press, 1951).

13. On the Law of Suspects and the institutionalization of the Terror, see Palmer, *Twelve Who Ruled*, chap. 3; Hugh Gough, *The Terror in the French Revolution* (New York: St. Martin's Press, 1998), 37–38; Hesse, "The Law of the Terror."

14. "Décret d'ordre du jour sur une pétition de la veuve Kolly, & relative aux enfans en bas-âge dont les peres & meres auront subi un jugement qui emporte la confiscation des biens," 15 Brumaire an II (November 5, 1793)," Collection Baudoin, accessed September 13, 2017, http://artflsrv02.uchicago.edu/cgi-bin/philologic/getobject.pl?c.25:122.baudouin0314.

15. On the general attitude of the French revolutionaries toward orphans and abandoned children, see Rachel Fuchs, *Abandoned Children: Foundlings and Child Welfare in Nineteenth-Century France* (Albany: State University of New York Press, 1984).

16. *AP*, 85:517, 519.

17. See Robert Schnerb, "Les lois de Ventôse et leur application dans le département du Puy-de-Dome," *AHRF* 11 (1934): 403–434. See also Mathiez, *French Revolution*, 449–455.

18. *A vendre, meubles de condamné. Département de Haute-Garonne. District de Toulouse*, 15 Thermidor, an III (August 2, 1794), ADHG, 1 S 84.

19. *Procès verbal de première enchère et adjudication définitive. Vente de Biens nationaux, provenant d'Emigres. Departement de Haute Garonne. District de Villefranche. Canton de Villefranche. Municipalité de Villefranche. Biens provenant de Charles Blanquet dit Rouville, condamné à la peine de mort. 25 jour du premier mois de l'an troisième, à dix heures le matin*, ADHG, Q 393, no. 275.

20. Marc Bouloiseau, *Le sequestre et la vente des biens des émigrés dans le district de Rouen, 1792—an X* (Paris: Maurice Lavergne, 1937), 145.

21. See Stephen C. Neff, *War and the Law of Nations: A General History* (Cambridge: Cambridge University Press, 2005).

22. See Dan Edelstein, "War and Terror: The Law of Nations from Grotius to the French Revolution," *FHS* 31, no. 2 (2008): 229–262.

23. Emmerich de Vattel, *Le droit des gens, ou, principes de la loi naturelle appliqués à la conduite & aux affaires des Nations & des Souverains*, 2 vols. (Neuchâtel: Droz, 1758), 2:134.

24. For an overview of legislation concerning the property of the émigrés, see Marc Bouloiseau, *Étude de l'émigration et de la vente des biens des émigrés (1792–1830). Instruction, sources, bibliographie, législation, tableaux* (Paris: Imprimerie nationale, 1963). On the revolutionary attitude to foreign nationals, see Sophie Wahnich, *L'impossible citoyen. L'étranger dans le discours de la Révolution* (Paris: Albin Michel, 1997).

25. "Mort Civil," *Dictionnaire critique de la langue française*, ARTFL Project, accessed September 16, 2017, https://artflsrv03.uchicago.edu/philologic4/publicdicos/query?report=bibliography&head=mort.

26. Vattel, *Le droit des gens*, 2:247.

27. *Petition d'André Toebaerts à la Convention nationale*, 29 Germinal, an III (April 18, 1795), AN, D III 98.

28. Joseph Pâris de l'Épinard, *Mon retour à la vie après quanze mois d'agonie* (n.p., c. 1794).

29. *Moniteur*, 25 Frimaire, an III (December 15, 1794), no. 85.

30. *Moniteur*, 23 Frimaire, an III (December 13, 1794), no. 83.

31. Ibid., 4 Germinal, an III (March 24, 1795), no. 184.

32. *Second tableau des prisons de Paris, sous le régne de Robespierre, pour servir de suite à l'Almanach des prisons, contenant différents anecdotes sur plusieurs prisonniers, avec les couplets, pieces de vers, lettres et testamens qu'ils ont faits* (Paris: Michel, 1794–1795).

33. See Douthwaite, *Frankenstein of 1790*, chap. 4.

34. See Alex Fairfax-Cholmeley, "The Victim Strikes Back? Print Culture after the Terror in France," paper presented at the annual meeting of the Society for French Historical Studies, Colorado Springs, Colorado, April 2015. The presentation can be viewed online at https://www.youtube.com/watch?v=Hnsk7Y497y8 (accessed September 22, 2017).

35. See Desan, "Reconstituting the Social after the Terror."

36. For example, *Charpentier, Veuve Saleure, son mari tombe sous la glaive de la loi*, 4 Pluviôse, an III (January 23, 1795), AN, D III 15*/1911; or *Berard, Veuve de Gigot-Boisbernier, condamné*, 18 Germinal, an III (April 7, 1795), AN, D III 26*/6255.

37. *Pétition de Marie-Anne Poirevesson, soeur de Pellegrin, à la Convention nationale*, 26 Nivôse, an III (January 15, 1795), AN, D III 161.

38. Olwen Hufton, "Women without Men: Widows and Spinsters in Britain and France in the Eighteenth Century," *Journal of Family History* 9, no. 4 (1984), 373.

39. *Petition de Marie Joseph Beguinet, Veuve Lamotte, aux citoyens membres du comité de législation près de l'assemblée nationale*, 23 Brumaire, an III (November 13, 1794), AN, D III 161. Addressing the petition to the National Assembly rather than to the National Convention suggests that the widow Lamotte had not kept abreast of revolutionary politics.

40. *Petition de Veuve Subrin, Cultivateur de Lyon, au Comité de Législation*, Frimaire, an III (c. December 1794), AN, D III 216.

41. *Petition de Marianne Edelmann, Veuve de Louis Edelmann, à la Convention nationale*, 4 Frimaire, an II (November 24, 1794), AN, D III 213.

42. *Petition de la section des Marchés en masse à la Convention nationale, le 21 ventôse, 3ème année républicaine, tenante, principalement, à rétablir honorablement la mémoire du citoyen Quatremere, marchand des draps, rue Denis, assassiné au tribunal révolutionnaire par les hommes de sang qui dominoient cette section* (Paris: Imprimerie de Pellier, 1795), 5.

43. "Restituer," *DAF*, ARTFL Project, accessed July 1, 2018, https://artflsrv03.uchicago.edu/philologic4/publicdicos/query?report=bibliography&head=restituer&start=0&end=0.

44. Robert Nye, *Masculinity and Male Codes of Honor in Modern France* (Berkeley: University of California Press, 1998), 29. See also Yves Castan, *Honnêteté et relations sociales en Languedoc, 1715–1780* (Paris: Presses universitaires de France, 1974).

45. On the notion of the French state as the institutor of social relations, see Pierre Rosanvallon, *L'état en France, de 1789 à nos jours* (Paris: Seuil, 1990).

46. See Gérard Walter, ed., *Actes du tribunal révolutionnaire* (Paris: Mercure de France, 1968), 139; Dupâquier, *Carrier*, 410–411.

47. See Laura Mason, "The 'Bosom of Proof': Criminal Justice and the Renewal of Oral Culture during the French Revolution," *JMH* 76, no. 1 (2004): 29–61.

48. See Guillaume-Alexandre Tronson-Ducoudray, *Mémoire pour les veuves et enfans des citoyens condamnés par le Tribunal révolutionnaire, antérieurement à la loi du 22 Prairial* (Paris: Imprimerie de Desenne, 1795).

49. *Petition de la citoyenne Felix, veuve d'Hélyot au citoyen Clauzel, président de la Convention*, 5 Nivôse, an III (December 25, 1794), AN, D III 91.

50. See the charges in the indictment against Le Bon in *Moniteur*, 4 Messidor, an III (June 22, 1795), no. 274.

51. Interestingly, we find similar concerns around the rehabilitation of victims in the Soviet Union after the death of Stalin. See Stephen G. Wheatcroft, *"Glasnost'* and Rehabilitations," in *Facing Up to the Past: Soviet Historiography after Perestroika*, ed. Takayuki Ito (Sapporo: Slavic Research Center, Hokkaido University, 1989), 199–218; and Kathleen E. Smith, *Remembering Stalin's Victims: Popular Memory and the End of the USSR* (Ithaca, N.Y.: Cornell University Press, 1996).

52. *Petition de Louis-François Mayoul au Comité de législation*, 18 Pluviôse, an III (February 6, 1795), AN, D III 198.

53. *Moniteur*, 2 Floréal, an III (April 21, 1795), no. 212. The mention of a "phrase by one of your colleagues" referred to a speech given by the Abbé Sieyès on March 21, 1795. See *Moniteur*, 5 Germinal, an III (March 25, 1795), no. 185.

54. For a study of the last letters written by victims of the Terror before their execution, see Olivier Blanc, *Last Letters: Prisons and Prisoners of the French Revolution, 1793–1794* (New York: Farrar, Straus and Giroux, 1989).

55. See *Pièces à l'appui de la pétition et du mémoire présentés par la citoyenne veuve GUSTAVE DECHÉZEAUX, à la Convention Nationale, le 29 Germinal, an 3, pour obtenir la réhabilitation de la mémoire de son malheureux époux, assassiné par le tribunal révolutionnaire établi à Rochefort, dont elle a ordonné l'impression et la renvoi au comité de législation, par décret du meme jour* (Paris: Imprimerie nationale, c. 1795).

56. The widow of another executed member of the Convention, Elie Guadet, also came to petition in person. See *Moniteur*, 25 Germinal, an III (April 14, 1795), no. 205. Both the Dechézeaux and Guadet cases were related to the purge of the Girondins, and the appearance of their widows before the Convention was related to the rehabilitation of this group after 9 Thermidor. On the reinstatement of the Girondins to the Convention, see Doyle, *Oxford History of the French Revolution*, 285, 290.

57. See Tackett, *Coming of the Terror*, 1.

58. See F. Charles Fensham, "Widow, Orphan, and the Poor in Ancient Near Eastern Legal and Wisdom Literature," *Journal of Near Eastern Studies* 21, no. 2 (1962): 129–139.

59. See Joseph Clarke, *Commemorating the Dead in Revolutionary France: Revolution and Remembrance, 1789–1799* (Cambridge: Cambridge University Press, 2007), 257–260.

60. See Eloise Ellery, *Brissot de Warville: A Study in the History of the French Revolution* (Boston: Houghton-Mifflin, 1915), 406–407. I am grateful to Bette Oliver for bringing this story to my attention.

61. *Arrêtés du parlement de Toulouse, séant en vacations, des 25 & 27 Septembre 1790* (n.p, n.d.), 7.

62. See Axel Duboul, *La fin du parlement de Toulouse* (Toulouse: Imprimerie F. Tardieu, 1890).

63. I could only make a partial estimate of the value of his property—land and real estate—at the time of his arrest. The total value came to about 162,000 livres. This was a considerable sum, but it paled in comparison to the wealth of *parlementaires* in Paris. I am very grateful to Hannah Callaway for sharing her expertise on the property of the émigrés with me. For her work on this subject, see Hannah Callaway, "Revolutionizing Property: The Confiscation of Émigré Wealth and the Problem of Property in the French Revolution" (PhD diss., Harvard University, 2015). The calcu-

lations that I have made of Blanquet-Rouville's property are based on the records of the public auction of his confiscated goods. See *Procès-verbal de première enchère et adjudication definitive, Vente de biens nationaux*, Vendemiaire–Brumaire, an III (September–October 1794), ADHG, Q 393, nos. 275–342.

64. "Décret relatif aux parcs maisons, etc., portant des armoiries," August 1, 1793, Collection Baudouin, accessed August 14, 2017, http://artflsrv02.uchicago.edu/cgi-bin/philologic/getobject.pl?c.38:25.baudouin0314.

65. *Le procureur general-syndic de department de Haute-Garonne au citoyen, le procureur-general syndic du district de Toulouse*, 16 Brumaire, an II (November 6, 1793), ADHG, 1 S AMT 89.

66. *Petition de la citoyenne Emilie Prax, veuve Blanquet-Rouville, au Comité de Salut Public*, 11 Prairial, an III (May 30, 1795), AN, D III 98.

67. Jean-Jacques Sacarau, *Au corps legislatif. Pétition et pièces relatives aux réclamations d'Émilie Prax, veuve de Charles Blanquet-Rouville, non condamné, mais assassiné* (Paris: Imprimerie Teulières, 1797), 9.

68. See Bodinier and Teyssier, *L'événement le plus important de la Révolution*, 398–405.

69. Sacarau, *Au corps législatif*, 22.

70. Antoine Claire Thibaudeau, *Rapport par Thibaudeau sur la pétition de la veuve Blanquet-Rouville, séance du 3 ventôse, l'an V* (Paris: Imprimerie nationale, 1797).

71. See Sacarau, *Au corps legislative*, 17.

72. Andrew Abbot, "The Historicality of Individuals," *Social Science History* 29, no. 1 (2005), 3.

73. See Teitel, *Transitional Justice*, 119; and Tyler Cowan, "How Far Back Should We Go? Why Restitution Should Be Small," in *Retribution and Reparation in the Transition to Democracy*, ed. Jon Elster (Cambridge: Cambridge University Press, 2006), 17–32.

74. On the *assignats*, see Seymour Harris, *The Assignats* (Cambridge, Mass.: Harvard University Press, 1930). For more recent scholarship on this subject, see Florin Aftalion, *The French Revolution: An Economic Interpretation* (Cambridge: Cambridge University Press, 1990); and Rebecca Spang, *Stuff and Money in the Time of the French Revolution* (Cambridge, Mass.: Harvard University Press, 2015).

75. *Moniteur*, 25 Frimaire, an III (December 15, 1794), no. 85.

76. *Moniteur*, 18 Floréal, an III (May 7, 1795), no. 228.

77. *Moniteur*, 29 Germinal, an III (April 18, 1795), no. 209.

78. *Moniteur*, 16 Floréal, an III (May 5, 1795), no. 226.

79. Ibid.

80. *Moniteur*, 30 Ventôse, an III (March 20, 1795), no. 180.

81. *Moniteur*, 16 Floréal, an III (May 5, 1795), no. 226.

82. In the original editions, the pamphlet was attributed to the Abbé Raynal, the famous author of *L'histoire des deux Indes* (1770). It was, however, written by Servan. A footnote to a later edition of Servan's works reads: "For reasons explained by the period in which he was writing, Servan thought it necessary to attribute this brochure to the name of Raynal, who, having descended not long before to his grave, had nothing to fear anymore from the enemies of the good; besides, Raynal, having matured with age and enlightened by experience, has manifested in his last years similar sentiments to those of our author." *Choix des oeuvres inédites de Servan, avocat général au Parlement de Grenoble*, 2 vols., ed. Xavier de Portets (Paris: Imprimérie de Jules Didot ainé,

1825), 2:367. Raynal actually died in 1796, but it is possible that he had been in hiding or in any case out of the public eye during the Terror and the last years of his life. I am grateful to Matthew J. Pagett for the reference to this edition of Servan's works.

83. Guillaume-Thomas Raynal, *Des assassinats et des vols politiques, ou des proscriptions et des confiscations, par Guillaume-Thomas Raynal* (London and Paris, chez Buisson, 1795), 19.

84. Ibid., 8–9, 78–79.

85. François d'Ivernois, *A Cursory View of the Assignats and the Remaining Resources of French Finance. September 5, 1795. Drawn from the Debates of the Convention. Translated from the Original French* (Dublin: P. Byrne, 1795), 3, 4, 12–13. On the significance of d'Ivernois's economic writings during the Thermidorian Reaction, see Livesey, *Making Democracy in the French Revolution*, 63–65.

86. *Moniteur*, 3 Germinal, an III (March 23, 1795), no. 183.

87. See Jeffrey Merrick and Dorothy Medlin, eds., *André Morellet (1727–1819) in the Republic of Letters and the French Revolution* (New York: Peter Lang, 1995).

88. André Morellet, *Mémoires de l'Abbé Morellet*, 2 vols. (Paris: à la librairie française, 1821), 2:132.

89. André Morellet, *Le cri des familles, ou discussion de la motion du représentant Lecointre, relativement à la révision des jugemens des tribunaux révolutionnaires* (Paris: Du Pont, 1794), 15.

90. *L'orateur du peuple par Fréron*, 25 Ventôse, an III (March 15, 1795), no. 91.

91. *Moniteur*, 24 Prairial, an III (June 12, 1795), no. 264; cf. *Loi qui determine le mode de restitution des biens des condamnés, du 21 Prairial, an troisième de la République française, une et indivisible* (Paris: Imprimerie du dépôt des lois, 1795).

92. *Pétition des parens des citoyens condamnés par la commission militaire de Bordeaux, à la Convention nationale*, 8 Floréal, an III (April 27, 1795), AN, D III 98.

93. On the reforms of criminal law after Thermidor, see Woloch, *New Regime*, 356–364; Howard Brown, *Ending the French Revolution*, chaps. 3–4; and Farcy, *Histoire de la justice française*, 364–387.

94. Robert Gordon, "Undoing Historical Injustice," in *Justice and Injustice in Law and Legal Theory*, ed. Austin Sarat and Thomas R. Kearns (Ann Arbor: University of Michigan Press, 1996), 35–36.

95. *Moniteur*, 24 Prairial, an III (June 12, 1795), no. 264.

96. D'Ivernois, *Cursory View of the Assignats*, 13.

97. *Moniteur*, 17 Floréal, an III (May 6, 1795), no. 227.

98. *La commission des revenus nationaux, à la Commission temporaire des arts réunie au Comité d'Instruction publique*, 27 Floréal, III (May 16, 1795), AN, F17 1048.

99. *La commission des revenus nationaux à la Commission temporaire des arts*, 15 Brumaire, an IV (November 6, 1795), AN, F17 1048.

100. Louis Teutey, ed., *Procès-verbaux de la Commission temporaire des arts*, 2 vols. (Paris: Imprimerie nationale, 1912–1917), 2:342.

101. *La Commission de revenus nationaux aux administrateurs dû département du Rhône à Lyon*, 18 Messidor, an III (July 6, 1795), ADR, 1 Q 1031.

102. A quantitative study of the actual state of restitution would have to be carried out in all the departmental archives of France. In some of them the specific series dealing with the national properties have been damaged or destroyed. This, for example, is the case with ADHG.

103. On religion as a new space for the political agency of women after 9 Thermidor, see Desan, *Reclaiming the Sacred*.

104. "Decrét concernant les biens des prêtres déportés," 22 Fructidor, an III (September 8, 1795), Collection Baudouin, accessed October 15, 2017, http://artflsrv02 .uchicago.edu/cgi-bin/philologic/getobject.pl?c.63:270.baudouin0314.

105. See Bouloiseau, *Étude de l'émigration et de la vente des biens des émigrés*.

106. See Almut Franke, "Le Millard des émigrés: The Impact of the Indemnity Bill of 1825 on French Society," in *The French Emigrés in Europe and the Struggle against Revolution, 1789–1814*, ed. Kirsty Carpenter and Philip Mansel (New York: St. Martin's Press, 1999), 124–137; and Elster, *Closing the Books*, 40–44.

107. See Cathy Caruth, "The Claims of the Dead: History, Haunted Property, and the Law," *Critical Inquiry* 28, no. 2 (Winter 2002): 419–441.

4. Remembrance

1. Honoré de Balzac, *Colonel Chabert*, trans. Carol Cosman (New York: New Directions, 1997), 19, 22, 24.

2. The "return of the repressed" is a concept in Freudian psychoanalysis. Freud believed that the content of the unconscious, which is repressed material, is never totally gone. It reemerges from time to time into consciousness in a variety of ways, and usually without our ability to recognize what is happening. This is the return of the repressed. See Laplanche and Pontalis, *Language of Psychoanalysis*, 398.

3. See Paul-Laurent Assoun, *Tuer le mort. Le désir révolutionnaire* (Paris: Presses Universitaires de France, 2015), 191–192.

4. *Ministère de l'Interieur à la Préfecture de Vaucluse*, November 16, 1830, ADV, 1 M art. 904.

5. *Le sous Commissaire d'Orange au Monsieur le Maire d'Orange*, May 28, 1848, AMO, M 1371.

6. Katherine Verdery, *The Political Lives of Dead Bodies: Reburial and Postsocialist Change* (New York: Columbia University Press, 1999), 25.

7. See Anon., *Orgie et testament de Mirabeau* (Paris: n.p., 1791).

8. Pierre Jean Georges Cabanis, *Journal de la maladie et de la mort d'Honoré-Gabriel-Victor Riquetti Mirabeau* (Paris: chez Grabit, 1791), 66.

9. See Jean-Claude Bonnet, *Naissance du Panthéon. Essai sur le culte de grands hommes* (Paris: Fayard, 1998); Mona Ozouf, "Le Panthéon. L'école normale des morts," in *Les liuex des mémoire*, 3 vols., ed. Pierre Nora (Paris: Gallimard, 1984), 1:139–166; Annie Jourdan, *Les monuments de la Révolution, 1770–1804. Une histoire de représentation* (Paris: Honoré Champion, 1997); Avner Ben-Amos, *Funerals, Politics, and Memory in Modern France, 1789–1996* (Oxford: Oxford University Press, 2000).

10. Antoine de Baecque, *Glory and Terror: Seven Deaths under the French Revolution* (New York: Routledge, 2001), 8.

11. See Philippe Ariès, *The Hour of Our Death* (Oxford: Oxford University Press, 1981); John McManners, *Death and the Enlightenment: Changing Attitudes to Death among Christians and Unbelievers in Eighteenth Century France* (Oxford: Oxford University Press, 1981).

12. Chevalier Louis de Jaucourt, "Mort," in *Encyclopédie, ou dictionnaire raisonné des sciences, des arts et des métiers, etc.*, ed. Denis Diderot and Jean le Rond d'Alembert,

ARTFL Encyclopédie, accessed October 30, 2017, http://artflsrv02.uchicago.edu/cgi
-bin/philologic/getobject.pl?c.9:2010.encyclopedie0416.

13. Thomas Kselman, *Death and the Afterlife in Modern France* (Princeton, N.J.: Princeton University Press, 1993), 176, 200. See also Ariès, *Hour of Our Death*, pt. 4; Richard Etlin, *The Architecture of Death: The Transformation of the Cemetery in Eighteenth Century Paris* (Cambridge, Mass.: MIT Press, 1984); David Charles Sloane, *The Last Great Necessity: Cemeteries in American History* (Baltimore: Johns Hopkins University Press, 1991).

14. Quoted Clarke, *Commemorating the Dead*, 59.

15. Quoted in Madeleine Lassère, *Villes et cimetières en France de l'ancien régime à nos jours. Le territoire des morts* (Paris: L'harmattan, 1997), 74.

16. Ibid., 75.

17. Quoted in Assoun, *Tuer le mort*, 65.

18. Ibid., 88.

19. Charles Dickens, *A Tale of Two Cities* (Boston: Houghton Mifflin, 1962), 255.

20. *Description des vêtements trouvés sur les deux cadavres du sexe masculin amenés au ci-devant cimetière Paul au sortir de la guillotine place de grève, le premier messidor an seconde de la république,* 1 Messidor, an II (June 19, 1794,) APP AA 70, document no. 574.

21. See Jean-Pierre Rémi, *Trésors et secrets du Quai d'Orsay. Une histoire inédite de la diplomatie française* (Paris: JC Lattès, 2001).

22. "Procès-verbal de l'inhumation de Louis Capet," reproduced in Soboul, *Le procès de Louis XVI*, 234–235.

23. *Transformation de la barrière Monceaux au cimetière,* an 2 (1793), APA, DQ10 715.

24. See Maurice Lever, *Sade: A Biography* (New York: Harcourt, 1994), 464–468. The opening scene of the French film *Sade* (2000, directed by Benoît Jacquot) depicts the arrival of carts carrying the corpses of the guillotined to Picpus, and the horror of the convalescents at this sight.

25. See G. Lenôtre, *Les pèlerinages de Paris révolutionnaire. Le jardin de Picpus* (Paris: Perrin, 1928); Lucien Lambeau, *Le cimetière de Picpus, 1794–1921* (Paris: Imprimerie municipal, Commission de vieux Paris, 1922).

26. See L'abbé S. Bonnel, *Les 332 victimes de la commission populaire d'Orange en 1794, d'après les documents officiels, avec reproduction du monument expiatoire de la Chappelle de Laplane et de quinze portraits,* 2 vols. (Carpentras: chez Tourrette, 1888); and Marianne Bignan, "La chapelle de Gabet," *Bulletin des amis d'Orange,* no. 127 (1994): 1–3.

27. See *Le monument religieux des Brotteaux. Historique, liste des victimes du siège de Lyon en 1793* (Lyon: Impressions de M. Audin et CIE, 1925); and Bruno Benoît, *L'identité politique de Lyon. Entre violences collectives et mémoires des élites, 1786–1905* (Paris: L'harmattan, 1999), 114–118.

28. See Michel Lagrée and Jeanne Roche, *Tombes de mémoire. La dévotion populaire aux victimes de la Révolution dans l'Ouest* (Rennes: Editions Apogée, 1993).

29. Jules Michelet, *Histoire de la Révolution française,* 2 vols. (Paris: Gallimard, 1952), 2:923.

30. Alain Corbin, *The Foul and the Fragrant: Odor and the French Social Imagination* (Cambridge, Mass.: Harvard University Press, 1986), 102.

31. Quoted in McManners, *Death and the Enlightenment*, 307.

32. Félix Vicq-d'Azyr, *Essai sur les lieux et les dangers des sepultures* (Paris: Didot, 1778), cxxix.

33. See Régis Bertrand, "Que faire des restes des exécutés?," in *L'exécution capitale. Une mort donnée en spectacle XVIe-XXe siècle*, ed. Régis Bertrand and Anne Carol (Aix-en-Provence: Publications de l'Université de Provence, 2003), 51.

34. See Sarah Tarlow, "Curious Afterlives: The Enduring Appeal of the Criminal Corpse," *Mortality* 21, no. 3 (2016): 210–228. See also Louise Christian Noble, *Medicinal Cannibalism in Early Modern English Literature and Culture* (Basingstoke, UK: Palgrave Macmillan, 2011); and Susan C. Lawrence, "Beyond the Grave—the Use and Meaning of Body Parts: A Historical Introduction," *Faculty Publications, Department of History* 37 (1998), accessed November 11, 2017, http://digitalcommons.unl.edu/cgi/viewcontent .cgi?article=1036&context=historyfacpub.

35. See Jordan, *King's Trial*, 220.

36. Emile Durkheim, *The Elementary Forms of Religious Life* (New York: Free Press, 1995), 414.

37. *Les citoyens habitans quartier du Picpus au comité de salut public*, 20 Messidor, an II (July 8, 1794), AN, F13 330.

38. *Rapport à la commission des travaux publics*, 14 Vendemiaire, an III (October 5, 1794), AN, F13 330.

39. See Brunel, "Bridging the Gulf of the Terror."

40. See Allen Feldman, "Violence and Vision: The Prosthetics and Aesthetics of Terror," *Public Culture* 10, no. 1 (1997): 24–60.

41. *Citoyen Riedain à la Convention nationale*, 28 Germinal, an III (April 17, 1795), AN, F13 524.

42. *Conseil municipale d'Orange. Registres des déliberations, 1790–1794*, 11 Brumaire, an III (November 1, 1794), AMO, D 705.

43. *Citoyen Poyet à la Commission des travaux publics*, 23 Fructidor, an III (September 9, 1795), AN, F13 524.

44. *Rapport, cimetière pour les suppliciés de Picpus*, 12 Brumaire, an IV (November 3, 1795), AN, F13 964.

45. G. G. Delammale, *L'enterrement de ma mere, ou reflexions sur les ceremonies des funérailles et le soin des sepultures et sur la moralité des institutions civiles en général* (Paris: Imprimerie de Boulard, 1794), 7, 9.

46. *Corps legislative. Conseil des Cinq-Cents. Rapport fait au nom d'une commission speciale, sur les inhumations, par Daubermesnil, séance du 21 Brumaire, an I* (Paris: Imprimerie nationale, 1796), 7.

47. Ariés, *Hour of Our Death*, 505.

48. Antoine François Fourcroy, *Notice sur la vie et les travaux de Lavoisier par A.-F. Fourcroy, précédée d'un discours sur les funérailles et suivie d'une ode sur l'immortalité de l'ame* (Paris: Imprimerie de la feuille du cultivateur, 1795), 3.

49. *Corps législatif. Conseil des Cinq-Cents. Rapport sur la violation des sepultures et des tombeaux, fait au nom de la commission de la classification et de la revision des lois, par Emm. Pastoret, séance du 26 Prairial, an IV* (Paris: Imprimerie nationale, 1796), 4.

50. *Rapport sur les sépultures, présenté à l'administration centrale du département de la Seine, par le citoyen Cambry, administratuer du département de la Seine, administrateur du prytanée François, et de l'académie des antiquaires de Cortone* (Paris: Imprimerie de Pierre Didot l'ainé, 1799), 12.

51. Kenneth Foote, *Shadowed Ground: America's Landscape of Violence and Tragedy* (Austin: University of Texas Press, 2003), 9.

52. See Philip Smith, "The Elementary Forms of Place and Their Transformations: A Durkheimian Model," *Qualitative Sociology* 22, no. 1 (1999): 13–36.

53. *Le Comission révolutionnaire au représentant du pueple Goupilleau*, 10 Brumaire, an III (October 30, 1794), ADV, 5 F 180.

54. Quoted in André Reyne and Daniel Brehier, *Les trente-deux religieuses, martyres d'Orange* (Avignon: Aubanel, 1995), 384–385.

55. See Dominique Javel, "La mémoire des 332 victimes d'Orange à l'époque contemporaine," in *Révolution et contre-révolution à Orange, 1794–1994*, ed. Philippe Gut (Orange: Colloque d'Orange, 1995), 59.

56. On the uprising of Lyon against the revolutionary government and its brutal repression by the revolutionary armies, see W. D. Edmonds, *Jacobinism and the Revolt of Lyon, 1789–1793* (Oxford: Clarendon, 1990); and M. Garden, "La Révolution et l'Émpire (1789–1815)," in *Histoire de Lyon et du Lyonnais*, ed. André Latreille (Toulouse: Privat, 1975), 285–314.

57. Antoine-François Delandine, *Tableau des prisons de Lyon, pour servir à l'histoire de la tyrannie de 1792 et 1793* (Lyon: chez Joseph Daval, 1797), 317–318.

58. *Le Journal de Lyon et du département du Rhône*, 13 Prairial, an III (June 1, 1795), no. 31 (hereafter cited as *Journal de Lyon*). On the gesture of the fraternal kiss, see Robert Darnton, *The Kiss of Lamourette: Reflections in Cultural History* (London: Faber and Faber, 1990), chap. 1.

59. See Stephen Clay, "Justice, vengeance, et passé révolutionnaire: les crimes de la Terreur blanche," *AHRF*, 350 (October–December 2007), 121.

60. Javogues's mission has been the subject of a detailed study by Colin Lucas. See Lucas, *Structure of the Terror*.

61. *Journal de Lyon*, 19 Prairial, an III (June 7, 1795), no. 33.

62. Delandine, *Tableau des prisons*, 323.

63. *Journal de Lyon*, 13 Prairial an III (June 1, 1795), no. 31.

64. See Richard Etlin, *Symbolic Space: French Enlightenment Architecture and Its Legacies* (Chicago: University of Chicago Press, 1995), chap. 1.

65. See Baczko, *Ending the Terror*; Howard Brown, *Ending the French Revolution*; Luzzatto, *L'automne de la Révolution*.; Luzzatto, *Mémoire de la Terreur*; Clarke, *Commemorating the Dead in Revolutionary France*; Emmanuel Fureix, *La France des larmes. Deuil politiques à l'âge romantique, 1814–1840* (Seyssel: Champ Vallon, 2009); Sheryl Kroen, *Politics and Theater: The Crisis of Legitimacy in Restoration France, 1815–1830* (Berkeley: University of California Press, 2000).

66. See Sutherland, *France 1789–1815*, 390–397; Louis Bergeron, *France under Napoleon* (Princeton, N.J.: Princeton University Press, 1981), 195–198.

67. See Philip Dwyer, "'It Still Makes Me Shudder': Memories of Massacres and Atrocities during the Revolutionary and Napoleonic Wars," *War in History* 16, no. 4 (2009): 381–405.

68. J.-J. Regnault-Warin, *Le cimetière de la Madeleine*, 4 vols. (Paris: chez Lepetit jeune, 1800–1801), 3:93.

69. Douthwaite, *Frankenstein of 1790*, 131.

70. *La décade philosophique, littéraire et politique*, 30 Ventôse, an IX (March 21, 1801), no. 18.

71. Jean François Villemain d'Abancourt, *Le cimetière de Mousseaux*, 2 vols. (Paris: Roux libraire, 1801), 1:15.

72. Jean François Villemain d'Abancourt, *Le cimetière de la Madeleine*, 2 vols. (Paris: Roux libraire, 1801), 1:1.

73. D'Abancourt, *Le cimetière de Mousseaux*, 1:52–53.

74. Danrton, *Kiss of Lamourette*, xii.

75. See Mikhail Bakhtin, *Rabelais and His World* (Bloomington: Indiana University Press, 1984).

76. See Kselman, *Death and the Afterlife in Modern France*, 169–170. See also Pascal Hintermeyer, *Politiques de la mort* (Paris: Payot, 1981).

77. *Rapport du ministère de la police générale*, October 14, 1808, APP, AA 435, document no. 678. Italics mine.

78. *La prefecture du département du Rhône au M. le Maire de la guillotière*, July 12, 1810, AML, 469 WP 013.

79. I am grateful to M. Chabot, guardian of the cemetery of Picpus, for calling my attention to this detail.

80. See Lagrée and Roche, *Tombes de mémoire*.

81. Quoted in Henri Welschinger, *La censure sous le premier empire* (Paris: Charavay Frères, 1882), 195.

82. *L'ami de la religion et du Roi. Journal ecclésiastique, politique, et littéraire*, June 1814, no. 18. The entire run of the newspaper has been collated in bound volumes. See *L'ami de la religion et du Roi. Journal ecclésiastique, politique, et littéraire*, 183 vols. (Paris: A. le Clère, 1814–1862), 1:282.

83. See Kroen, *Politics and Theater*, 96.

84. See Fureix, *La France des larmes*, 26–32.

85. Ibid., 442.

86. See Kroen, *Political and Theater*, chap. 1.

87. Assoun, *Tuer le mort*, 218.

88. Fureix, *La France des larmes*, 21.

89. *Notice historique et pièces relatives au monument religieux élevé à Feurs, aux victimes de l'anarchie de 1793, dans le département de la Loire, rédigées et réunies par le maire de Feurs, pour servir à l'histoire du pays pendant la crise révolutionnaire, et comme compte rendu a MM. les souscripteurs* (Tours: Imprimerie de A. Mame, 1829), 75, 77–78.

90. *Lettre à M. le Prefet de Police*, April 8, 1818, APP 435, Dossier of Madeleine.

91. *Fontaine, architecte de la chapelle expiatoire, au M. le duc de Doudeauville, Pair de France*, April 13, 1818, reproduced in Georges Hartmann, "Une lettre de l'architecte Fontaine, au sujet du cimetière de la Madeleine et de la chapelle expiatoire," in *Mélanges, Emile le Senne*, ed. Albert Vuaflart (Paris: Société historique et archéologique des VIII et XVII arrondissements de Paris, 1915–1916), 94.

92. *M. le Vicomte de Montmorency au prefet de Police*, April 9, 1818, APP 435, Dossier of Madeleine.

93. Chevalier Louis de Jaucourt, "Expiation," ARTFL Encyclopédie, accessed July 2, 2018, https://artflsrv03.uchicago.edu/philologic4/encyclopedie1117/navigate/6/719.

94. Fureix, *La France des larmes*, 221.

95. *Fondation de la chapelle funéraire de Picpus* (Paris: Imprimerie de Lottin de S.-Germain, 1814), 1.

96. See Alfred Fierro, *Vie et histoire du XIIe arrondissement* (Paris: Editions Hervas, 1988).

97. *Fondation de la chapelle funéraire de Picpus*, 6.

98. *M. le Duc de Damas au préfet de Police*, September 11, 1823, APP, AA 435, 10 bis.

99. Famille de Baudus, private archive. Only fragments of de Baudus's journal have survived. They are fragile, unpaginated, and often difficult to read. This quotation consists of fragments that are in different sections of the original journal. I am grateful to Florence de Baudus for allowing me to consult these documents and for her generous hospitality. For more on the involvement of this family in Picpus, see Florence de Baudus, *Le lien de Sang* (Paris: Editions Rocher, 2000).

100. Jonathan Dewald, "French Nobles and the Historians, 1820–1960," in *The French Nobility in the Eighteenth Century: Reassessments and New Approaches*, ed. Jay M. Smith (University Park: Pennsylvania State University Press, 2006), 311.

101. See in this regard Paul de Noailles, *Anne-Paul-Dominique de Noailles, Marquise de Montagu* (Paris: Dentu, 1861); see also the list of owners of the property in Lenôtre, *Les pèlerinages de Paris révolutionnaire*, 190–191.

102. *Première et seconde listes des souscriptions et dons pour la construction du monument religieux à élever aux Brotteaux à la mémoire des victimes du siège de Lyon*, October 16, 1814, and November 16, 1814, ADR, 4 T 32.

103. To give a sense of what this means, consider that the average wage of a skilled worker in this period was between 1.5 and 3 francs a day. See Paul Louis, *Histoire de la classe ouvrière en France de la Révolution à nos jours. La condition matérielle de travaielleurs, les salaires, et le coût de la vie* (Paris: M. Rivière, 1927).

104. *Liste nominative des personnes qui ont souscrit dans l'arrondissement de Carpentras pour le monument d'Orange*, May 16, 1825, AMO, 1 M 904.

105. *Annales Lyonnais; ou, observations sur les moeurs et les usages, sur l'état des arts, des sciences, de la literature, du Barreau, et des théatres de la ville de Lyon*, October 22, 1814, no. 18.

106. *Extrait du journal de Lyon ou bulletin administrative et politique du département du Rhône*, October 25, 1814, no. 84, AML, 1 II 0254 1 4.

107. *Extrait des registres des déliberations et arêtes du conseil générale d'administration des Hopitaux civils de Lyon*, July 28, 1814, ADR, 4 T 32.

108. *Journal de Lyon*, June 1, 1819, no. 148.

109. *Monument expiatoire élevé aux Brotteaux*, C. 1824, BML, The Jean-Antoine-Louis Coste Collection of Manuscripts and Prints, print no. 458.

110. See Assoun, *Tuer le mort*, chap. 1. See also Verdery, *Political Lives of Dead Bodies*, 38.

111. *Le lieutenant de la police générale du departément du Rhône au M. le prefet du departément du Rhône*, October 1, 1821, BML, The Jean-Antoine-Louis Coste Collection of Manuscripts and Prints, Mss. 710, no. 43.

112. *Rapport sur l'exhumation des corps des victimes du siège Lyonnais*, March 6, 1823, AML, WP 013 1.

113. See Alan Spitzer, *Old Hatreds and Young Hopes: The French Carbonari against the Bourbon Restoration* (Cambridge, Mass.: Harvard University Press, 1971); and Laqueur, *History of Terrorism*.

114. *Ministère de l'Interieur à la Préfecture de Vaucluse*, November 16, 1830, ADV, 1 M art. 904.

115. *Le sous Commissaire d'Orange au Monsieur le Maire d'Orange*, May 28, 1848, AMO, M 1371.

116. The notion that the mass violence of the past gets embedded somehow in the physicality of certain places is intriguing, but not within the purview of this chapter. See Thomas F. Gieryn, "A Space for Place in Sociology," *Annual Review of Sociology* 26 (2000): 463–496. See also Maria Tumarkin, *Traumascapes: The Power and Fate of Places Transformed by Tragedy* (Melbourne: Melbourne University Press, 2005). This brings to mind a personal anecdote. When I visited the site at Picpus in 2006, the guardian of the place inquired about my interests there. When he discovered that I am originally from Israel, he put his hand on my shoulder, leaned toward me, and whispered in my ear: "You know, our Robespierre was like your Hitler."

5. Haunting

1. Minow, *Between Vengeance and Forgiveness*, 4.

2. Baczko, *Ending the Terror*, 115.

3. Avery Gordon, *Ghostly Matters*, 7.

4. See Raymond Williams, *The Long Revolution* (Orchard Park, N.Y.: Broadview Press, 2001), esp. chap. 2.

5. *Correspondance des vivans et des morts* (Paris: chez Desenne, chez Petit, et au Bureau du Courrier-Universel, 1795), 5.

6. Ibid., 6–7.

7. See Morris Slavin, "Jacques Roux: A Victim of Vilification," *FHS* 3, no. 4 (1964): 525–537; and Morris Slavin, "Jean Varlet as Defender of Direct Democracy," *JMH* 39, no. 4 (1967): 387–404. See also Daniel Guerin, *La lutte de classes sous la première république. Bourgeois et "bras nus," 1793–1797* (Paris: Gallimard, 1946).

8. See Laura Mason, *Singing the French Revolution: Popular Culture and Politics, 1787–1799* (Ithaca, N.Y.: Cornell University Press, 1996), chap. 5; see also Alphonse Aulard, *Paris pendant la réaction thermidorienne et sous le directoire*, 5 vols. (Paris: Léopold Cerf, 1898–1902), 1:414–415.

9. See Jainchill, *Reimagining Politics after the Terror*.

10. This is, of course, a very common view of the Revolution now. See Furet, *Interpreting the French Revolution*; Baker, *Inventing the French Revolution*; Hunt, *Politics, Culture, and Class in the French Revolution*.

11. See Andreasen, "Posttraumatic Stress Disorder"; and "Post-Traumatic Stress Disorder," AllPsych, http://allpsych.com/disorders/anxiety/ptsd.html,http://allpsych.com/disorders/anxiety/ptsd.html.

12. See Alexander, *Cultural Trauma and Collective Identity*; Leys, *Trauma*; Young, *Harmony of Illusions*; Rothberg, "Decolonizing Trauma Studies"; Micale and Lerner, *Traumatic Pasts*.

13. Herman, *Trauma and Recovery*, 37.

14. See Bessel van der Kolk and Rita Fisler, "Dissociation and the Fragmentary Nature of Traumatic Memories: Overview and Exploratory Study," *Journal of Traumatic Stress* 8, no. 4 (1995): 505–525. See also Veena Das, "Language and Body: Transactions in the Construction of Pain," in *Violence in War and Peace: An Anthology*, ed. Nancy Scheper-Hughes and Philippe Bourgeois (Oxford: Blackwell, 2004), 327–333.

15. See Susan Brison, *Aftermath: Violence and the Remaking of a Self* (Princeton, N.J.: Princeton University Press, 2002).

16. Cathy Caruth, *Unclaimed Experience: Trauma, Narrative, and History* (Baltimore: Johns Hopkins University Press, 1996), 91–92.

17. Leys, *Trauma*, 268.

18. See Yoav Di-Capua, "Trauma and Other Historians: An Introduction," *Historical Reflections/Réflexions historiques* 41, no. 3 (2015): 1–13; see also Saul Friedländer, ed., *Probing the Limits of Representation: Nazism and the Final Solution* (Cambridge, Mass.: Harvard University Press, 1992). See especially the series of books on the subject by Dominic LaCapra, *Representing the Holocaust: History, Theory, Trauma* (Ithaca, N.Y.: Cornell University Press, 1996); and *Writing History, Writing Trauma*.

19. See Steinberg, "Somber Historiographies."

20. See Wolfgang Schivelbusch, *The Railway Journey: The Industrialization of Time and Space in the Nineteenth Century* (Berkeley: University of California Press, 1986), chap. 9.

21. See Barry Shapiro, *Traumatic Politics: The Deputies and the King in the Early French Revolution* (University Park: Pennsylvania State University Press, 2009); Patrice Higonnet, "Terror, Trauma, and the 'Young Marx' Explanation of Jacobin Politics," *Past and Present* 191 (May 2006): 121–164.

22. See Linton, *Choosing Terror*; and William Reddy, *The Navigation of Feeling: A Framework for the History of Emotions* (Cambridge: Cambridge University Press, 2001).

23. Raymond Williams, *Marxism and Literature* (Oxford: Oxford University Press, 1977), 131.

24. See Ian Buchanan, *Oxford Dictionary of Critical Theory* (Oxford: Oxford University Press, 2010), 454–455.

25. See Williams, *Marxism and Literature*, 135.

26. I wish to clarify that the link I am trying to draw between these different texts or cases from the postrevolutionary context and the modern concept of trauma is not a direct one. I am not arguing that the French revolutionaries invented the concept of trauma, or that this term emerged somehow necessarily from the process of coming to terms with the Terror. I am implying that there is something in the revolutionary experience of rupture, in the modern attitudes toward time that emerge from the revolutionary era, which makes the concept of trauma possible. This is an implication that I have yet to work out fully. For a more developed version of this argument, see Ronen Steinberg, "Trauma and the Effects of Mass Violence in Revolutionary France: A Critical Inquiry," *Historical Reflections/Réflexions historiques* 41, no. 3 (2015): 28–46.

27. The Marquis de Sade, "Reflections on the Novel," in *Marquis de Sade: The 120 Days of Sodom and Other Writings*, ed. Austryn Wainhouse and Richard Seaver (New York: Grove Press, 1966), 108–109.

28. See Ronald Paulson, *Representations of Revolution, 1789–1820* (New Haven, Conn.: Yale University Press, 1983); Robert Miles, "The 1790s: The Effulgence of the Gothic," in *The Cambridge Companion to Gothic Fiction*, ed. Jerrold E. Hogle (Cambridge: Cambridge University Press, 2002), 41–62.

29. See E. J. Clery, *The Rise of Supernatural Fiction, 1762–1800* (Cambridge: Cambridge University Press, 1999).

30. See Crawford, *Gothic Fiction and the Invention of Terrorism*.

31. Jan Bondeson, *Buried Alive: The Terrifying History of Our Most Primal Fear* (New York: Norton, 2001), 93.

32. L.-A. Beffroy de Reigny, ed., *Dictionnaire néologique des hommes et des choses*, 2 vols. (Paris: Moutardier, 1801), 1:319.

33. See Eugene Weber, *Peasants into Frenchmen: The Modernization of Rural France, 1870–1914* (Stanford, Calif.: Stanford University Press, 1976), 15.

34. Shane McCorristine, *Specters of the Self: Thinking about Ghosts and Ghost-Seeing in England, 1750–1920* (Cambridge: Cambridge University Press, 2010), 31–40.

35. Laurent Mannoni, *The Great Art of Light and Shadow: An Archaeology of the Cinema* (Exeter: University of Exeter Press, 2000), 136.

36. This general account is based on Françoise Levie, *Étienne-Gaspard Robertson. La vie d'un phantasmagore* (Longeuill, Quebec: Le préambule, 1990).

37. See Hoffman, *Inside Terrorism*, chap. 5.

38. W. J. T. Mitchell, *Cloning Terror: The War of Images, 9/11 to the Present* (Chicago: University of Chicago Press, 2011), 57. See Feldman, "Violence and Vision."

39. *Journal of Natural Philosophy, Chemistry and the Arts*, by William Nicholson, 41 vols. (1797–1813), vol. 1, January–August 1802, pp. 148–149, accessed October 25, 2018, https://archive.org/stream/journalofnatural01lond#page/148/mode/2up.

40. See Jack Censer and Lynn Hunt, "Imaging the French Revolution: Depictions of the French Revolutionary Crowd," *AHR* 110, no. 1 (2005): 38–45.

41. Terry Castle, *The Female Thermometer: 18th Century Culture and the Invention of the Uncanny* (Oxford: Oxford University Press, 1995), 144.

42. Etienne-Gaspard Robertson, *Mémoires récréatifs, scientifiques, et anecdotiques du physicien-aéronaute*, 2 vols. (Paris: chez l'auteur et à la librairie Wurtz, 1831), 1:144.

43. See Keith Thomas, *Religion and the Decline of Magic* (London: Weidenfeld and Nicolson, 1971), 588–605; and Jean Delumeau, *La peur en occident, XIVe-XVIIIe siècles. Une cité asiégée* (Paris: Fayard, 1978), 75–87.

44. Robertson, *Mémoires*, 1:87.

45. Ibid., 1:106.

46. Ibid., 1:150.

47. *Affiches, Annonces et avis divers, ou Journal général de France*, 17 Pluviôse, an VI (February 5, 1798), no. 137.

48. *L'ami des lois, par le représentant Poultier, et autres gens de lettres, sous la direction des frères Sibuet, propriétaires*, 8 Germinal, an VI (March 28, 1798), no. 955.

49. *Affiches, Annonces et Avis divers*, 1 Pluviôse, an VI (January 20, 1798), no. 121.

50. See Marcello Pera, *The Ambiguous Frog: The Galvani-Volta Controversy on Animal Electricity* (Princeton, N.J.: Princeton University Press, 1992), 86–90.

51. See Robert Darnton, *Mesmerism and the End of Enlightenment in France* (Cambridge, Mass.: Harvard University Press, 1968).

52. See Jan Goldstein, *The Post-Revolutionary Self: Politics and Psyche in France, 1750–1850* (Cambridge, Mass.: Harvard University Press, 2005), 58.

53. Robertson, *Mémoires*, 1:365. On scientific experiments as a mode of entertainment in eighteenth century France, see Barbara Stafford, *Artful Science: Enlightenment, Entertainment, and the Eclipse of Visual Education* (Cambridge, Mass.: MIT Press, 1994).

54. See Ernst Benz, *The Theology of Electricity: On the Encounter and Explanation of Theology and Science in the 17th and 18th Centuries* (Allison Park, Pa.: Pickwick Publications, 1989), 10.

55. Robertson, *Mémoires*, 1:276.

56. *L'ami des Lois*, no. 955.

57. Ibid.

58. See Peter Buse and Andrew Stott, "Introduction: A Future for Haunting," in *Ghosts: Deconstruction, Psychoanalysis, History*, ed. Peter Buse and Andrew Stott (New York: St. Martin's Press, 1999), 1–17.

59. Leslie A. Fiedler, *Love and Death in the American Novel* (New York: Stein and Day, 1966), 129.

60. John Borneman, *Political Crime and the Memory of Loss* (Bloomington: Indiana University Press, 2011), 33.

61. Mannoni, *Great Art of Light and Shadow*, 21. Interestingly, magic lanterns are commonly attributed to Athanasius Kircher, a seventeenth-century man of science and Jesuit. I mention this because Jesuits of course were highly interested in finding ways to make the invisible, intangible presence of God visible and tangible. See Mark Waddell, "The World, as It Might Be: Iconography and Probabilism in the *Mundus subterraneus* of Athanasius Kircher," *Centaurus* 48, no. 1 (2006): 3–23.

62. Benz, *Theology of Electricity*, 19–21.

63. Tom Gunning, "Phantasmagoria and the Manufacturing of Illusions and Wonder: Towards a Cultural Optics of the Cinematic Apparatus," in *The Cinema: A New Technology for the 20th Century*, ed. Andre Gaudreault et al. (Lausanne: Payot, 2004), 34.

64. Mannoni, *Great Art of Light and Shadow*, 136.

65. *L'ami des Lois*, no. 955.

66. See X. Theodore Barber, "Phantasmagorical Wonders: The Magic Lantern Ghost Show in Nineteenth-Century America," *Film History* 3, no. 2 (1989): 73–86.

67. Robertson, *Mémoires*, 1:212.

68. Ibid., 1:214.

69. See Vincent Barras, "Le laboratoire de la décapitation," in Bertrand and Carol, *L'exécution capitale*, 59–70. See also Daniel Arasse, *The Guillotine and the Terror* (London: Penguin, 1989), 37–42. This debate continued in fits and starts well into the twentieth century. See Daniel Gerould, *Guillotine: Its Legend and Lore* (New York: Blast Books, 1992), 53–57.

70. Antoine Louis, *Lettres sur la certitude des signes de la mort, où l'on rassure les citoyens de la crainte d'etre enterrés vivans, avec des observations et des expériences sur les noyés* (Paris: Chez Michel Lambert, 1752). See also Bondeson, *Buried Alive*, chap. 4.

71. See Alister Kershaw, *A History of the Guillotine* (New York: Barnes and Noble, 1993), 33–37.

72. Paul Loye, *La mort par la décapitation* (Paris: Bureaux du progress medical, 1888), 33–34.

73. "Sur le supplice de la guillotine, par le professeur Soemmering. Oelsner aux rédacteurs du Magasin Encyclopédique," *Extrait du Magasin Encylopédique: ou journal des sciences, des lettres et des arts*, May 20, 1795, BHVP, 8086, 469.

74. *Opinion du chirurgien Sue, professeur de Medicine et de Botanique, sur le supplice de la guillotine* (Paris, Brumaire an IV [1796]), 7.

75. Mercier, *Paris pendant la Révolution*, 1:193.

76. See *Anécdotes sur les décapités, par Auberive* (Paris: chez J. F. Sobry, 1797); and Mutel, *La guillotine, ou Réflèxions physiologiques sur ce genre de supplice, par D. Ph. Mutel, docteur en médecine* (Paris: Paulin, 1834), 3–4.

77. See Jean-Pierre Bonnafont, *Décapitation du Marabout et du Cheik de la Tribu d'El-Oufia en 1834. Histoire de deux-têtes par le docteur Bonnafont. Extrait du journal d'hygiène* (Paris: Imprimerie Chaix, 1885).

78. "Sur les supplice . . . par Soemmering," 474.

79. Jean-Pierre-Georges Cabanis, *Note sur la supplice de la guillotine* (Périgueux: Éditions Fanlac, 2002 [1795]), 11.

80. Quoted in Arasse, *Guillotine and the Terror*, 46. On Cabanis's brushes with revolutionary authorities during the Terror, see Martin S. Staum, *Cabanis: Enlightenment and Medical Philosophy in the French Revolution* (Princeton, N.J.: Princeton University Press, 1980), 192–193.

81. "Sur le supplice . . . par Soemmering," 465.

82. *Anécdotes sur les décapités*, 17.

83. *Réflèxions historiques et physiologiques sur le supplice de la Guillotine, par Sédillot le jeune, Docteur en médecine de la ci-devant Académie de Chirurgie de Paris, membre du Lycée des Arts* (Paris: Debray, 1795), 24–25.

84. See Paul Henri Stahl, *Histoire de la décapitation* (Paris: Presses Universitaires de France, 1986).

85. Regina Janes, "Beheadings," *Representations*, no. 35 (Summer 1991), 21.

86. Julia Douthwaite, *The Wild Girl, Natural Man, and the Monster: Dangerous Experiments in the Age of Enlightenment* (Chicago: University of Chicago Press, 2002), 194.

87. Giovanni Aldini, *Essai théorique et experimental sur le galvanisme, avec une série d'expériences* (Paris: Imprimerie de Fournier Fils, 1804), 124.

88. Ibid., 122. The emphasis on sudden and violent death was important. Aldini maintained that the bodies of people who had died from diseases were not useful for experiments in galavanism because in these bodies the disease had already destroyed the nerve fibers and the power of electricity prior to death. For this reason, he insisted on conducting his experiments on bodies of people who had just been guillotined. Indeed, he obtained permission from the authorities in Bologna to collect the bodies immediately after execution, and situated his laboratory right next to the site of execution.

89. Ibid., 128.

90. "Lettre de M. Ferry, professeur de physique et de chimie, adressée au professeur Aldini," reproduced in Aldini, *Essai théorique*, 257.

91. Sean M. Quinlan, "Physical and Moral Regeneration after the Terror: Medical Culture, Sensibility, and Family Politics in France, 1794–1804," *Social History* 29, no. 2 (2004), 141.

92. See de Baecque, *Body Politic*, 314; and Dorinda Outram, *The Body and the French Revolution: Sex, Class, and Political Culture* (New Haven, Conn.: Yale University Press, 1989), 50–51.

93. Marc-Antoine Petit, "Discours sur l'influence de la Révolution française sur la santé publique," in *Essai sur la médecine du coeur* (Lyon: chez Garnier, 1806), 116.

94. Ibid., 128.

95. See Neria, *9/11*; and NATAL, Israeli Trauma Center for Victims of Terror and War, http://www.natal.org.il/English/?CategoryID=160 (accessed March 1, 2014).

96. Biographical details about Petit are drawn from the *Biographie universelle (Michaud) ancienne et moderne*, 45 vols. (Paris: Madame C. Desplaces, 1854–1865), 32:598.

97. See Elizabeth A. Williams, *A Cultural History of Medical Vitalism in Enlightenment Montpellier* (Aldershot, UK: Ashgate, 2003), 265.

98. See Daniel Wickberg, "What Is the History of Sensibilities? On Cultural Histories, Old and New," *AHR* 112, no. 3 (2007): 661–684. See also Carolyn Purnell, *The Sensational Past: How the Enlightenment Changed the Way We Use Our Senses* (New York: Norton, 2017).

99. See Antonie Luyendijk-Elshout, "Of Masks and Mills: The Enlightened Doctor and His Frightened Patient," in *The Languages of Psyche: Mind and Body in Enlightenment Thought*, ed. G. S. Rousseau (Berkeley: University of California Press, 1990), 224.

100. See Roseleyne Rey, *The History of Pain* (Cambridge, Mass.: Harvard University Press, 1995), 129.

101. Petit, "Discours," 153.

102. Ibid., 132.

103. The author of this pamphlet is identified only by the initials J.-F. and his last name.

104. J.-F. Guitard, *Mémoire qui a remporté le prix au jugement de L'académie des sciences, arts et belles-lettres de Caen, dans sa séance publique du 3 Juillet 1811, sur la question proposée en ces termes: Quels sont les effets de la Terreur sur l'économie animale?* (Bordeaux: Lawalle Jeune, 1811), 30. Such arguments bring to mind very recent work that is being done on the concept of posttraumatic growth, that is, positive change that is experienced as a result of a struggle with traumatic life events. See "Posttraumatic Growth Research Group," University of North Carolina, Charlotte, Department of Psychology, http://ptgi.uncc.edu (accessed March 1, 2014).

105. On the difficulties of the republican left with the legacies of the Terror, see François Furet, *La gauche et la Révolution française*.

106. See Goldstein, *Post-Revolutionary Self*.

107. See Reddy, *Navigation of Feeling*, esp. chap. 6.

108. See Jan Goldstein, "The Hysteria Diagnosis and the Politics of Anticlericalism in Late Nineteenth Century France," *JMH* 54, no. 2 (1982): 209–239.

109. Quoted in Françoise Jacob, "Faire la Révolution, est ce devenir fou? Les alienistes français du XIXe siècle jugent 1789," in *L'image de la Révolution française*, ed. Michelle Vovelle, 4 vols. (Paris: Pergamon Press, 1990), 3:2057.

110. A. Briérre de Boismont, "De l'influence de la civilisation sur le développement de la folie," *Annales d'hygiène publique et de médecine légale*, ser. 1, no. 21 (1839), 242, 245. Italics mine.

111. Philippe Pinel, *Traité medico-philosophique sur l'aliénation mentale, ou la manie* (Paris: chez Richard, Caille et Ravier, 1801), 66–67. I first encountered this story in Jan Goldstein, *Console and Classify: The French Psychiatric Profession in the Nineteenth Century* (Chicago: University of Chicago Press, 1987), 82.

112. See Alain Corbin, "Backstage," in *A History of Private Life, Vol. 4: From the Fires of Revolution to the Great War*, ed. Michelle Perrot (Cambridge, Mass: Harvard University Press, 1990), 515.

113. See Benoît Chabert, "Sur la peine de mort en France de la Restauration au début de la IIIe République," In *Victor Hugo contre la peine de mort*, ed. Jérome Picon and Isabel Violante, (Paris: Textuel, 2001), 169–173. See also Jean Imbert, *La peine de mort* (Paris: Presses Universitaires de France, 1993); and Julie le Quang Sang, *La loi et le bourreau. La peine de mort en débats, 1870–1985* (Paris: Harmattan, 2001).

114. See Daniel P. Resnick, *The White Terror and the Political Reaction after Waterloo* (Cambridge, Mass.: Harvard University Press, 1966).

115. On this problem for liberals under the Restoration, see Mellon, *Political Uses of History*.

116. See François Guizot, *De la peine de mort en matière politique* (Paris: Chez Béchet ainé, 1822).

117. Élisabeth-Félicie Bayle-Mouillard, *Aux Femmes. Quelques mots sur la peine de mort* (Paris: Paul Dupont et compagnie, 1836), 10.

118. Charles Claude Pierquin de Gembloux, *De la peine de mort et de son influence sur la santé publique* (Paris: Imprimerie de Veuve Thuau, 1830), 38.

119. Ibid., 63.

120. In the early 1800s, it seems, noble pregnant women were still being wheeled around the Louvre so that they might gaze at portraits of those whom they wished their future children to resemble. See Jan Bondeson, *A Cabinet of Medical Curiosities* (Ithaca, N.Y.: Cornell University Press, 1997), 155.

121. See Andrew Aisenberg, *Contagion: Disease, Government and the "Social Question" in Nineteenth Century France* (Stanford, Calif.: Stanford University Press, 1999).

122. J.-B. F. Descuret, *La médicine des passions, ou les passions considerées dans leurs rapports avec les maladies, les lois et la religion* (Paris: Labé, 1844), 430.

123. Pirequin de Gembloux, *De la peine de mort*, 34.

124. Ibid., 37.

Conclusion

1. Pierre-Charles-Louis Baudin, *Rapport fait à la Convention nationale, et projet de décret, présenté dans la séance du 2 brumaire, an 4, au nom de la Commission des onze, par P.C.L. Baudin, député de la departément des Ardennes, sur l'abolition de la peine de mort, et l'amnistie pour les faits relatifs à la révolution* (Paris: Imprimerie nationale, 1795), 9.

2. See Bodinier and Teyssier, *L'événement le plus important de la Révolution*.

3. See Luzzatto, *Mémoire de la Terreur*, 162. Siân Reynolds is currently completing a project on children of the revolutionaries. I am grateful to her for a very illuminating conversation we had in Paris in January 2017 and to the several exchanges over e-mail, which followed that meeting.

4. See Emile Le Bon, *Joseph Le Bon, dans sa vie privée et dans sa carrière politique* (Paris: E. Dentu, 1861).

5. Edmond and Jules de Goncourt, *Journal des Goncourt. Mémoires de la vie littéraire*, 9 vols. (Paris: Bibliothèque-Charpentier, 1851–1895), 2:82. See also Geoffrey Wall, *The Enlightened Physician: Achille-Cléophas Flaubert, 1784–1846* (Oxford: Peter Lang, 2013).

6. Fureix, *La France des larmes*, 201.

7. Susan Nagel, *Marie-Thérèse, Child of Terror: The Fate of Marie Antoinette's Daughter* (New York: Bloomsbury, 2008), 364. I am grateful to my student Heidi Fluck for calling my attention to this story.

8. James Dawes, *Evil Men* (Cambridge, Mass.: Harvard University Press, 2013), 14–15.

9. Pumla Gobodo-Madikizela, *A Human Being Died That Night: A South African Woman Confronts the Legacy of Apartheid* (New York: Mariner Books, 2003), 86.

10. See Jürgen Kocka, *Capitalism: A Short History* (Princeton, N.J.: Princeton University Press, 2016); and Joyce Appleby, *The Relentless Revolution: A History of Capitalism* (New York: Norton, 2011).

11. On the emergence of science and medicine as distinct loci of authority in the modern era, see Michel Foucault, *Power/Knowledge: Selected Interviews and Other Writings, 1972–1977*, ed. Colin Gordon (New York: Pantheon Books, 1980), esp. chaps. 5–6.

12. Linton, *Choosing Terror*, 4.

13. Agonism is a political theory that sees certain forms of conflict as positive to, and indeed, constitutive of healthy democracies. See Chantal Mouffe, *The Democratic Paradox* (London: Verso, 2005); and Adam Phillips, *Equals* (New York: Basic Books, 2002).

14. Quinet, *La Révolution*, 2:832.

15. Ruti Teitel, "Transitional Justice Genealogy," *Harvard Human Rights Journal* 16 (2003): 69–94.

16. See Samuel Moyn, *Human Rights and the Uses of History* (New York: Verso, 2014), chap. 6.

17. Alex Boraine, "Transitional Justice: A Holistic Interpretation," *Journal of International Affairs* 60, no. 1 (2006), 18.

18. Minow, *Between Vengeance and Forgiveness*, esp. chap. 6.

19. See Francis Fukuyama, *The End of History and the Last Man* (New York: Free Press, 1992).

20. For a recent study that questions whether transitional justice is necessary for the establishment of a robust political culture in the wake of repressive and authoritarian regimes, see Omar G. Encarnación, *Democracy without Justice in Spain: The Politics of Forgetting* (Philadelphia: University of Pennsylvania Press, 2014).

21. See Zinaida Miller, "Effects of Invisibility: In Search of the 'Economic' in Transitional Justice," *International Journal of Transitional Justice* 2, no. 3 (2008): 266–291; and Tafadzwa Pasipanodya, "A Deeper Justice: Economic and Social Justice as Transitional Justice in Nepal," *International Journal of Transitional Justice* 2, no. 3 (2008): 378–397.

22. See Haim Burstin, *La Révolution à l'oeuvre. Le faubourg Saint-Marcel, 1789–1794* (Seyssel: Champ Vallon, 2005); William H. Sewell, *A Rhetoric of a Bourgeois Revolution: The Abbé Sieyes and What Is the Third Estate?* (Durham, N.C.: Duke University Press, 1994); and, of course, the classic work by Georges Lefebvre, *Questions agraires au temps de la Terreur* (La Roche-sur-Yon: Potier, 1954).

23. See Wendy Brown, *States of Injury*; Asad Haider, *Mistaken Identity: Race and Class in the Age of Trump* (New York: Verso, 2018).

24. See Fassin and Rechtman, *Empire of Trauma*.

25. Torpey, *Making Whole What Has Been Smashed*, 41.

26. See Confino, *Foundational Pasts*; and Samuel Moyn, *The Last Utopia: Human Rights in History* (Cambridge, Mass.: Harvard University Press, 2010).

27. Keith M. Baker, ed., *The Old Regime and the French Revolution* (Chicago: University of Chicago Press, 1987), 1.

28. Lindet, *Rapport fait à la Convention nationale dans la séance du 4ème des Sans-Culottides de l'an 2ème*, 22.

Bibliography

Primary Sources

Archival Sources

Archives Nationales

Comité de Législation

D III 5
D III 90
D III 91
D III 98
D III 161
D III 191
D III 198
D III 213
D III 216
D III 240
D III 320
D III 15*–27*

Police Générale, affaire Lebon

F7 4772
F7 4773
F7 4774/1
F7 4774/2
F7 4774/3
F7 4774/4–5
F4 4774/6

Bâtiments Civils

F13 330
F13 524
F13 964

Instruction Publique

F17 1048
F17 1051

F17 1240
F17 1253

Ministére de la Justice, affaires criminels, dossier Lebon
BB3 29

ARCHIVES DE PARIS
5 Mi 1/87
DQ 10 715

ARCHIVES DE LA PRÉFECTURE DE POLICE
Série Ancienne
AA 70
AA 71
AA 173
AA 220
AA 435

ARCHIVES DÉPARTEMENTALES DU RHÔNE
Affaires culturelles, monument de Brotteaux
4T 32

Biens nationaux, restitutions
1 Q 284
1 Q 808
1 Q 1031–1041

ARCHIVES MUNICIPALES DE LYON
4 II 159 E (Papers of the architect Claude Cochet)
2066 WP 323 (Administration of Cemeteries)
475 WP 008 (Public Monuments)
14 II 421 P (Papers of the architect Cyr Decrénice)
468 WP 013 1 (Public Monuments)
1 II 0254 1 4 (Papers of the Morand de Jouffrey Family)
1 II 0255 1 (Papers of the architect Jean Antoine Morand de Jouffrey)
14 II 040 1 (Papers of the archite)
4 WP 057 1 (Local police, district of La guillotière)

BIBLIOTHÈQUE MUNICIPALE DE LYON
Manuscript Collection of Jean-Louis-Antoine Coste

ARCHIVES DÉPARTEMENTALES DE LA HAUTE GARONNE
Q 393
Q 546

1 S 84
1 S AMT 89
1 L 200
1 L 372
1 L 374

ARCHIVES DÉPARTEMENTALES DU PAS-DE-CALAIS

4 L 3
4 L 17
4 L 26
4 L 5
4 L 18

ARCHIVES DÉPARTEMENTALES DE VAUCLUSE

1 L 135–136*
8 L 21
7 L 57
5 F 182*
3 L 170
7 L 37*
5 F 180
1 M 904

ARCHIVES MUNICIPALES D'ORANGE

M 1371
D 705

ARCHIVES DÉPARTEMENTALES DE LA SOMME

L 975
L 3311
DA 981
L 1245
L 4650

PRIVATE ARCHIVE

Papers of the De Baudus Family

Newspapers and Journals

    Affiches, Annonces et avis divers, ou Journal général de France
    Annales Lyonnais
    Archives parlementaires
    Décade philosophique, littéraire et politique
    Journal de Lyon et du département du Rhône
    Journal of Natural Philosophy, Chemistry & the Arts, by William Nicholson
    L'ami de la religion et du Roi. Journal ecclésiastique, politique, et littéraire

L'ami des lois, par le représentant Poultier
L'orateur du peuple, par Fréron
Patriot François
Réimpression de l'ancien Moniteur
Sentinelle du Nord

Print Sources

Aldini, Giovanni. *Essai théorique et experimental sur le galvanisme, avec une série d'expériences* (Paris: Imprimerie de Fournier Fils, 1804).

Anonymous. *Correspondance des vivans et des morts* (Paris: chez Desenne, chez Petit, et au Bureau du Courrier-Universel, 1795).

———. *Fondation de la chapelle funéraire de Picpus* (Paris: Imprimerie de Lottin de S. Germain, 1814).

———. *La confession générale de Joseph Lebon et bande, ou prédiction de Jean Sans Peur, applicable à tous les autres bouveurs de sang et complices du terrorisme* (Arras: Imprimerie du grand Pain d'épice d'Arras, n.d.).

———. *Orgie et testament de Mirabeau* (Paris: n.p., 1791).

———. *Sur les moyens de communiquer sur-le-champ au peuple, occupant le dehors du lieu où se tient l'Assemblée, les délibérations qui y sont prises* (Paris: Imprimerie de Vve. Hérissant, 1789).

Arrêtés du parlement de Toulouse, séant en vacations, des 25 & 27 Septembre 1790 (n.p., n.d).

Auberive. *Anécdotes sur les décapités, par Auberive* (Paris: chez J. F. Sobry, 1797).

Babeuf, Gracchus. *La guerre de la Vendée et le système de dépopulation* (Paris: Tallandier, 1987).

Barère, Bertrand. *Rapport fait au nom du Comité de Salut Public, sur les pétitions faites à raison des opérations de Joseph Lebon, Représentant du peuple dans les départements du Pas de-Calais at du Nord, dans la séance du 21 Messidor, l'an 2 de la République française, une & indivisible, par Barère* (Paris: Imprimerie nationale, 1794).

Baudin, Pierre-Charles-Louis. *Rapport fait à la Convention nationale, et projet de décret, présenté dans la séance du 2 brumaire, an 4, au nom de la Commission des onze, par P.C.L. Baudin, député de la departément des Ardennes, sur l'abolition de la peine de mort, et l'amnistie pour les faits relatifs à la révolution* (Paris: Imprimerie nationale, 1795).

Baudot, Marc-Antoine. *Notes historiques sur la Convention nationale, le Directoire, l'Empire, et l'exil des votants* (Genève: Slatkine-Megariotis, 1974 [1893]).

Bayle-Mouillard, Élisabeth-Félicie. *Aux Femmes. Quelques mots sur la peine de mort* (Paris: Paul Dupont et compagnie, 1836).

Beffroy de Reigny, L.-A. *Dictionnaire néologique des hommes et des choses.* 2 vols. (Paris: Moutardier, 1801).

Boissy d'Anglas, François-Antoine. *Essai sur la vie, les écrits, et les opinions de M. de Malesherbes, adressé à mes enfans.* 3 vols. (Paris: chez Treuttel et Wurtz, 1819).

Bonnafont, Jean-Pierre. *Décapitation du Marabout et du Cheik de la Tribu d'El-Oufia en 1834. Histoire de deux-têtes par le docteur Bonnafont. Extrait du journal d'hygiène* (Paris: Imprimerie Chaix, 1885).

Briérre de Boismont. "De l'influence de la civilisation sur le développement de la folie." *Annales d'hygiène publique et de médecine légale,* ser. 1, no. 21 (1839).

Buchez, P.-J.-B.. and P.-C. Roux, eds. *Histoire parlementaire de la Révolution française*. 40 vols. (Paris: J. Hetzel, 1834–1838).

Cabanis, Pierre-Jean-George. *Journal de la maladie et de la mort d'Honoré-Gabriel-Victor Riquetti Mirabeau* (Paris: chez Grabit, 1791).

———. *Note sur la supplice de la guillotine* (Périgueux: Éditions Fanlac, 2002 [1795]).

Cambry, Jacques. *Rapport sur les sépultures, présenté à l'administration centrale du département de la Seine, par le citoyen Cambry, administratuer du département de la Seine, administrateur du prytanée François, et de l'académie des antiquaires de Cortone* (Paris: Imprimerie de Pierre Didot l'aîné, 1799).

Courtois, Edme-Bonaventure. *Rapport fait au nom de la Commission chargée de l'examen des papiers trouvés chez Robespierre et ses complices par E. B. Courtois, député du département de l'Aube, dans la séance du 16 Nivôse, an III* (Paris: chez Maret, 1795).

Croker, John Wilson. "The Guillotine." Review of *Notice Historique et Physiologique sur le Supplice de la Guillotine* by Guyot de Fère and of *Recherches Historiques et Phsyiologiques sur la Guillotine; et détails sur Sanson, ouvrage rédigé sur pieces officiels* by Louis de Bois, *Quarterly Review* 73, no. 145 (December 1843): 235–280.

D'Alemebrt, Jean le Rond, and Denis Diderot, eds. *Encyclopédie, ou dictionnaire raisonné des sciences, des arts et des métiers, par une société des gens de lettres* (Genève, Paris, Neufchastel: chez Brisson, 1754–1772). University of Chicago: ARTFL Encyclopédie Project (Autumn 2017 ed.), edited by Robert Morrissey and Glenn Roe.

Daubermesnil, François Antoine. *Corps legislative. Conseil des Cinq-Cents. Rapport fait au nom d'une commission speciale, sur les inhumations, par Daubermesnil, séance du 21 Brumaire, an V* (Paris: Imprimerie nationale, 1796).

Dauchez, Jean-Baptiste. *Rapport fait au nom d'une commission spéciale, par Dauchez (d'Arras), représentant du peuple, relativement à la suppression des prénoms révolutionnaires donnés aux enfans dont la naissance a été constatée pendant le régime de la terreur: séance du 6 messidor, an V* (Paris: Imprimerie nationale, 1797).

Delamalle, G. G. *L'enterrement de ma mere, ou reflexions sur les ceremonies des funérailles et le soin des sepultures et sur la moralité des institutions civiles en général* (Paris: Imprimerie de Boulard, 1794).

Descuret, J.-B. *La médicine des passions, ou les passions considerées dans leurs rapports avec les maladies, les lois et la religion* (Paris: Labé, 1844).

D'Ivernois, François. *A Cursory View of the Assignats and the Remaining Resources of French Finance. September 5, 1795. Drawn from the Debates of the Convention. Translated from the Original French* (Dublin: P. Byrne, 1795).

———. *Tableau historique et politique des pertes que la Révolution et la guerre ont causées au peuple français dans sa population, son agriculture, ses colonies, ses manufactures et son commerce* (London: Imprimerie de Baylis, 1799).

Duval, Georges. *Souvenirs thermidoriens*. 2 vols. (Paris: Victor Magen, 1844).

Épinard, Joseph Pâris de l'. *Mon retour à la vie après quanze mois d'agonie* (n.p., c. 1794).

Fourcroy, Antoine François. *Notice sur la vie et les travaux de Lavoisier par A.-F. Fourcroy, précédée d'un discours sur les funérailles et suivie d'une ode sur l'immortalité de l'ame* (Paris: Imprimerie de la feuille du cultivateur, 1795).

Goncourt, Edmond de. *Journal des Goncourt. Mémoires de la vie littéraire*. 9 vols. (Paris: Bibliothèque-Charpentier, 1851–1895).

Guffroy, Armand. *Censure républicain ou lettre d'A.-B.-J. Guffroy, représentant du peuple, aux françois habitans d'Arras et des communes environnantes, à la Convention nationale, et à l'opinion publique* (Paris: Imprimerie de Rougyff, n.d.).

Guitard, J.-F. *Mémoire qui a remporté le prix au jugement de L'académie des sciences, arts et belles-lettres de Caen, dans sa séance publique du 3 Juillet 1811, sur la question proposée en ces termes: Quels sont les effets de la Terreur sur l'économie animale?* (Bordeaux: Lawalle Jeune, 1811).

Guizot, François. *De la peine de mort en matière politique* (Paris: chez Béchet ainé, 1822).

Jacob, Louis. *La défense du conventionnel Joseph Le Bon, présentée par lui-même* (Paris: Mellottée, 1934).

Histoire du terrorisme dans la commune d'Arles, servant de suite au mémoire publié pour cette commune, le 8 Floréal (Paris: Imprimerie de Guffroy, 1795).

Le Bon, Emile. *Joseph Le Bon dans sa vie privée et dans sa carrière politique, par son fils Émile Le Bon, juge au Tribunal de 1ère instance de Chalon-sur-Saône* (Paris: E. Dentu, 1861).

Lecointre, Laurent. *Les Crimes de sept membres des anciens Comités de salut public et de sûreté générale, ou, Dénonciation formelle à la Convention nationale contre Billaud-Varennes, Barère, Collot-d'Herbois, Vadier, Vouland, Amar et David, suivie de pièces originales existantes dans les comités, preuves et temoins indiqués à l'appui des faits* (n.p., 1795).

Lezay-Marnésia, Adrien de. *Des causes de la Révolution et de ses résultats* (Paris: L'imprimerie du journal d'Économie publique, 1797).

Lindet, Robert. *Rapport fait à la Convention nationale dans la séance du 4ème des Sans Culottides de l'an 2ème, au nom des Comités de salut public, de sûretè générale et de législation, réunis, sur la situation interieure de la république, par Robert Lindet, Représentant du peuple, et membre du comité de salut public* (Montauban: chez Fontanel, imprimeur de la société populaire, 1794).

Liste generale des individus condamnés par jugemens, ou mis hors de la Loi par Decrets, et dont les biens ont été déclarés confisqués au profit de la République (Paris: Imprimerie des domaines nationaux, 1794).

Liste générale et alphabetique des noms, ages, qualités, emplois et demeurs de tous les conspirateurs qui ont été condamnés à mort par le Tribunal Revolutionnaire, établi à Paris par la loi du 17 Aout 1792, et par le second Tribunal, établi à Paris par la loi du= 10 Mars, 1793, pour juger tous les ennemis de la Patrie (London: J. Johnson, St. Paul's Church-Yard, 1795).

Liste, par ordre alphabétique, des noms des citoyens deputés à la convention nationale, avec leurs demeurs au second mois de l'an 2 de la République (Paris: Imprimerie nationale, 1794).

Loi qui determine le mode de restitution des biens des condamnés, du 21 Prairial, an troisième de la République française, une et indivisible (Paris: Imprimerie du dépôt des lois, 1795).

Louis, Antoine. *Lettres sur la certitude des signes de la mort, où l'on rassure les citoyens de la crainte d'etre enterrés vivans, avec des observations et des expériences sur les noyés* (Paris: chez Michel Lambert, 1752).

Loye, Paul. *La mort par la décapitation* (Paris: Bureaux du progress medical, 1888).

Méhée de la Touche, Jean-Claude-Hippolyte. *La queue de Robespierre, ou les Dangers de la liberté de la presse* (Paris: Imprimerie de Rougyff, 1794).

Mercier, Louis-Sebastien. *Paris pendant la Revolution.* 2 vols. (Paris: Poulet-Malassis, 1862).

Michelet, Jules. *Histoire de la Révolution française.* 2 vols. (Paris: Gallimard, 1952).

Montgey et Poirier. *Atrocités commises envers les citoyennes, ci devant détenues dans la Maison d'Arrêt, dite la Providence, à Arras, par Joseph Lebon et ses Adhérens, pour servir de suite aux angoisses de la mort ou idées des horreurs des prisons d'Arras, par les citoyens Montgey et Poirier de Dunkerque* (Paris: chez les Marchands des nouvautés, 1795).

Morellet, André. *Mémoires de l'Abbé Morellet.* 2 vols. (Paris: à la librairie française, 1821).

——. *Le cri des familles, ou discussion de la motion du représentant Lecointre, relativement à la révision des jugemens des tribunaux révolutionnaires* (Paris: Du Pont, 1794).

Mutel (D.-Ph.). *La guillotine, ou Réflèxions physiologiques sur ce genre de supplice, par D. Ph. Mutel, docteur en médecine* (Paris: Paulin, 1834).

Noailles, Paul de. *Anne-Paul-Dominique de Noailles, Marquise de Montagu* (Paris: Dentu, 1861).

Notice historique et pièces relatives au monument religieux élevé à Feurs, aux victimes de l'anarchie de 1793, dans le département de la Loire, rédigées et réunies par le maire de Feurs, pour servir à l'histoire du pays pendant la crise révolutionnaire, et comme compte rendu a MM. les souscripteurs (Tours: Imprimerie de A. Mame, 1829).

Pastoret, Emmanuel. *Rapport sur la violation des sepultures et des tombeaux, fait au nom de la commission de la classification et de la revision des lois, par Emm. Pastoret, séance du 26 Prairial, an IV* (Paris: Imprimerie nationale, 1796).

Peltier, Jean-Gabriel. *Paris pendant l'année.* 15 vols. (London: Baylis, 1795–1801).

Petit, Marc-Antoine. *Essai sur la médecine du coeur* (Lyon: chez Garnier, 1806).

Pétition à la Convention nationale des citoyens de la Commune d'Avignon, victimes de la faction Robespierre, sur les atrocités commises dans cette commune et dans le département de Vaucluse, par les agens et les complices de cette faction (Avignon: V. Raphel, 1794).

Petition de la section des Marchés en masse à la Convention nationale, le 21 ventôse, 3ème année républicaine, tenante, principalement, à rétablir honorablement la mémoire du citoyen Quatremere, marchand des draps, rue Denis, assassiné au tribunal révolution-naire par les hommes de sang qui dominoient cette section (Paris: Imprimerie de Pellier, 1795).

Pièces à l'appui de la pétition et du mémoire présentés par la citoyenne veuve GUSTAVE DECHÉZEAUX, à la Convention Nationale, le 29 Germinal, an 3, pour obtenir la réhabilitation de la mémoire de son malheureux époux, assassiné par le tribunal révolutionnaire établi à Rochefort, dont elle a ordonné l'impression et la renvoi au comité de législation, par décret du meme jour (Paris: Imprimerie nationale, c. 1795).

Pierquin de Gembloux, Charles Claude. *De la peine de mort et de son influence sur la santé publique* (Paris: Imprimerie de Veuve Thuau, 1830).

Pinel, Philippe. *Traité medico-philosophique sur l'aliénation mentale, ou la manie* (Paris: chez Richard, Caille et Ravier, 1801).

Prudhomme, Louis-Marie. *Histoire générale et impartiale des erreurs, des fautes, et des crimes commis pendant la Révolution française, à dater du 24 août 1787, contenant le nombre des individus qui ont péri par la Révolution, de ceux qui ont émigré, et les intrigues des factions qui pendant ce tems ont désolé la France.* 6 vols. (Paris: n.p., 1796–1797).

Quinet, Edgar. *La Révolution.* 2 vols. (Paris: Belin, 1987).

Quoniam Bonus. *L'anniversaire ou le libera de Joseph Lebon, éxécuté à Amiens, le 23 Vendémiaire, an 4, ou le 14 Octobre 1795, dédié à Arras et Cambrai* (n.p., 1796).

Raynal, Guillaume-Thomas. *Des assassinats et des vols politiques, ou des proscriptions et des confiscations, par Guillaume-Thomas Raynal* (London and Paris: chez Buisson, 1795).

Regnault-Warin, J. -J. *Le cimetière de la Madeleine* (Paris: chez Lepetit jeune, 1800–1801).

Richardson, Samuel. *The Paths of Virtue Delineated, or the History in Miniature of the Celebrated Clarissa Harlowe, Familiarised and Adapted to the Capacities of Youth* (Philadelphia: W. Woodhouse, 1791).

Robertson, Etienne-Gaspard. *Mémoires récréatifs, scientifiques, et anecdotiques du physician aéronaute.* 2 vols. (Paris: chez l'auteur et à la librairie Wurtz, 1831).

Robespierre, Maximilien. *Oeuvres de Maximilien Robespierre.* 10 vols., edited by Marc Bouloiseau et al. (Paris: Presses Universitaires de France, 1910–).

Roederer, P. L. *Oeuvres du Comte P. L. Roederer.* 8 vols., edited by A. M. Roederer (Paris: Firmin Didot Frères, 1853–1859).

Sacarau, Jean-Jacques. *Au corps legislatif. Pétition et pièces relatives aux réclamations d'Émilie Prax, veuve de Charles Blanquet-Rouville, non condamné, mais assassiné* (Paris: Imprimerie Teulières, 1797).

Saint-Just, Louis Antoine. *Oeuvres completes.* 2 vols., edited by Charles Vellay (Paris: Charpentier et Fasquelle, 1908).

Second tableau des prisons de Paris, sous le régne de Robespierre, pour servir de suite à l'Almanach des prisons, contenant différents anecdotes sur plusieurs prisonniers, avec les couplets, pieces de vers, lettres et testamens qu'ils ont faits (Paris: Michel, 1794–1795).

Sedilot, Jean. *Réflèxions historiques et physiologiques sur le supplice de la Guillotine, par Sédillot le jeune, Docteur en médecine de la ci-devant Académie de Chirurgie de Paris, membre du Lycée des Arts* (Paris: Debray, 1795).

Söemmerring, Samuel Thomas von. *Sur le supplice de la guillotine, par le professeur Soemmering. Oelsner aux rédacteurs du "Magasin encyclopédique"* [Letter to M. Oelsner] (Paris: imprimerie du Magasin encyclopédique, n.d.).

Sue, Jean-Joseph. *Opinion du chirurgien Sue, professeur de Medicine et de Botanique, sur le supplice de la guillotine* (Paris: 1796).

Tallien, Jean-Lambert. *La vérité sur les événemens du 2 septembre* (Paris: n.p., 1792).

Teutey, Louis, ed. *Procès-verbaux de la Commission temporaire des arts.* 2 vols. (Paris: Imprimerie nationale, 1912–1917).

Thibaudeau, Antoine Claire. *Rapport par Thibaudeau sur la pétition de la veuve Blanquet-Rouville, séance du 3 ventôse, l'an V* (Paris: Imprimerie nationale, 1797).

Tisset, François-Barnabé. *Compte rendu aux sans-culottes de la République française par très haute, très-puissante, et très-expeditive Dame Guillotine.* 2 vols. (Paris: De l'Imprimerie du Calculateur Patriote, au corps sans tête, 1794).

Tronson-Ducoudray, Guillaume-Alexandre. *Mémoire pour les veuves et enfans des citoyens condamnés par le Tribunal révolutionnaire, antérieurement à la loi du 22 Prairial* (Paris: Imprimerie de Desenne, 1795).

Varlé. *Procès de Joseph Lebon, membre de la députation du Département du Pas-de-Calais à la Convention nationale, condamné à la peine de mort par le Tribunal Criminel du Département de la Somme, Recueilli audit Tribunal, par la Citoyenne Varlé*. 2 vols. (Amiens: n.p., 1795).

Vattel, Emmerich de. *Le droit des gens, ou, principes de la loi naturelle appliqués à la conduit & aux affaires des Nations & des Souverains*. 2 vols. (Neuchâtel: Droz, 1758).

Vicq-d'Azyr, Félix. *Essai sur les lieux et les dangers des sepultures* (Paris: Didot, 1778).

Villemain d'Abancourt, Jean-François. *Le cimetière de Mousseaux* (Paris: Roux libraire, 1801).

———. *Le cimetière de la Madeleine* (Paris: Roux libraire, 1801).

Vve Lallart. *Encore un crime de Joseph Le Bon, représentant du peuple, La veuve Lallart, demeurant à Arras, à la Convention nationale* (Paris: Imprimerie de Rougyff, 1795).

Selected Secondary Sources

Abbot, Andrew. "The Historicality of Individuals." *Social Science History* 29, no. 1 (2005): 1–13.

Aftalion, Florin. *The French Revolution: An Economic Interpretation* (Cambridge: Cambridge University Press, 1990).

Alexander, Jeffrey, et al. *Cultural Trauma and Collective Identity* (Berkeley: University of California Press, 2004).

Allen, Robert. *Les tribunaux criminels sous la Révolution et l'Empire, 1792–1811* (Rennes: Presses Universitaires de Rennes, 2005).

Alpaugh, Micah. *Non-Violence and the French Revolution: Political Demonstrations in Paris, 1787–1795* (Cambridge: Cambridge University Press, 2015).

Andress, David. *The Terror: Civil War in the French Revolution* (London: Little, Brown, 2005).

———, ed. *The Oxford Handbook of the French Revolution* (Oxford: Oxford University Press, 2015).

Arasse, Daniel. *The Guillotine and the Terror* (London: Penguin, 1989).

Arendt, Hannah. *Eichmann in Jerusalem: A Report on the Banality of Evil* (New York: Penguin, 1963).

Ariès, Philippe. *The Hour of Our Death* (Oxford: Oxford University Press, 1981).

Assoun, Paul-Laurent. *Tuer le mort. Le désir révolutionnaire* (Paris: Presses Universitaires de France, 2015).

Astbury, Katherine. *Narrative Responses to the Trauma of the French Revolution* (London: Magenta, 2012).

Aston, Nigel. *Religion and Revolution in France, 1780–1804* (Washington D.C.: Catholic University of America Press, 2000).

Baczko, Bronislaw. *Ending the Terror: The French Revolution after Robespierre* (Cambridge: Cambridge University Press, 1994).

———. *Politiques de la Révolution française* (Paris: Gallimard, 2008).

Baecque, Antoine de. *The Body Politic: Corporeal Metaphor in Revolutionary France, 1770–1800* (Stanford, Calif.: Stanford University Press, 1997).

——. *Glory and Terror: Seven Deaths under the French Revolution* (New York: Routledge, 2001).

Baker, Keith M. *Condorcet: From Natural Philosophy to Social Mathematics* (Chicago: University of Chicago Press, 1974).

——. "Enlightenment and the Institution of Society: Notes for a Conceptual History." In *Main Trends in Cultural History: Ten Essays*, edited by Willem Melching and Wyger Velema (Amsterdam: Rodopi, 1994), 95–120.

——. *Inventing the French Revolution: Essays on French Political Culture in the Eighteenth Century* (Cambridge: Cambridge University Press, 1990).

Baker, Keith M., et al., eds. *The French Revolution and the Creation of Modern Political Culture.* 4 vols. (New York: Pergamon Press, 1987–1994).

Barkan, Elazar. *The Guilt of Nations: Restitution and Negotiating Historical Injustices* (New York: Norton, 2000).

Ben-Amos, Avner. *Funerals, Politics, and Memory in Modern France, 1789–1996* (Oxford: Oxford University Press, 2000).

Benz, Ernst. *The Theology of Electricity: On the Encounter and Explanation of Theology and Science in the 17th and 18th Centuries* (Allison Park, Pa.: Pickwick Publications, 1989).

Bergeron, Louis. *France Under Napoleon* (Princeton, N.J.: Princeton University Press, 1981).

Bertrand, Régis, and Anne Carol, eds. *L'exécution capitale. Une mort donnée en spectacle XVIe XXe siècle* (Aix-en-Provence: Publications de l'Université de Provence, 2003).

Bevernage, Berber. "The Past Is Evil/Evil Is Past: On Retrospective Politics, Philosophy of History, and Temporal Manichaeism." *History and Theory* 54, no. 3 (2015): 333–352.

Biard, Michel *Missionaires de la République. Les représentants du peuple en mission* (Paris: CTHS, 2002).

——, ed. *Les politiques de la Terreur, 1793–1794* (Rennes: Presses Universitaires de Rennes, 2008).

Blanc, Olivier. *Last Letters: Prisons and Prisoners of the French Revolution, 1793–1794* (New York: Farrar, Straus and Giroux, 1989).

Blanchot, Maurice. *The Writing of the Disaster* (Lincoln: University of Nebraska Press, 1986).

Blaufarb, Rafe. *The Great Demarcation: The French Revolution and the Invention of Modern Property* (Oxford: Oxford University Press, 2016).

Blum, Carol. *Rousseau and the Republic of Virtue: The Language of Politics in the French Revolution* (Ithaca, N.Y.: Cornell University Press, 1986).

Bodinier, Bernard, and Éric Teyssier. *L'événement le plus important de la Révolution. La vente des biens nationaux, 1789–1867* (Paris: Société des Études Robespierristes et Editions du CTHS, 2000).

Borneman, John. *Political Crime and the Memory of Loss* (Bloomington: Indiana University Press, 2011).

Bouloiseau, Marc. *Étude de l'émigration et de la vente des biens des émigrés (1792–1830). Instruction, sources, bibliographie, législation, tableaux* (Paris: Imprimerie nationale, 1963).

Bourdin, Philippe, ed. *La Révolution, 1789–1871. Écriture d'une histoire immediate* (Clermont Ferrand: Presses Universitaires Blaise-Pascal, 2008).

Brison, Susan. *Aftermath: Violence and the Remaking of a Self* (Princeton, N.J.: Princeton University Press, 2002).

Brooks, Peter. *The Melodramatic Imagination: Balzac, Henry James, Melodrama, and the Mode of Excess* (New Haven, Conn.: Yale University Press, 1976).

Brown, Howard. *Ending the Revolution: Violence, Justice, and Repression from the Terror to Napoleon* (Charlottesville: University of Virginia Press, 2006).

———. "Robespierre's Tail: The Possibilities of Justice after the Terror." *Canadian Journal of History* 45, no. 3 (2010): 503–535.

Brown, Howard, and Judith Miller, eds. *Taking Liberties: Problems of a New Order from the French Revolution to Napoleon* (Manchester: Manchester University Press, 2003).

Brown, Wendy. *States of Injury: Power and Freedom in Late Modernity* (Princeton, N.J.: Princeton University Press, 1995).

Brunel, Françoise. *Thermidor. La chute de Robespierre* (Brussels: Editions Complexes, 1989).

Burson, Jeffrey, and Ulrich Lehner, eds. *Enlightenment and Catholicism: A Transnational History* (South Bend, Ind.: University of Notre Dame Press, 2014).

Burton, Richard. *Blood in the City: Violence and Revelation in Paris: 1789–1945* (Ithaca, N.Y.: Cornell University Press, 2001).

Buruma, Ian. "The Joys and Perils of Victimhood." *New York Review of Books* 46, no. 6 (April 1999): 1–9.

Carpenter, Kirsty, and Philip Mansel, eds. *The French Emigrés in Europe and the Struggle against Revolution, 1789–1814* (New York: St. Martin's Press, 1999).

Caruth, Cathy. "The Claims of the Dead: History, Haunted Property, and the Law." *Critical Inquiry* 28, no. 2 (Winter 2002): 419–441.

———. *Unclaimed Experience: Trauma, Narrative, and History* (Baltimore: Johns Hopkins University Press, 1996).

Castle, Terry. *The Female Thermometer: 18th Century Culture and the Invention of the Uncanny* (Oxford: Oxford University Press, 1995).

Censer, Jack, and Lynn Hunt. "Imaging the French Revolution: Depictions of the French Revolutionary Crowd." *American Historical Review* 110, no. 1 (2005): 38–45.

Chaliand, Gérard, and Arnaud Blin. *The History of Terrorism, from Antiquity to Al Qaeda* (Berkeley: University of California Press, 2007).

Chartier, Roger. *The Cultural Origins of the French Revolution* (Durham, N.C.: Duke University Press, 1991).

Clarke, Joseph. *Commemorating the Dead in Revolutionary France: Revolution and Remembrance, 1789–1799* (Cambridge: Cambridge University Press, 2007).

Clay, Stephen. "Vengeance, Justice, and Reactions in the Revolutionary Midi." *French History* 23, no. 1 (2009): 22–46.

Cobb, Richard. *Reactions to the French Revolution* (Oxford: Oxford University Press, 1972).

Cole, Joshua. *The Power of Large Numbers: Population, Politics, and Gender in Nineteenth Century France* (Ithaca, N.Y.: Cornell University Press, 2000).

Collectif. *La Vendée. Après la Terreur, la reconstruction. Actes du colloque ténu à la Roche-sur Yon les 25, 25, et 27 Avril 1996* (Paris: Perrin, 1997).

Confino, Alon. *Foundational Pasts: The Holocaust as Historical Understanding* (Cambridge: Cambridge University Press, 2011).

Corbin, Alain. *The Foul and the Fragrant: Odor and the French Social Imagination* (Cambridge, Mass.: Harvard University Press, 1986).

——. *The Village of Cannibals: Rage and Murder in France, 1870* (Cambridge, Mass.: Harvard University Press, 1992).

Crawford, Joseph. *Gothic Fiction and the Invention of Terrorism: The Politics and Aesthetics of Fear in the Age of the Reign of Terror* (London: Bloomsbury, 2013).

Crook, Malcolm. *Elections in the French Revolution: An Apprenticeship in Democracy, 1789 1799* (Cambridge: Cambridge University Press, 1996).

Crouzet, Denis. *Les guerriers de Dieu. La violence au temps des troubles de religion.* 2 vols. (Paris: Champ Vallon, 1990).

Darnton, Robert. *The Forbidden Best-Sellers of Pre-Revolutionary France* (London: Fontana, 1997).

——. "The History of Reading." In *New Perspectives on Historical Writing*, edited by Peter Burke (Cambridge: Polity Press, 1991), 157–186.

——. *Mesmerism and the End of Enlightenment in France* (Cambridge, Mass.: Harvard University Press, 1968).

——. *Reflections in Cultural History* (London: Faber and Faber, 1990).

Davidson, Denise. "Making Society 'Legible': People-Watching in Paris after the Revolution." *French Historical Studies* 28, no. 2 (2005): 265–296.

Davis, Natalie Zemon. "The Rites of Violence: Religious Riot in Sixteenth Century France." *Past and Present* 59 (1973): 51–91.

Dawes, James. *Evil Men* (Cambridge, Mass.: Harvard University Press, 2013).

Delumeau, Jean. *La peur en occident, XIVe-XVIIIe siècles. Une cité asiégée* (Paris: Fayard, 1978).

Desan, Suzanne. "Reconstituting the Social after the Terror: Family, Property, and the Law in Popular Politics." *Past and Present* 164 (August 1999): 81–121.

——. *Reclaiming the Sacred: Lay Religion and Popular Politics in Revolutionary France* (Ithaca, N.Y.: Cornell University Press, 1990).

Di-Capua, Yoav. "Trauma and Other Historians: An Introduction." *Historical Reflections/Reflexions historiques* 41, no. 3 (2015): 1–13.

Douthwaite, Julia. *The Frankenstein of 1790 and Other Lost Chapters from Revolutionary France* (Chicago: University of Chicago Press, 2012).

——. *The Wild Girl, Natural Man, and the Monster: Dangerous Experiments in the Age of Enlightenment* (Chicago: University of Chicago Press, 2002).

Doyle, William. *The Oxford History of the French Revolution* (Oxford: Oxford University Press, 1989).

Durkheim, Emile. *The Elementary Forms of Religious Life* (New York: Free Press, 1995).

Edelstein, Dan. "War and Terror: The Law of Nations from Grotius to the French Revolution." *French Historical Studies* 31, no. 2 (2008): 229–262.

——. *The Terror of Natural Right: Republicanism, the Cult of Nature, and the French Revolution* (Chicago: University of Chicago Press, 2009).

Edmonds, W. D. *Jacobinism and the Revolt of Lyon, 1789–1793* (Oxford: Clarendon, 1990).

Elias, Norbert. *The Civilizing Process: Sociogenetic and Psychogenetic Investigations* (Oxford: Blackwell, 1994).

Elster, Jon. *Closing the Books: Transitional Justice in Historical Perspective* (Cambridge: Cambridge University Press, 2004).

——, ed. *Retribution and Reparation in the Transition to Democracy* (Cambridge: Cambridge University Press, 2006).

Etlin, Richard. *The Architecture of Death: The Transformation of the Cemetery in Eighteenth Century Paris* (Cambridge, Mass.: MIT Press, 1984).

Farcy, Jean-Claude. *Histoire de la justice française de la Révolution à nos jours. Trois décennies de recherches* (Paris: Presses Universitaires de France, 2001).

Fassin, Didier, and Richard Rechtman. *The Empire of Trauma: An Inquiry into the Condition of Victimhood* (Princeton, N.J.: Princeton University Press, 2009).

Feitlowitz, Marguerite. *A Lexicon of Terror: Argentina and the Legacies of Torture* (Oxford: Oxford University Press, 1998).

Feldman, Allen. "Violence and Vision: The Prosthetics and Aesthetics of Terror." *Public Culture* 10, no. 1 (1997): 24–60.

Felman, Shoshana. *The Juridical Unconscious: Trials and Traumas in the Twentieth Century* (Cambridge, Mass.: Harvard University Press, 2002).

Foote, Kenneth. *Shadowed Ground: America's Landscape of Violence and Tragedy* (Austin: University of Texas Press, 2003).

Ford, Caroline. *Divided Houses: Religion and Gender in Modern France* (Ithaca, N.Y.: Cornell University Press, 2005).

Foucault, Michel. *The Order of Things: An Archaeology of the Human Sciences* (New York: Vintage, 1970).

——. *Power/Knowledge: Selected Interviews and Other Writings, 1972–1977*. Edited by Colin Gordon (New York: Pantheon Books, 1980).

Friedland, Paul. *Revolutionary Actors: Representative Bodies and Theatricality in the Age of the French Revolution* (Ithaca, N.Y.: Cornell University Press, 2002).

——. *Seeing Justice Done: The Age of Spectacular Capital Punishment in France* (Oxford: Oxford University Press, 2012).

Fritzsche, Peter. *Stranded in the Present: Modern Time and the Melancholy of History* (Cambridge, Mass.: Harvard University Press, 2004).

Fukuyama, Francis. *The Origins of Political Order: From Prehuman Times to the French Revolution* (New York: Farrar, Straus and Giroux, 2011).

Fureix, Emmanuel. *La France des larmes. Deuil politiques à l'âge romantique, 1814–1840* (Seyssel: Champ Vallon, 2009).

Furet, François. *Interpreting the French Revolution* (Cambridge: Cambridge University Press, 1981).

——. *La gauche et la Révolution au milieu du XIXe siècle. Edgar Quinet et la question du jacobinisme, 1865–1870* (Paris: Hachette, 1986).

——. *Revolutionary France, 1770–1880* (Oxford: Blackwell, 1995).

Furet, François, and Denis Richet. *La Révolution française* (Paris: Fayard, 1973).

Furet, François, and Mona Ozouf, eds. *A Critical Dictionary of the French Revolution* (Cambridge, Mass.: Harvard University Press, 1989).

Gelbart, Nina Rattner. "Death in the Bathtub: Charlotte Corday and Jean-Paul Marat." In *The Human Tradition in Modern Times*, edited by Steven K. Vincent and Alison Klairmont Lingo (Lanham, Md.: Rowman and Littlefield, 2000), 17–32.

Gendron, François. *The Gilded Youth of Thermidor* (Montreal: McGill-Queen's University Press, 1993).

Gieryn, Thomas. "A Space for Place in Sociology." *Annual Review of Sociology* 26 (2000): 463–496.

Gobodo-Madikizela, Pumla. *A Human Being Died That Night: A South African Woman Confronts the Legacy of Apartheid* (New York: Mariner Books, 2003).

Godineau, Dominique. *The Women of Paris and Their French Revolution* (Berkeley: University of California Press, 1998).

Goldhammer, Jesse. *Headless Republic: Sacrificial Violence in Modern French Thought* (Ithaca, N.Y.: Cornell University Press, 2005).

Goldstein, Jan. *Console and Classify: The French Psychiatric Profession in the Nineteenth Century* (Chicago: University of Chicago Press, 1987).

——. "The Future of French History in the United States: Unapocalyptic Thoughts for the New Millennium." *French Historical Studies* 24, no. 1 (2001): 1–10.

——. "The Hysteria Diagnosis and the Politics of Anticlericalism in Late Nineteenth Century France." *Journal of Modern History* 54, no. 2 (1982): 209–239.

——. *The Post-Revolutionary Self: Politics and Psyche in France, 1750–1850* (Cambridge, Mass.: Harvard University Press, 2005).

Gomez-Le Chevanton, Corinne. "Le procés Carrier. Enjeux politiques, pédagogie collective et construction mémorielle." *Annales historiques de la Révolution française*, no. 343 (January–March 2006): 73–92.

Goodman, Dena. *The Republic of Letters: A Cultural History of the French Enlightenment* (Ithaca, N.Y.: Cornell University Press, 1996).

Gordon, Avery. *Ghostly Matters: Ghosts and the Sociological Imagination* (Minneapolis: University of Minnesota Press, 1997).

Gordon, Robert. "Undoing Historical Injustice." In *Justice and Injustice in Law and Legal Theory*, edited by Austin Sarat and Thomas R. Kearns (Ann Arbor: University of Michigan Press, 1996), 35–66.

Greer, Donald. *The Incidence of the Emigration during the French Revolution* (Cambridge, Mass.: Harvard University Press, 1951).

——. *The Incidence of the Terror during the French Revolution: A Statistical Interpretation* (Cambridge, Mass.: Harvard University Press, 1935).

Gueniffey, Patrice. *La politique de la Terreur. Essai sur la violence révolutionnaire, 1789–1794* (Paris: Fayard, 2000).

——. *Le nombre et la raison. La Révolution française et les élections* (Paris: EHESS, 1993).

Hanson, Paul. *The Jacobin Republic under Fire: The Federalist Revolt in the French Revolution* (University Park: Pennsylvania State University Press, 2003).

Harder, Mette. "A Second Terror: The Purges of French Revolutionary Legislators after Thermidor." *French Historical Studies* 38, no. 1 (2015): 33–60.

Harrison, Carol. *Romantic Catholics: France's Postrevolutionary Generation in Search of a Modern Faith* (Ithaca, N.Y.: Cornell University Press, 2014).

Hazan, Eric. *A People's History of the French Revolution* (London: Verso, 2014).

Hazareesingh, Sudhir. *From Subjects to Citizens: The Second Empire and the Emergence of Modern French Democracy* (Princeton, N.J.: Princeton University Press, 1998).

Habermas, Jürgen. *The Structural Transformation of the Public Sphere: An Inquiry into a Category of Bourgeois Society* (Cambridge, Mass.: the MIT Press, 1989).

Herman, Judith. *Trauma and Recovery: The Aftermath of Violence—from Domestic Abuse to Political Terror* (New York: Basic Books, 1992).

Hesse, Carla. "The Law of the Terror." *Modern Language Notes* 114, no. 4 (1999): 702–718.

Heuevel, Gerd van der. "Terreur, Terroriste, Terrorisme." In *Handbuch politisch-sozialer Grundbegriffe in Frankreich, 1680–1820*, 21 vols., edited by Rolf Reichardt and Eberhard Schmitt (Munich: Oldenbourg, 1985–), 3:89–132.

Higonnet, Patrice. "Terror, Trauma, and the 'Young Marx' Explanation of Jacobin Politics." *Past and Present* 191 (May 2006): 121–164.

Hintermeyer, Pascal. *Politiques de la mort* (Paris: Payot, 1981).

Hobson, Marian. *The Object of Art: The Theory of Illusion in Eighteenth Century France* (Cambridge: Cambridge University Press, 1982).

Hoffman, Bruce. *Inside Terrorism* (New York: Columbia University Press, 2006).

Huet, Marie-Hélène. *Mourning Glory: The Will of the French Revolution* (Philadelphia: University of Pennsylvania Press, 1997).

Hufton, Olwen. "Women without Men: Widows and Spinsters in Britain and France in the Eighteenth Century." *Journal of Family History* 9, no. 4 (1984): 355–376.

Hunt, Lynn. "The Experience of Revolution." *French Historical Studies* 32, no. 4 (2009): 671–678.

——. *The Family Romance of the French Revolution* (Berkeley: University of California Press, 1992).

——. *Politics, Culture, and Class in the French Revolution* (Berkeley: University of California Press, 1984).

——. "The World We Have Gained: The Future of the French Revolution." *American Historical Review* 108, no. 1 (2003): 1–19.

——. *Writing History in the Global Era* (New York: Norton, 2014).

Jainchill, Andrew. *Reimagining Politics after the Terror: The Republican Origins of French Liberalism* (Ithaca, N.Y.: Cornell University Press, 2008).

Janes, Regina. "Beheadings." *Representations*, no. 35 (Summer 1991): 21–51.

Jones, Colin. "The Great Chain of Buying: Medical Advertisement, the Bourgeois Public Sphere, and the Origins of the French Revolution." *American Historical Review* 101, no. 1 (1996): 13–40.

Jordan, David. *The King's Trial: Louis XVI vs. the French Revolution* (Berkeley: University of California Press, 1979).

Jouanna, Arlette. *The Saint-Bartholomew Day Massacre: The Mysteries of a Crime of State* (Manchester: Manchester University Press, 2015).

Jourdan, Annie. "Les discours de la terreur à l'époque révolutionnaire (1776–1798): Etude comparative sur une notion ambiguë." *French Historical Studies* 36, no. 1 (2013): 51–81.

——. *Les monuments de la Révolution, 1770–1804. Une histoire de représentation* (Paris: Honoré Champion, 1997).

Kafka, Benjamin. "The Demon of Writing: Paperwork, Public Safety, and the Reign of Terror." *Representations* 98, no. 1 (2007): 1–24.

Kaplan, Ann. *Trauma Culture: The Politics of Terror and Loss in Media and Literature* (New Brunswick, N.J.: Rutgers University Press, 2005).

Kingston, Ralph. *Bureaucrats and Bourgeois Society: Office Politics and Individual Credit in France, 1789–1848* (Basingstoke, UK: Palgrave Macmillan, 2012).

Kritz, Neil ed. *Transitional Justice: How Emerging Democracies Reckon with Former Regimes*. 3 vols. (Washington D.C.: United States Institute of Peace, 1995).

Kroen, Sheryl. *Politics and Theater: The Crisis of Legitimacy in Restoration France, 1815–1830* (Berkeley: University of California Press, 2000).

Kselman, Thomas. *Death and the Afterlife in Modern France* (Princeton, N.J.: Princeton University Press, 1993).

Kwass, Michael. *Contraband: Louis Mandrin and the Making of a Global Underground* (Cambridge, Mass.: Harvard University Press, 2014).

LaCapra, Dominick. *Writing History, Writing Trauma* (Baltimore: Johns Hopkins University Press, 2000).

Lagrée, Michel, and Jeanne Roche. *Tombes de mémoire. La dévotion populaire aux victimes de la Révolution dans l'Ouest* (Rennes: Editions Apogée, 1993).

Landes, Joan. *Women and the Public Sphere in the Age of the French Revolution* (Ithaca, N.Y.: Cornell University Press, 1988).

Laqueur, Walter. *A History of Terrorism* (New Brunswick, N.J.: Transaction, 2001).

Lassère, Madeleine. *Villes et cimetières en France de l'ancien régime à nos jours. Le territoire des morts* (Paris: L'harmattan, 1997).

Lefebvre, Georges. *The Thermidorians and the Directory: Two Phases of the French Revolution* (New York: Random House, 1964).

Levie, Françoise. *Étienne-Gaspard Robertson. La vie d'un phantasmagore* (Longeuill, Quebec: Le préambule, 1990).

Lewis, Gwynne, and Colin Lucas, eds. *Beyond the Terror: Essays in French Regional and Social History, 1794–1815* (Cambridge: Cambridge University Press, 1983).

Leys, Ruth. *Trauma: A Genealogy* (Chicago: University of Chicago Press, 2000).

Linton, Marisa. *Choosing Terror: Virtue, Friendship, and Authenticity in the French Revolution* (Oxford: Oxford University Press, 2013).

——. *The Politics of Virtue in Enlightenment France* (Basingstoke, UK: Macmillan, 2001).

Livesey, James. *Making Democracy in the French Revolution* (Cambridge, Mass.: Harvard University Press, 2001).

Lucas, Colin. "Revolutionary Violence, the People, and the Terror." In *The French Revolution and the Creation of Modern Political Culture*, 4 vols., edited by Keith M. Baker et al. (New York: Pergamon Press, 1987–1994), 4:57–80.

——. *The Structure of the Terror: The Example of Javogues and the Loire* (Oxford: Oxford University Press, 1972).

——. "The Theory and Practice of Denunciation in the French Revolution." *Journal of Modern History* 68, no. 4 (1996): 768–785.

Luzzatto, Sergio. *L'automne de la Révolution. Luttes et cultures politiques dans la France thermidorienne* (Paris: Champion, 2001).

——. *Mémoire de la Terreur. Vieux montagnards et jeune républicains au XIXe siècle* (Lyon: Presses Universitaires de Lyon, 1991).

Maier, Charles S. "Overcoming the Past? Narrative and Negotiation, Remembering, and Reparation: Issues at the Interface of History and the Law." In *Politics and the Past: On Repairing Historical Injustices*, edited by John Torpey (New York: Rowman and Littlefield, 2003), 295–304.

Mannoni, Laurent. *The Great Art of Light and Shadow: An Archaeology of the Cinema* (Exeter: University of Exeter Press, 2000).

Martin, Jean-Clément. *Violence et Révolution. Essai sur la naissance d'un mythe nationale* (Paris: Seuil, 2006).

Mason, Laura. "The 'Bosom of Proof': Criminal Justice and the Renewal of Oral Culture during the French Revolution." *Journal of Modern History* 76, no. 1 (2004): 29–61.

———. *Singing the French Revolution: Popular Culture and Politics, 1787–1799* (Ithaca, N.Y.: Cornell University Press, 1996).

——, ed. "Thermidor and the French Revolution." Special Forum. *French Historical Studies* 38, no. 1 (2015) and 39, no. 3 (2016).

Mathiez, Albert. *After Robespierre: The Thermidorian Reaction* (New York: Grosset and Dunlap, 1965).

———. *The French Revolution* (New York: Russell and Russell, 1962).

Maza, Sarah. *The Myth of the Bourgeoisie: An Essay on the Social Imaginary, 1750–1850* (Cambridge, Mass.: Harvard University Press, 2005).

———. *Private Lives and Public Affairs: The Causes Célèbres of Prerevolutionary France* (Berkeley: University of California Press, 1995).

Mazeau, Guillaume. *Le bain de l'histoire: Charlotte Corday et l'attentat contre Marat (1793 2009)* (Seysell: Champ Vallon, 2009).

McCorristine, Shane. *Specters of the Self: Thinking about Ghosts and Ghost-Seeing in England, 1750–1920* (Cambridge: Cambridge University Press, 2010).

McManners, John. *Church and Society in Eighteenth Century France.* 2 vols. (Oxford: Oxford University Press, 1998).

———. *Death and the Enlightenment: Changing Attitudes to Death among Christians and Unbelievers in Eighteenth Century France* (Oxford: Oxford University Press, 1981).

McPhee, Peter. *Liberty or Death: The French Revolution* (New Haven, Conn.: Yale University Press, 2016).

Mellon, Stanley. *The Political Uses of History: A Study of Historians in the French Restoration* (Stanford, Calif.: Stanford University Press, 1958).

Melton, James Van Horn. *The Rise of the Public in Enlightenment Europe* (Cambridge: Cambridge University Press, 2001).

Meyer, Arno. *The Furies: Violence and Terror in the French and Russian Revolutions* (Princeton, N.J.: Princeton University Press, 2001).

Micale, Mark S., and Paul Lerner, eds. *Traumatic Pasts: History, Psychiatry, and Trauma in the Modern Age, 1870–1930* (Cambridge: Cambridge University Press, 2001).

Michaud, Yves. *La violence apprivoisée* (Paris: Hachette, 1996).

Miles, Robert. "The 1790s: the Effulgence of the Gothic." In *The Cambridge Companion to Gothic Fiction*, edited by Jerrold E. Hogle (Cambridge: Cambridge University Press, 2002), 41–62.

Miller, Mary Ashburn. *A Natural History of the French Revolution: Violence and Nature in the French Revolutionary Imagination, 1789–1794* (Ithaca, N.Y.: Cornell University Press, 2011).

Minow, Martha. *Between Vengeance and Forgiveness: Facing History after Genocide and Mass Violence* (Boston: Beacon Press, 1998).

Mitchell, W. J. T. *Cloning Terror: The War of Images, 9/11 to the Present* (Chicago: University of Chicago Press, 2011).

Mouffe, Chantal. *The Democratic Paradox* (London: Verso, 2005).

Mowery, Richard Andrews. *Law, Magistracy, and Crime in Old Regime Paris, 1735–1789: Volume 1, the System of Criminal Justice* (Cambridge: Cambridge University Press, 1994).

Nora, Pierre, ed. *Les liuex des mémoire*. 3 vols. (Paris: Gallimard, 1984).

Nye, Robert. *Masculinity and Male Codes of Honor in Modern France* (Berkeley: University of California Press, 1998).

Oliver, Bette. *Surviving the French Revolution: A Bridge across Time* (Lanham, Md.: Lexington Books, 2013).

Ophir, Adi. *Divine Violence: Two Essays on God and Disaster* [Hebrew] (Tel-Aviv: Hakibbutz Hameuchad, 2013).

Outram, Dorinda. *The Body and the French Revolution: Sex, Class, and Political Culture* (New Haven, Conn.: Yale University Press, 1989).

Palmer, R. R. *Twelve Who Ruled: The Year of the Terror in the French Revolution* (Princeton, N.J.: Princeton University Press, 1941).

Popkin, Jeremy. *Revolutionary News: The Press in France, 1789–1799* (Durham, N.C.: Duke University Press, 1990).

Postone, Moishe, and Eric Santner, eds. *Catastrophe and Meaning: The Holocaust and the Twentieth Century* (Chicago: University of Chicago Press, 2003).

Purnell, Carolyn. *The Sensational Past: How the Enlightenment Changed the Way We Use Our Senses* (New York: Norton, 2017).

Quinlan, Sean. "Physical and Moral Regeneration after the Terror: Medical Culture, Sensibility, and Family Politics in France, 1794–1804." *Social History* 29, no. 2 (2004): 139–164.

Reddy, William. *The Navigation of Feeling: A Framework for the History of Emotions* (Cambridge: Cambridge University Press, 2001).

Resnick, Daniel. *The White Terror and the Political Reaction after Waterloo* (Cambridge, Mass.: Harvard University Press, 1966).

Rey, Roseleyne. *The History of Pain* (Cambridge, Mass.: Harvard University Press, 1995).

Roht-Arriaza, Naomi, and Javier Mariezcurrena, eds. *Transitional Justice in the Twenty-First Century: Beyond Truth versus Justice* (Cambridge: Cambridge University Press, 2006).

Rosanvallon, Pierre. *L'état en France, de 1789 à nos jours* (Paris: Seuil, 1990).

Rosenberg, Tina. "Tipping the Scales of Justice." *World Policy Journal* 12, no. 3 (1995): 55–64.

Rosenfeld, Sophia. *A Revolution in Language: The Problem of Signs in Late Eighteenth Century France* (Stanford, Calif.: Stanford University Press, 2001).

Rothberg, Michael. "Decolonizing Trauma Studies: A Response." *Studies in the Novel* 40, nos. 1–2 (2008): 224–234.

Ruff, Julius. *Violence in Early Modern Europe, 1500–1800* (Cambridge: Cambridge University Press, 2001).

Scarry, Elaine. *The Body in Pain: The Making and Unmaking of the World* (Oxford: Oxford University Press, 1985).

Schama, Simon. *Citizens: A Chronicle of the French Revolution* (New York: Knopf, 1989).

Sewell, William H., Jr. "Historical Events as Transformations of Structures: Inventing Revolution at the Bastille." *Theory and Society* 25, no. 6 (1996): 841–881.

——. *Work and Revolution in France: The Language of Labor from the Old Regime to 1848* (Cambridge: Cambridge University Press, 1980).

Shapiro, Barry. *Traumatic Politics: The Deputies and the King in the Early French Revolution* (University Park: Pennsylvania State University Press, 2009).

Sheehan, Jonathan. "Enlightenment, Religion, and the Enigma of Secularization: A Review Essay." *American Historical Review* 208, no. 4 (2003): 1061–1080.

Singer, Brian C. J. *Society, Theory, and the French Revolution* (New York: St. Martin's Press, 1986).

Smith, Jay M., ed. *The French Nobility in the Eighteenth Century: Reassessments and New Approaches* (University Park: Pennsylvania State University Press, 2006).

Smith, Philip. "The Elementary Forms of Place and Their Transformations: A Durkheimian Model." *Qualitative Sociology* 22, no. 1 (1999): 13–36.

Soboul, Albert. *The French Revolution 1787–1799: From the Storming of the Bastille to Napoleon* (New York: Random House, 1974).

——. *The Sans-Culottes: The Popular Movement and Revolutionary Government, 1793–1794* (Princeton, N.J.: Princeton University Press, 1972).

Soll, Jacob. *The Reckoning: Financial Accountability and the Rise and Fall of Nations* (New York: Basic Books, 2014).

Spang, Rebecca. *The Invention of the Restaurant: Paris and Modern Gastronomic Culture* (Cambridge Mass.: Harvard University Press, 2000).

——. *Stuff and Money in the Time of the French Revolution* (Cambridge, Mass.: Harvard University Press, 2015).

Spitzer, Alan. *The French Generation of 1820* (Princeton, N.J.: Princeton University Press, 1987).

——. *Old Hatreds and Young Hopes: The French Carbonari against the Bourbon Restoration* (Cambridge, Mass.: Harvard University Press, 1971).

Stafford, Barbara. *Artful Science: Enlightenment, Entertainment, and the Eclipse of Visual Education* (Cambridge, Mass.: MIT Press, 1994).

Staum, Martin. *Cabanis: Enlightenment and Medical Philosophy in the French Revolution* (Princeton, N.J.: Princeton University Press, 1980).

Steinberg, Ronen. "Somber Historiographies: The French Revolution, the Holocaust, and Alon Confino's Concept of Foundational Pasts." *Storia della storiografia* 66, no. 2 (2014): 87–100.

——. "Trauma and the Effects of Mass Violence in Revolutionary France: A Critical Inquiry." *Historical Reflections/Reflexions historiques* 41, no. 3 (2015): 28–46.

Sutherland, Donald M. G. *France 1789–1815: Revolution and Counter-Revolution* (Oxford: Oxford University Press, 1986).

——, ed. "Violence and the French Revolution." Special Issue. *Historical Reflections/Réflexions historiques* 29, no. 3 (2003).

——. *Murder in the Aubagne: Lynching, Law, and Justice during the French Revolution* (Cambridge: Cambridge University Press, 2009).

Tackett, Timothy. *The Coming of the Terror in the French Revolution* (Cambridge, Mass.: Harvard University Press, 2015).

——. *Religion, Revolution, and Regional Culture in Eighteenth-Century France: The Ecclesiastical Oath of 1791* (Princeton, N.J.: Princeton University Press, 1986).

Taussig, Michael. *The Nervous System* (New York: Routledge, 1992).

Teitel, Ruti. *Transitional Justice* (Oxford: Oxford University Press, 2000).

Thomas, Keith. *Religion and the Decline of Magic* (London: Weidenfeld and Nicolson, 1971).

Torpey, John. *Making Whole What Has Been Smashed: On Reparation Politics* (Cambridge, Mass.: Harvard University Press, 2006).

Trouillot, Michel-Rolph. *Silencing the Past: Power and the Production of History* (Boston: Beacon Press, 1997).

Turner, Victor. *Dramas, Fields, and Metaphors: Symbolic Action in Human Society* (Ithaca, N.Y.: Cornell University Press, 1974).

——. *The Ritual Process: Structure and Anti-Structure* (New Brunswick, N.J.: Transaction, 1969).

Van Klay, Dale. "Christianity as Causality and Chrysalis of Modernity: The Problem of Dechristianization in the French Revolution." *American Historical Review* 108, no. 4 (2003): 1081–1104.

Verdery, Katherine. *The Political Lives of Dead Bodies: Reburial and Postsocialist Change* (New York: Columbia University Press, 1999).

Vovelle, Michel, ed. *Le tournant de l'an III. Réaction et Terreur blanche dans la France révolutionnaire* (Paris: CTHS, 1997).

——. *L'image de la Révolution française*. 4 vols. (Paris: Pergamon Press, 1990).

Wahnich, Sophie. *In Defence of the Terror: Liberty or Death in the French Revolution* (London: Verso, 2012).

——. *L'impossible citoyen. L'étranger dans le discours de la Révolution* (Paris: Albin Michel, 1997).

Walton, Charles. *Policing Public Opinion in the French Revolution: The Culture of Calumny and the Problem of Free Speech* (Oxford: Oxford University Press, 2009).

Walzer, Michael. *Regicide and Revolution: Speeches at the Trial of Louis XVI* (Cambridge: Cambridge University Press, 1974).

Wickberg, Daniel. "What Is the History of Sensibilities? On Cultural Histories, Old and New." *American Historical Review* 112, no. 3 (2007): 661–684.

Williams, Raymond. *Marxism and Literature* (Oxford: Oxford University Press, 1977).

Woloch, Isser. *The New Regime: Transformations of French Civic Order, 1789–1820s* (New York: Norton, 1994).

Woronoff, Denis. *The Thermidorean Regime and the Directory, 1794–1799* (Cambridge: Cambridge University Press, 1984).

Wright, Gordon. *Between the Guillotine and Liberty: Two Centuries of the Crime Problem in France* (Oxford: Oxford University Press, 1985).

Young, Allan. *The Harmony of Illusions: Inventing Post Traumatic Stress Disorder* (Princeton, N.J.: Princeton University Press, 1995).

Zizek, Joseph. "'Plumes de fer': Louis-Marie Prudhomme Writes the French Revolution." *French Historical Studies* 26, no. 4 (2003): 619–660.

INDEX

Italicized page numbers indicate illustrations. Page numbers followed by n indicate notes.

Abbot, Andrew, 82
Accountability: derivation of word, 47; types of ministerial accountability, 45
Accountability, as fundamental principle of Revolution, 13, 15, 43–64, 148; denunciations and retributive turn, 51–54; inviolability and accountability after Terror, 48–51; Le Bon, accusations against and theme of virtue, 43, 49, 56–62, 58; Le Bon's defense at trial, 43, 44–45, 54, 61–64, 117–18; Le Bon's execution, 43, 64; Le Bon's work as *représentant en mission* in North, 43, 54–56; pre-revolutionary transitional justice and, 44–48; pre-Revolution judicial practices, 46–47
Aldini, Giovani, 136–38, 191n88
Algeria, 135
Almanach des prisons, 73
Alpaugh, Micah, 24
Ami de la religion et du Roi, L' (newspaper), 108
Ami du peuple, L' (newspaper), 27
Amnesty: National Convention decrees and, 14, 43, 146; restitution and, 83
Annulment (*cassation, annulation*), rehabilitation and, 76–77
Arendt, Hannah, 48
Ariès, Philippe, 93, 100
Assoun, Paul-Laurent, 95, 109
Austria, 20, 68–69

Babeuf, Gracchus, 53
Baczko, Bronislaw, 8–9, 13, 28, 44, 52, 118
Baker, Keith, 15
Bakhtin, Mikhail, 106
Balzac, Honoré de, 89, 90–91
Barère, Bertrand, 28, 59, 133
Barnave, Antoine, 24–25
Bastille, storming of: commemoration of, 93–94; violence and, 6, 7, 19, 23–24

Baudin, Pierre, 146
Bayle-Mouillard, Elizabeth-Félicie, 143
Beauharnais, vicomte de, 107
Beccaria, Cesare, 26, 142
Belisarius Begging for Alms (David), 87
Berry, duc de, 108, 142
Bertier de Sauvigny, Louis Bénigne François, 24, 106
Biard, Michel, 61
Bibliothèque bleue (pamphlets), 22
Biens des condamnés. See Restitution, for *les biens des condamnés*
Biens nationaux de deuxième origine (second-round properties), 68–69
Biens nationaux de premiére origine (first-round properties), 67–68
Blanchot, Maurice, 41
Blanquet-Rouville, Charles, 79
Blaufarb, Rafe, 68
Boissy d'Anglas, François Antoine de, 65–66, 84–85
Bonfils, J. F., 141
Boraine, Alex, 149–50
Bordeu, Théophile de, 140
Borges, Jorge Luis, 38
Bornemen, John, 132
Boullée, Étienne-Louis, 102
Bourdon de l'Oise, 83
Boverie, Joseph Golvan Thouault de la, 26
Brièrre de Boismont, Alexandre Jacques François, 141
Brillat-Savarin, Jean-Antelme, 25–26
Brissot, Jacques Pierre, 78
Brontë, Emily, 123
Brossard, Julien Fructidor, 40
Brotteaux, cenotaph at, 101–2, *103*, 111–12, *113*, 116
Brown, Harold, *9*, 44, 47
Brown, Wendy, 151

Burke, Edmund, 24, 46
"Burocratie," 31–32

Cabanis, Pierre Jean George, 135
Cabarrus, Thérésia, 29
Café des Chartres, 119, 120
Cahiers de doléances (lists of grievances), 45, 68
Caligula, references and comparisons to, 28, 61
Cambacérès, Jean-Jacques, 109
Cambon, Pierre-Joseph, 53, 133
Capital responsibility, 45
Capuchin Convent, Robertson's phantasmagoria and, 125, 127, 130
Carbonari, 114
Carnot, Lazare, 81
Carrier, Jean-Baptiste: indictment of, 77; trial of, 13, 52–53, 56; wolf story about, 124–25
Caruth, Cathy, 121
Castle, Terry, 128
Cataclysmic events, pre-Revolutionary attitudes toward, 19–23, 42
Catholic cult of the dead, 93
Celestial Emporium of Benevolent Knowledge (Borges), 38
Chamber of Peers, 65, 110
Charles X, king, 89
Chénier, André, 73
Chénier, Marie-Joseph, 73
Chevalier, Madame, 129
Children: foster care and, 69; named during Revolution, 39; property restoration and, 66–67, 68, 72, 75–76, 85; renamed after Revolution, 14, 40–41, 147
Chinard, Joseph, 102
Choderlos de Laclos, Pierre, 96
Church lands, confiscation and sale of, 67–68, 86
Cimetière de la Madeleine, Le (Regnault-Warin), 104–5, 106
Cimetière de la Madeleine, Le (Villemain d'Abancourt), 105–6
Cimetière de Mousseaux, Le (Villemain d'Abancourt), 105–6
Cimetières des suppliciés (cemeteries of the punished): locations of, 95–97; reactions of Parisians to, 97–98
Civil responsibility, 45
Clarissa (Richardson), 57
Cobb, Richard, 157n44
Cochet, Claude, 102, 113
Colonel Chabert, Le (Balzac), 89, 90–91
Committee of General Security, 49

Committee of Public Safety, 27, 28, 43, 49, 55, 59, 65, 69, 81, 133, 151
Compte Rendu (Necker), 22, 47
Compte rendu aux sans-culottes (Tisset), 35
Condé, prince of, 69
Conduit politique, of writers, 73
Confino, Alan, 10–11
Consciousness. See Decapitation and consciousness, debates about
Constituent Assembly, 33, 45, 67–68
Constitution of 1791, 45, 48, 50
Contagion, theories of, 143–44
Corbin, Alain, 24, 27, 166n103
Corday, Charlotte, 134–35
Correspondance entre les vivans et les morts (pamphlet), 117–21
Council of Five Hundred, 40, 78, 79, 81, 99–100
Courtois, E. B., 61
Crawford, Joseph, 14, 124
Cri des familles, Les (pamphlet), 85
Criminal or penal responsibility, 45
Crocker, John Wilson, 6

Damas, duc de, 111
d'Angoulême, duchesse, 112
Danton, Georges, 45, 49, 96
d'Artois, comte, 112
Daubermesnil, François Antoine, 99
Dauchez, Jean-Baptist, 40–41
David, Jacques-Louis, 87
Davidson, Denise, 40
Death, remembrance and transformation of attitudes about, 93–94
Death penalty: abolished for political crimes, 141; debates about, 12, 25–26, 142–44; National Convention rejects abolition of, 146. See also Executions
de Baecque, Antoine, 92
de Baudus, Amable, 111
Decapitation and consciousness, debates about, 133–38, 137, 144
Dechézeaux, widow of Gustave, 78
DeChristianization campaign, in Year II, 94
Declaration of the Rights of Man and Citizen, 47
Delamalle (citizen), 99
Delandine, Antoine-François, 101–2
de Salm-Kyrburg, Amélie, 107
Desan, Suzanne, 74
Descuret, Jean-Baptiste-Félix, 143–44
Desmoulins, Camille, 96
Dickens, Charles, 95, 123
Dictionnaire de l'Académie française, 24, 47, 76

Difficult past, Terror seen as, 2, 17–42; ambivalence toward violence and, 19, 25, 42, 95, 98; attitudes toward violence and cataclysmic events before Revolution, 19–23, 27, 42; "coming to terms" with past, 41, 168n131; debates about violence during Revolution, 23–26, 42; ideology and preoccupation with names, 39–41; instability after, and need to define Terror, 2, 17–19; language and violence, 30–32; Prudhomme's catalogue of Revolution's crimes, 32–38, 35, 37; Revolution as rupture in symbolic order, 31, 166n91; Revolution's meaning transformed, 27–30

Directory, 9, 32, 81, 99, 104

d'Ivernois, François, 36, 84, 87

Divine will versus human action, pre-Revolution attitudes toward violence and, 19, 21, 23

Double-entry bookkeeping, accountability and, 46

Douthwaite, Julia, 105, 136

Droit des gens, Le (Vattel), 70–71

Dubbary, Jean-Baptist, 70

Dufour, Louis, 40

Dupont, Felicité, 78

Durkheim, Emil, 98

Dussault, Jean-Joseph, 17

Duval, Georges, 17

Émigrés, seizure of property of, 68–69, 70–71

Edelman, Frèderic, 75–76

Edelman, Louis, 75–76

Emile (Rousseau), 63

Encyclopédie, 85, 93, 110

Enlightenment: cast as original sin, 108; death and, 93–94, 97; guillotine and, 136; internal pathology of ghosts and, 125, 128–29, 138, 144; political culture of Revolution, and, 98; pre-Revolution attitudes toward violence and, 20; violence and, 148

Enragés, 119, 120

Épinard, Joseph Pâris de l,' 72

Errancis cemetary, 96

Estates-General, 39, 45, 68

Executions: lynchings during Revolution, 24–25; ordered by Le Bon, 53, 56; Terror's need for, 18. *See also* Death penalty

Exhumations and reburials, 91, 94–95, 108–9, 114–16, 118, 147

Fassin, Didier, 12

Fauvety, Jean, 53–54

Fear, Tallien and Terror's use of, 18

Feeling. *See* Structure of feeling

Feldman, Allen, 126

Féraud, Jean-Bertrand, 65

Fiedler, Leslie, 131

"Fields of care," mass graves turned into, 100

Fiscal accountability, 46

Flaubert, Gustave, 147

Foote, Kenneth, 100

Foucault, Michel, 38

Foullon de Doué, Joseph, 106

"Foundational pasts," 10–11

Fouquier-Tinville, Antoine, 28, 50, 53, 80

Fourcroy, Antoine François, 100

Foy, General, 109

Frankenstein (Shelley), 138

Franklin, Benjamin, 132

Fréron, Stanislas, 60, 61–62, 85–86

Friedland, Paul, 26

Fureix, Emmanuel, 109

Furet, François, 44, 48

Galvani, Luigi, 130, 136

Galvanism, 130, 136, 137, 143, 191n88

Gazzette du département du Nord, 72

Gembloux, Claude Charles Pierquin de, 143–44

General and Impartial History of the Errors, Offenses, and Crimes Committed during the French Revolution (Prudhomme), 33–38, 35, 37

General responsibility, 45

"General Table of the Disasters of the French Revolution, A". *See General and Impartial History of the Errors, Offenses, and Crimes Committed during the French Revolution* (Prudhomme)

General Will principle, of Rousseau, 6

Ghostly presence, of Terror, 15, 117–45; concept of trauma and, 118–19, 121–22; in *Correspondance entre les vivans et les morts*, 117–21; debates about death penalty, 142–44; debates about decapitation and consciousness, 133–38, 137; physicians and mental and public health issues, 138–42; visual culture and, 124–33, 127; Williams's "structure of feeling" and, 119, 122–23

Girey-Dupré, mother of Jean-Marie, 72–73

Girondins, 27, 40, 52, 73, 78, 87, 96, 109, 132

Glass harmonica, phantasmagoria and, 132

Gobodo-Madikizela, Pumla, 147
Goldstein, Jan, 11, 141
Gomez-Le Chevanton, Corinne, 44
Goncourt, Edmund and Jules, 147
Gordon, Avery, 12, 118
Gordon, Robert, 86
Gothic, the: fiction and, 124–25; phantasmagoria and, 130–32; severed head and, 136
Goujon (*conventionnel*), 49
Goupilleau, Jean-François, 101
Great Fear of 1789, 49
Guffroy, Armand, 54–55, 58–59
Guillotine, 1, 54, 165n83; cemeteries and, 95–96, 101, 109; LeBon and, 56, 60, 64; National Convention and, 14, 146; Tisset and, 35; visual culture and coming to terms with, 124, 126, 131. *See also* Decapitation and consciousness, debates about
Guitard, J.-F., 140
Guizot, François, 143
Guyomar, Pierre, 83

Habermas, Jürgen, 21–22
Harder, Mette, 29
Hastings, Warren, 46
Haunting. *See* Ghostly presence, of Terror
Hélyot (widow), 77
Hemey d'Auberive, Philibert Nicolas, 135
Henry IV, king, 94
Hérault de Séchelles, Marie-Jean, 45
Herman, Judith, 121
History, Prudhomme's lists and new way of writing, 34–36
Hoffman, Bruce, 126
Holocaust, 10–13, 116, 122, 149, 151
Hufton, Olwen, 75
Hunt, Lynn, 4, 11, 15, 23

Innocents, Les, 97
Inviolability, justice and, 48, 49–50, 85
Islam, Algeria and, 135

Jacobins, 29, 83, 94, 102, 125, 129; repression and, 52, 53, 58, 61, 73; White Terror and, 13, 132–33, 142; widows' pensions and, 78
Jainchill, Andrew, 59
James, Regina, 136
Jaucort, Chevalier Louis de, 93
Javogues, Claude, 102
Jeunesse dorée, 120
Josephine, empress, Robertson's phantasmagoria and, 125
Jourdan, Annie, 18, 29

Kolly, Paul Pierre, 69
Krug, Wilhelm Traugott, 8

Lacan, Jacques, 166n91
Lafayette, Madame, 107
Laïcité, 21
Lamoignon de Malesherbes, Guillaume-Chrétien de, 65–66
Lamotte (widow), 75
Language, instability of and Terror as difficult past, 30–32
Lanjuinais, Jean-Denis, 109
Lavoisier, Antoine, 100, 131
Lavoisier, widow of Antoine, 87
Law of Suspects, 14, 69, 87
Le Bon, Emile, 147
Le Bon, Joseph, 13, 50, 51, 146; accusations against and theme of virtue, 43, 49, 56–62, 58; defense at trial, 43, 44–45, 54, 61–64, 117–18; execution of, 43, 64; pre-Revolutionary life, 54–55; work as *représentant en mission* in North, 43, 54–56
Lecointre, Laurent, 49, 82
Legendre, Louis, 49
Lewis, Matthew, 124
Lezay-Marnésia, Adrien de, 6
"Liberal authoritarianism," 9
Liberal democracy, transitional justice and, 150
Lindet, Robert, 50, 151–52
Linton, Marisa, 148
Lisbon Earthquake (1755), pre-Revolution attitudes toward violence and, 20, 21
Literacy, seventeenth and eighteenth century rates of and ties to emergence of public sphere, 22–23
Louis, Antoine, 134
Louis XIV, king, 5, 94
Louis XVI, king, 87, 147; burial of, 96; execution of, 65, 98; exhumation and reburial of, 91, 108, 109; monument at La Madeleine, 109–10; renamed Louis Capet, 39, 87; Robertson's phantasmagoria and, 131; trial of, 47–48
Louis XVIII, king, 66, 108–9, 112
Loustalot, Elysée, 24
Louvet, Jean-Baptiste, 87
Loye, Paul, 134
Lucas, Colin, 55
Luzzatto, Sergio, 59
Lycanthropy (belief in the transformation of humans into wolves), 125

Lynching, Revolutionary violence and, 24–25. *See also* Executions

Lyon, 91, 96; cenotaph at Brotteaux and commemorations of dead, 101–2, *103*, 107, 109, 111–13, *113*; effects of bombardment of, 39, 138–39; renaming after Revolution, 39

Madeleine, La, burials and exhumations at, 91, 95–96, 104–6, 108, 109–10

Magic lanterns, 132, 190n61

Maier, Charles, 66

Mannoni, Laurent, 132

Marat, Jean-Paul: assassination of, 24, 27; exhumation and reburial of, 52, 92; Robertson's phantasmagoria and, 125, 131

Marie-Antoinette, queen: burial of, 96; execution of, 129; exhumation and reburial of, 91, 108; monument at La Madeleine, 109–10

Marie-Thérèse, 147

Martin, Jean-Clément, 5, 11, 29

Marxist theory, structure of feeling and, 122–23

Mass graves, remembrance and, 14, 15, 90–116; *cimetières des suppliciés* (cemeteries of the punished), 95–98; criminal corpses and, 97–98; expiatory chapels constructed during Restoration, 91–92, 108–16; first commemorations of, 99–102, *103*, 115; history before Terror, 95–96; Napoleonic era and, 91, 104–8, 115; politicization of memories of dead and transformation of attitudes toward death, 92–95; visual culture and coming to terms with, 126

Maternal impression, theory of, 143

Matthieu, Jean-Baptiste, 49, 83

Mathiez, Albert, 43–44

Mayoul, Louis François, 77–78

Medicine: and debate on decapitation, 133–38, *137*; and effects of Terror on mental and public health, 138–42

Méhée de la Touche, Jean-Claude-Hippolyte, 17

Mémoires d'un détenu, 73

Mercier, Louis-Sébastien, 7, 32, 134

Mesmer, Anton, 130

Metempsychosis, (belief in the transmigration of souls), 125

Michelet, Jules, 53, 96–97

Millard des émigrés, 89

Minow, Martha, 11, 118, 150

Mirabeau, Count Honoré Gabriel Riqueti, 92

Mitchell, W.J.T., 126

Moeurs (moral habits), accountability and, 45

Monceaux, burials at, *95*, *96*, 100, 106

Moniteur, Le, 57, *58*, 104

Monk, The (Lewis), 124

Montagu, Marquise de, 107

Moral accountability, 46

Moral responsibility, 45

Morellet, Abbé, 85

Mouffe, Chantal, 149

Muscadins, 30, 52

My Return to Life after Fifteen Months of Pain (Épinard), 72

Mysteries of Udolpho, The (Radcliffe), 124

Names: changing of, 39, 87, 147; difficult past of Terror, ideology, and preoccupation with, 39–41

Napoleon, marriage to Josephine, 107

Napoleonic era: effects of Terror and, 140; memory and mass graves, 91, 104–8, 115–16

National Assembly, 23, 25, 39, 79, 92–94

National Convention, 3, 8; accountability and, 48–51; Boissy and, 65; first actions of, 8–9, 14, 17, 28, 43; inability to impose silence about Revolution, 149; last session of, 14, 146; Le Bon and, 55, 56–61; restitution and, 65–66, 67, 69, 71–73, 75–87; trial of Louis XVI and, 47–48

Natural disasters, pre-Revolution attitudes toward violence and, 20, 21

Necker, Jacques, 22, 46, 47

Negative responsibility, 45

Neiman, Susan, 20

Ney, Maréchal, 108

Night Thoughts on Life, Death and Immortality (Young), 130

9 Thermidor. *See* Thermidorian Reaction

Nuremberg Trials, 149, 150

Nye, Robert, 76

October Days, 24, 25

Ölsner, Konrad Engelbert, 135

On Assassination and Political Theft (Servan), 84

On Crimes and Punishments (Beccaria), 142

On the Means to Communicate Immediately with the People (pamphlet), 23

On the Necessity to Make the Crimes of Tyrants Known during Their Reign (Prudhomme), 32–33

Orange: burials in, 91, 93, 99, 101; expiatory monument in, 112, 114; Popular Commission of Orange, 53, 96
Orateur du peuple, L' (newspaper), 60, 61–62, 85–86
Order of Things, The (Foucault), 38
Ozouf, Mona, 33–34

Pantheon (Church of Sainte-Geneviève), 92
Paris pendant la Révolution (Mercier), 32
Particular responsibility, 45
Pastoret, Claude-Emmanuel, 100
Patriot français, Le (newspaper), 73
Pecuniary responsibility, 45
Pellegrin, Jean-Baptist, 74
Peltier, Jean-Gabriel, 30–31
Pemberton, Thomas, 139
Pensions, for widows, 7, 72–73, 75–76, 78, 93
Perturbation, therapeutics of, 140
Pétion, Jérome, 25
Petit, Marc-Antoine, 138–40
Petit, Michel-Edme, 30
Phantasmagoria, 125–33, *127*, 144, 147; the Gothic and, 130–32; origins of, 128; science and, 128–30; visual culture and, 132–33
Philosophes, 20, 47, 85, 93, 94
Picpus: first commemorations at, 99, 107, 108; funeral chapel constructed at, 110–11; Holocaust and, 116; mass graves at, 95, 98
Pièces justificatives, 73
Pindray (citizen), 31–32
Pinel, Philippe, 142
Place de la Concord, 14, 96, 146
Place de la Révolution, 14, 96, 146
Poirevesson, Marie-Anne, 74
Political power, double-entry bookkeeping and, 46
Politics, modern, Revolution's invention of, 148–49
Pombal, marquis of, 21
Pompadour, marquise de, 125
Popkin, Jeremy, 23
Popular Commission of Orange, 53, 96
Popular sovereignty: accountability and, 14; democratization of responsibility and, 48; Revolution and population's transformation from subjects to citizens, 3–4
Positive responsibility, 45
Post-traumatic stress disorder (PTSD), 1, 12, 19, 141–42, 144
Poyet (architect), 99

Prax, Emilie, 79–82
Précy, comte de, 113, 114
Property restoration. *See* Restitution, for *les biens des condamnés*
Prudhomme, Louis-Marie, 32–38, *35*, *37*
Prussia, 68–69
Psychiatry, rise of, 141–42, 144
Public health, effects of Terror on, 138–40, 144
Public sphere: emergence of and attitudes toward violence, 19, 20, 21–23, 42; as metaphor, 22

Queue de Robespierre, La (Méhée de la Touche), 17
Quinet, Edgar, 3–5, 149

Radcliffe, Ann, 124
Raffron, Nicolas, 83
Reburials. *See* Exhumations and reburials
Rechtman, Richard, 12
Redistributive justice, focus on future and, 150–51
Regnault-Warin, Jean Joseph, 104–5, 106
Regulus, Le Bon's use of story of, 62
Reign of Terror: conditions during, 1; modernity, violence, and varying interpretations of, 5–8; Quinet on French Revolution's democratization and need to address, 3–5; shadow of Holocaust and, 10–13, 116, 122, 149, 151. *See also* Thermidorian Reaction
Religion. *See* Secularization
Remembrance. *See* Mass graves, remembrance and
Reparatory justice, 82–83, 85, 87, 89
Représentants en mission, responsibility and, 43–44, 48–49, 50, 54–56, 58, 61, 117–18
Repressed, concept of return of, 91, 181n2
Republican Calendar, names changed in, 39
"Republican marriages," 53
Responsibility: derivation of word, 47; kinds of, 45
Restitution, for *les biens des condamnés*, 13–14, 65–89, 147, 148; arguments against, 82–83; arguments for, 83–86; confiscation and distinction between power and property and, 67–68, 88; debates about, 82–86; Emilie Prax and, 79–82; law of restitution, 86–88; *les bien des condamnés* as past that has not passed, 67; memoires and petitions of victims, 71–78; pensions for widows, 7, 72–73,

75–76, 78, 93; posthumous exoneration
and, 76–78; property already resold and,
75, 79, 81; rehabilitation of memory, 66,
67, 75–81, 86; reparatory justice, 82–83,
85, 87, 89; restorative justice, 13, 81–82,
149–50; retribution and accountability,
51–54; retrospective nature of, 88;
seizures from church, 67–68, 89; seizures
from émigrés, 68–69, 70–71, 86, 89;
seizures from victims of Terror, 65–69,
71–78; social order and, 71, 88; varying
confiscatory practices, 69–70; women
and, 66–67, 72–73, 74–75, 76, 78–82,
88–89
Restoration, of Bourbons, 69; impact of
Terror and, 140; remembrance and,
90–92, 104, 108–14, 115, 147
Restorative justice, 13, 81–82, 149–51
Retributive justice, 13, 15, 51–54, 102,
149–50
Revision (révision), rehabilitation and, 76–77
Révolution, La (Quinet), 3–5
Revolutionary Society of Nogent-sur-
Marne, 147
Revolution of 1830, 89, 91
Revolution of 1848, 89, 91, 114
Révolutions de Paris (newspaper), 32
Rex non potest peccare (king can do no
wrong) principle, 48
Richardson, Samuel, 57
Richet, Denis, 44
Ricoeur, Paul, 30
Riouffe, Honoré de, 73
Robec, Magdelaine Françoise de, 69
Robertson (Robert), Etienne-Gaspard, 125,
128–33, 144
Robespierre, Augustin, 54–55
Robespierre, Maximilien: arguments against
death penalty, 26; burial site, 96; mass
graves and, 98; Robertson's phantasmago-
ria and, 125; and Terror's political goals,
27–28, 29–30
Roederer, Pierre-Louis, 165n83
Romme, Gilbert, 93–94
Rosenfeld, Sophia, 31
Rougyff, Le (newspaper), 58–59
Rousseau, Jean-Jacques, 6, 62–63

Sade, Marquis de, 96, 124
Saint Bartholomew's Day Massacre (1572),
21
Saint-Denis basilica: burials at, 91, 94–95,
108; exhumation of royal cadavers, 94–95

Saint-Fargeau, Lepeletier de, 92
Saint-Just, Louis Antoine de, 27, 69–70, 76, 96
"Sanguinocratie," 31–32
Schama, Simon, 24
Science, phantasmagoria and, 128–30
Secularization: internal pathology of ghosts
and, 125; language use and, 31; pre-
Revolution attitudes toward violence and,
19, 20–21, 23, 42
Sédillot, Jean the Younger, 135–36
September Massacres of 1792, 7, 108
Servan, Joseph, 84
Servan, Michel Antoine, 84, 179n82
Seven Years War (1756–1763), pre-
Revolution attitudes toward violence
and, 20
Shelley, Mary, 138
Shklar, Judith, 62
Shock therapy, 139–40
Soboul, Albert, 44
Socialists, 140–41
Social reflexivity, 15
Sömmering, Samuel Thomas von, 134–36
Structure of feeling, 119, 122–23, 136, 145
Sue, Jean-Joseph, 134
Sulla, Lucius Cornelius, 3

Tackett, Timothy, 6–7, 55
Tale of Two Cities, A (Dickens), 95
Talleyrand, Charles-Maurice de, 54
Tallien, Jean-Lambert, 17–19, 25, 29–30,
49–50
Tallien, Madame, 125
Talma, François-Joseph, 109
Teitel, Ruti, 149
Terrorisme, Tallien's use of word, 18
Théophilanthropie, 14
Thermidorian Reaction: basic rhetoric
about Terror, 28–30; challenges of past
and future and, 8–10; mourning and
remembrance after 9 Thermidor, 12, 91,
98–99, 104, 115, 117, 125; narratives of
Terror and, 19, 33; perceptions and
naming of Terror after 9 Thermidor,
28–29, 34, 169–70n9, 171n33; problems
facing Republic after 9 Thermidor, 9–10,
125, 138–39, 148; recent reevaluation of,
9–10; redress and restoration for victims
of Terror, 73, 78, 85, 87. See also
Accountability, as fundamental principle
of Revolution; Difficult past, Terror
seen as; Restitution, for les biens des
condamnés

Thermidorians: accountability and attempts at justice, 44, 49, 59–60, 62; lack of political strategy, 9; perception of Terror, 28–29, 41; redress and restoration of property and, 78

Thibaudeau, Antoine Claire, 81, 147

Thionville, Merlin de, 9

Thirty Years War (1618–1648), pre-Revolution attitudes toward violence and, 20

Tisset, François-Barnabé, 35

Toebaerts, André, 71–72

Torpey, John, 2

Transitional justice: accountability in early Revolution and, 44–48; challenges of Terror and, 12, 15; concept of, 11; liberal democracy and, 150; similarities and differences with recent cases, 147, 149–51; trauma and, 11–12; violence and, 122

Trauma: aftermath of Reign of Terror and, 12; as assault on meaning, 147; concept of, 11–12; "General Table of the Disasters of the French Revolution," 144; "ghosts" of Terror and concept of, 118–19, 121–22; as historic concept, 122; mental health and, 141–42; as particular attitude toward time, 121, 142; Petit and therapeutic effects of Terror, 138–40; rise of psychiatry and, 141–42; twenty-first century concept of, 2; visual culture and coming to terms with, 126

Treatise of Insanity (Pinel), 142

Treatise on Crime and Punishments (Beccaria), 26

Trial by jury, transitional justice before Revolution and, 47–48

Tronson-Ducoudray, Guillaume-Alexandre, 75–76

Turenne, marshal of France, 94

Turner, Victor, 166n91

Turreau, Louis Marie, 52

Tutu, Archbishop Desmond, 149

Vainqueurs de la Bastille, funerals and, 93–94

Vattel, Emmerich de, 70–71

Vengeance. *See* Retributive justice

Ventôse Decrees (1794), 55, 69–70

Verdery, Katherine, 92

Vergangenheitsbewältigung, 12–13

Vicq-d'Azyr, Félix, 97

Vidaud, Gabriel de, 112

Villemain d'Abancourt, Jean-François, 105–6

Violence: ambivalence toward, 19, 25, 42, 95, 98; debates about during Revolution, 23–26, 42; language and representations of, 30–32; need for reckoning with, 45–47; popular violence accepted as part of Revolution, 24–25; preoccupation with ghosts and, 124, 131–33, 136, 138, 140, 142, 144; pre-Revolution attitudes toward, 19–23, 27, 42; storming of Bastille and, 6, 7, 19, 23–24, 93–94; transitional justice and trauma and, 11–12, 122; twenty-first century reactions to, 1–2, 3. *See also* Death penalty; Executions

Viot (prosecutor), 53–54

Virtue: allegations against Le Bon and theme of, 43, 56–62, *58*; as understood by Le Bon, 62–64

Visual culture, ghost of Terror and, 124–33, *127*, 145

Vitalism, 139–40, 144

Volney, comte de, 96

Voltaire, 92, 97

Walton, Charles, 61

Walzer, Michael, 48

War of Spanish Succession (1701–1713), 20

War of the Austrian Succession (1740–1748), 20

Weber, Max, 20, 32

White Terror, 13, 52, 102, 132, 142–43, 158n66

Widows. *See* Women

Williams, Raymond, 119, 122–23

Wolves, visual culture and, 124–25

Women: effects of Terror on, 133, 140, 143; pensions for widows and children, 7, 72–73, 75–76, 78, 93; redress and restoration of property and, 66–67, 72–73, 74–75, 76, 78–82, 88–89, 118; in Revolutionary urban riots, 25

Young, Edward, 130

Ysabeau, Claude-Alexandre, 72, 82

Zizek, Joseph, 34